Economic Growth with Equity

Economic Growth with Equity

Challenges for Latin America

Edited by Ricardo Ffrench-Davis and José Luis Machinea

palgrave
macmillan

ECLAC

Softcover reprint of the hardcover 1st edition 2007 978-0-230-01893-8

First published 2007 by
PALGRAVE MACMILLAN
Houndmills, Basingstoke, Hampshire RG21 6XS and
175 Fifth Avenue, New York, N.Y. 10010
Companies and representatives throughout the world

PALGRAVE MACMILLAN is the global academic imprint of the Palgrave Macmillan division of St. Martin's Press, LLC and of Palgrave Macmillan Ltd. Macmillan® is a registered trademark in the United States, United Kingdom and other countries. Palgrave is a registered trademark in the European Union and other countries.

ISBN 978-1-349-28520-4 ISBN 978-0-230-80091-5 (eBook)
DOI 10.1057/9780230800915

This book is printed on paper suitable for recycling and made from fully managed and sustained forest sources.

A catalogue record for this book is available from the British Library.

A catalogue record for this book is available from the Library of Congress.

12 11 10 9 8 7 6 5 4
16 15 14 13 12 11 10 09 08

Transferred to Digital Printing 2011

Contents

Part IV Trade for Growth

List of Tables

List of Figures

Preface

From time to time, Latin American countries experience growth spurts, like in the period 2004–05, when the region achieved the highest biennial growth rate of the past 25 years. However, sustained growth has been elusive in the last quarter of a century, and this elusive growth has come hand-in-hand with notorious economic and social inequalities.

Concerned by these twin failures, on September 1–2, 2005, the Economic Commission for Latin America and the Caribbean (ECLAC) convened an outstanding group of economists to review the state of the art in the fields of policy and development, with the aim of establishing the best available knowledge regarding how development can get started and how it can then evolve into a sustained trend.

Ten papers were prepared for the seminar and revised for the present volume edited by ECLAC. An overview chapter, covering the main issues of growth and equity in the region, opens the volume. The following three chapters tackle the challenge of reviewing recent development experiences, discussing the alternative interpretations of the sources of success stories and failures in both Latin America and other emerging economies.

Although development is associated with many branches of public policy, economic and social policies are often designed and implemented independently, without accounting for the complex relationship among them. The following two chapters examine this relationship from the perspective of social policies and their potential impact on growth and poverty. The final aim of these chapters is to establish how policy makers and societies can adopt pro-growth social policies.

The last four chapters analyze the policy areas that were two of the main targets of Washington Consensus reforms: respectively, finance and trade. The chapters covering the former focus on domestic capital markets and productive investment, on the one hand, and on the management of the capital account for a development-friendly financial environment, on the other. The chapters covering trade concentrate on the external environment faced by the countries, the impact of the composition of trade on the economies, and the effects of the diversity and stability of exports on aggregate economic growth.

The subject of this volume and the topics covered have been at the core of ECLAC's research and policy work throughout its history, as witnessed by the significant contributions made over the years to the study of the determinants of economic development. The Commission has recently emphasized the need to put back public policies at the center of the development agenda, and has insisted on the importance of an integrated approach to social and economic policy issues. The objective of these recommendations is to allow the countries of the region to achieve sustained growth and, at the same time, to be able to distribute more equitably the resulting benefits of this process.

This volume, which constitutes a continuation of ECLAC's line of thought, has been produced in the context of growing concern and interest on the inequality prevailing in Latin American societies. Economies with average per-capita GDP of about one-fifth that of developed countries must tackle the challenge of equitable growth, since this appears to be a requisite for reducing the development gap with richer economies. The purpose of the set of papers in this volume on growth-with-equity is to contribute to the debate and action in that direction.

We appreciate the contributions of all the authors of the chapters in this book, as well as the revisions of the drafts presented in the September seminar, and the efforts made to incorporate the comments received during and after that event. Naturally, all authors are fully responsible for the content of their respective chapters, which do not necessarily represent the point of view of any of the institutions represented in this volume.

We acknowledge the valuable contributions of the discussants and chairpersons that participated in the seminar. The group includes Nancy Birdsall (President, Center for Global Development, Washington, DC), Roberto Bouzas (Professor, Universidad de San Andrés, Buenos Aires), Vittorio Corbo (President, Central Bank of Chile), Robert Devlin (Integration, Trade & Hemispheric Affairs Division, IDB), Fábio Eber (Professor, Instituto de Economía, Federal University of Río de Janeiro, Brazil), Joao Carlos Ferraz (Director, Production Productivity and Management Division, ECLAC), Alejandro Foxley (Minister of Foreign Affairs of Chile, former Senator), Daniel Heymann (Expert, ECLAC Buenos Aires Office), Jorge Katz (Professor of Economics, University of Chile; former Director of the Production Productivity and Management Division, ECLAC), Claudio Loser (Interamerican Dialogue, Washington, DC), Manuel Marfán (Member of the Board, Central Bank of Chile), Juan Antonio Morales (President, Central Bank of Bolivia), Guillermo Perry (Chief Economist for Latin America and the Caribbean, World Bank), Joseph Ramos (Dean, School of Economics, University of Chile), Andrés Solimano (Regional Adviser, ECLAC), Augusto de la Torre (Regional Adviser on Finance, World Bank), Andras Uthoff (Chief, Social Division, ECLAC), Dorotea Werneck (former Minister of Industry and Trade and of Labor of Brazil), Roberto Zahler (Former President, Central Bank of Chile).

Rodrigo Heresi, Rafael López-Monti and Miguel Torres assisted in the revision of drafts. Lenka Arriagada and Marcela Osses worked efficiently in the presentation and formatting of files.

The seminar and the publication of this book were made possible by the generous contributions of the Ford Foundation and the German Federal

Ministry for Economic Cooperation and Development (BMZ). The funds of the latter institution are managed by the "Deutsche Gesellschaft für Technische Zusammenarbeit" (GTZ).

Ricardo Ffrench-Davis
Senior Advisor
Economic Commission for Latin America
and the Caribbean (ECLAC)

José Luis Machinea
Executive Secretary
Economic Commission for Latin America
and the Caribbean (ECLAC)

April 2006

Notes on the Contributors

José Luis Machinea, Executive Secretary of the Economic Commission for Latin America and the Caribbean (CEPAL/ECLAC), United Nations. Former Minister of Economics and President of the Central Bank of Argentina. He holds a Ph.D. in Economics from the University of Minnesota.

Osvaldo Luis Kacef, Officer in charge of the Economic Development Division of CEPAL/ECLAC. Former Under-Secretary of Macroeconomic Programming of the Ministry of Economics, Argentina. He holds an M.A. from the Catholic University of Rio de Janeiro.

Dani Rodrik, Professor of International Political Economy at the John F. Kennedy School of Government, Harvard University. He holds a Ph.D. in Economics and a MPA from Princeton University, and an A.B. (summa cum laude) from Harvard College.

William Easterly, Professor of Economics (Joint with African Studies Program), New York University. Former Senior Adviser at the World Bank. He holds a Ph.D. in Economics from the Massachusetts Institute of Technology (MIT).

José Antonio Ocampo, Under-Secretary-General for Economic and Social Affairs of the United Nations. Former Executive Secretary of the Economic Commission for Latin America and the Caribbean (ECLAC), and Minister of Finance and of Planning of Colombia. He holds a Ph.D. in Economics from Yale University.

María Angela Parra, Advisor to the Under-Secretary-General for Economic and Social Affairs of the United Nations. Former Advisor to the Executive Secretary of CEPAL (ECLAC). She is doing her Ph.D. in Economics at the New School University in New York.

François Bourguignon, Chief Economist and Senior Vice-President of the World Bank. Member of the Conseil d'Analyze Economique (France), Professor of Economics at the Ecole des Hautes Etudes en Sciences Sociales. He earned a postgraduate degree in Applied Mathematics from the University of Paris, a Ph.D. from the University of Western Ontario, and a Doctorate in Economics from the University of Orleans.

Michael Walton, Lecturer in International Development at the John F. Kennedy School of Government, Harvard University. He previously worked at the World Bank, and was co-director for the 2006 World Development Report on Equity. He holds a M. Phil. in Economics from Oxford University.

Miguel Székely, Under-Secretary for Planning and Evaluation at the Ministry of Social Development of Mexico, 2002–2006. Former Chief of Regional Development at the Office of the President of Mexico, and Research Economist at the Inter American Development Bank. He holds a Ph.D. in Economics from Oxford University.

Armando Castelar Pinheiro, Senior Researcher at the Instituto de Pesquisa Econômica Aplicada (IPEA) and Professor at the Instituto de Economia of the Universidade Federal do Rio de Janeiro. He holds a Ph.D. in Economics from the University of California, Berkeley.

Regis Bonelli, Research Associate at the Instituto de Pesquisa Econômica Aplicada (IPEA), Rio de Janeiro. Former Executive Director of the Banco Nacional de Desenvolvimento Econômico e Social of Brazil (BNDES). Ph.D. in Economics from the University of California, Berkeley.

Ricardo Ffrench-Davis, Senior Advisor of CEPAL (ECLAC), and Professor of Economics, Universidad de Chile. Former Director of Research of the Central Bank of Chile. In 2005 was awarded the Chilean National Prize for the Humanities and Social Sciences. Ph.D. in Economics from the University of Chicago.

Manuel R. Agosin, Professor, Department of Economics, Universidad de Chile. Until January 2006, Chief Economist for Central America, Mexico, Dominican Republic and Haiti, Inter-American Development Bank. Consultant to international organizations and national governments. He holds a Ph.D. in Economics from Columbia University.

Marcelo de Paiva Abreu, Professor of Economics, Pontifical Catholic University of Rio de Janeiro, and former Chair of the Department of Economics. He holds a Ph.D. in Economics from Cambridge University.

1
Growth and Equity: In Search of the "Empty Box"

José Luis Machinea and Osvaldo L. Kacef

Introduction

Nearly a decade and a half ago, the renowned ECLAC economist Fernando Fajnzylber had a simple but profound idea. He constructed a double-entry table for use in categorizing the countries of Latin America according to their performance in terms of income concentration and growth rates (Fajnzylber, 1992). When it was completed, only one of the four boxes in that table remained empty, and that was the one that combined high growth with low levels of inequality. Hence the idea of the "empty box" as a metaphor for the region's shortcomings in this respect, which continue to pose a challenge for analysts and policy-makers.

Fajnzylber's keen eye detected several traits of Latin American societies that he associated with their comparatively poor performance: the region's contribution to gross world product (GWP) was less than its share of world population, and its share of industrial output was even smaller. Moreover, if we were to disaggregate this last variable further, we would find that the region's shares of the world totals for capital-goods production, engineers and scientists, and the resources made available to them are, in decreasing order, smaller still.

The region's development has been marked by low rates of technical progress, by low levels of value added to its natural resources and by the use of imported technologies, all of which reflects a reliance on imitation rather than original thought. Thus, the significance of this empty box cannot be fully understood without reference to the region's inability to open what Fajnzylber referred to as the "black box" of technical progress. This inability stems, in its turn, from the history of the continent and from the individual and institutional mentalities and behavioral patterns gradually formed through centuries of conquest and colonization. The result was a legacy of highly concentrated assets, societies built on a caste structure, and States that were strong on ensuring the maintenance of such a scheme, but weak when it came to providing public goods such as health, education or a stable, impartial legal system.

The region's deficits in terms of growth and equality cannot be explained without reference to their historical roots. The bureaucratic structure of the colonial government, designed to extract taxes and deliver them to the Crown, was succeeded by the predominance of European elites and their descendants, who accumulated real assets, access to education and control of public administration. Comparing the development of Latin America and the Caribbean in colonial times with the early European settlements on the east coast of North America, Engermann and Sokoloff (2002) showed that the latter's factor endowments encouraged the establishment of a production system based on small-scale family farms that had little access to economies of scale.

Thus, the societies of the North, with their less unequal distribution of wealth (especially in terms of land, political rights and public education), developed much faster than the more polarized societies of the South. This was partly because, under conditions of extreme inequality, elites will tend to be more reluctant to share political rights, which can be used to redistribute power and to open up access to economic opportunities and basic education for the majority. The reason for this lies in the power of knowledge as a source of political mobilization, together with the fact that the burden of providing the requisite financing necessarily falls on the wealthier sectors of society.

The region's recent history has exacerbated its chronic difficulty in sustaining a growth process whose benefits are shared more fairly. In fact, over the past 25 years the region's pace of growth has been slow and volatile,

Figure 1.1 GDP per capita and poverty in Latin America, 1980–2004

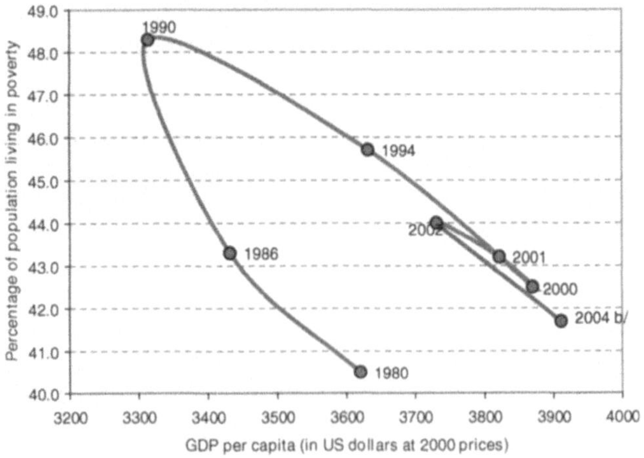

and income distribution has worsened.[1] As a result, poverty levels in the region have increased both in absolute terms and as a percentage of the total population (see Figure 1.1).

The rapid economic liberalization process that took place in the early 1990s within a context of appreciating real exchange rates made foreign capital goods cheaper relative to local labor. This, in turn, provided an incentive for the adoption of technologies that made intensive use of capital goods and imported inputs. Meanwhile, increased foreign direct investment brought with it new forms of work organization and more advanced product and process technologies. The combination of these factors caused businesses' human resource structures to shift towards more highly skilled labor. At around this same time, the dismantling of tariff and non-tariff barriers heightened competition between domestic goods and imported substitutes, a large part of which came from countries with an abundant endowment of unskilled, low-paid labor.

This had the effect of sharply increasing the production structure's heterogeneity and gave rise to the formation of a "three-speed" model. The first component of that model was made up of large capital-intensive firms using state-of-the-art technologies. The second comprised small and medium-sized labor-intensive enterprises that were losing their linkages as suppliers to the first group and as producers of consumer goods due to rising competition from imports. These firms had also serious difficulties in gaining access to capital and credit markets. The third and last component was composed of a growing number of informal microenterpriises, which were, to a great extent, one of the many manifestations of the countries' social fragmentation.

In a low-growth setting, economic reforms triggered an increase in the region's unemployment and informal employment levels and widened the wage gap between high- and low-skilled workers.[2] These impacts stand in sharp contrast to the Eastern Asian countries' experiences in the 1960s and 1970s.

Apart from the two liberalization processes' different styles,[3] the differentiating factor between the experiences of the four Asian "tigers" and of the

[1]Per capita growth between 1980 and 2005 has been roughly 11%, and regional output has been twice as volatile as the global economy and most of the developing world (ECLAC, 2006).

[2]In 2000, 54% of labor income among the poorest 40% of households and 63% of their employment came from the informal sector. At the same time, whereas in 1990 the average income of an employed worker in the formal sector was roughly 60% higher than that of an informal worker, 10 years later the difference had grown to 72%.

[3]See Agosin (2001) or Ffrench-Davis and Ocampo (2001).

Latin American countries probably has less to do with unequal endowments of other factors of production in the two regions (e.g., greater abundance of arable land in Latin American countries) and more to do, as Wood (1997) argues, with the fact that large-scale exporters from low-income countries were entering world markets just when the Latin America economies were being opened up.

As Wood points out, 50 percent of the world's population, much of it unskilled labor, lives in just five low-income Asian countries: China, India, Pakistan, Indonesia and Bangladesh. Their competition with middle-income Latin American countries on world markets altered the competitive position of the latter (whose ratio between low- and high-skilled labor is above the world average but below that of the new Asian exporters), skewing their comparative advantages towards the production of goods of intermediate skill intensity.

Thus, the region's liberalization process of the late 1980s and early 1990s led to a contraction of both the most skill-intensive sectors (as a result of competitive pressure from developed-country products) and the least skill-intensive production sectors (which had to compete with products from low-income countries). The net result was an increase in the skill premium (and in unemployment).

Moreover, drawing on some of the arguments made by Rodrik (1997) in his analysis of globalization's impact on developed economies, it can be argued that greater economic integration per se increased the elasticity of the labor-demand function. Growing economic integration also exposed less-skilled workers to more direct competition from products made by their counterparts in countries with a similar per capita income or development level, thereby making it much harder for them to defend earlier social conquests or to sustain their wage levels.

In sum, in view of the fact that Fajnzylber's box remains empty today, in this analysis we intend, first, to explore the feasibility of filling that box in Latin American developing countries and, second, consider how we might go about doing so. In the next section we will look at the interaction between equity and growth, before going on to analyse the lessons that can be learned from other experiences in this area. We then discuss a number of economic policy options that we believe could help the region to grow more and distribute the benefits of that growth better.

Equity and growth: Antagonistic or complementary processes?

From the very outset, the concepts of equity and growth have had a complex and changing relationship within economic development theory. In the post-war period, when economists began to think about ways to increase per capita GDP in less developed economies on a systematic basis, greater inequality seemed to be an almost inevitable by-product of growth.

A classic exposition of this idea can be found in Arthur Lewis' model of economic development with unlimited supplies of labor (Lewis, 1954).

In economies where the population is so large relative to capital and natural resource stocks that in some sectors the marginal productivity of labor is negligible or nil, increasing inequality is an outcome of the model and a constituent element of the development process. Most of the benefits reaped by the modern sector are channelled into saving, and all saving is invested in reproductive capital. Development is viewed as consisting of a shift in proportions between the modern sector, which is necessarily more unequal, and the traditional sector, which is more equitable but technologically stagnant. Inequality, in this view, is simply the price to be paid for modernization.

This pattern of growth with increasing inequality reaches a turning point, however, when the source of surplus labor is exhausted. When this occurs, wages will start to rise and growth will begin to become more equitable.[4] [5] This succession of phases was consistent with one of development theory's most popular and controversial empirical regularities, namely the Kuznets curve (Kuznets, 1955). Nowadays, empirical research tends to mistrust the idea of a universal law that determines the path to be followed in all cases, given the diversity of factor endowments, ownership structures, historical backgrounds and economic policy experiments that can be found in each society.[6]

Latin America emerged from the 1980s with a per capita income that was 10 percent lower than it had been at the start of the decade and with 47 percent more people living in poverty. The succession of external shocks in the region, and the ensuing adjustment policies aimed at making a dual transfer viable,[7] triggered abrupt contractions in activity levels and employment. These contractions were, with few exceptions, followed by unstable recoveries and then, in some cases, untenable or chaotic adjustments that plunged a number of economies into hyperinflation (Bolivia, Peru, Argentina).

---

[4]This brief description does not pretend to do justice to the richness of the original model formulated by Lewis, nor to the literature to which it gave rise. Fields (2005) provides an interesting review of the influence of Lewis' thesis on the analysis of labor markets.

[5]This new phase can take quite some time to arrive if domestic labor supply is augmented by international labor as a consequence of the increasing mobility of goods or labor.

[6]A World Bank review (2005) of the recent empirical literature indicates that no systematic relationship exists between changes in income inequality and per capita GDP growth.

[7]From the private sector (which was the main generator of foreign exchange in most countries of the region) to the public sector (which held the bulk of external debt) and thence abroad. See, for example, Ros (2001).

Cuts in social spending made as part of the countries' adjustment policies, rising unemployment and informality, and bouts of high inflation led to steep increases in inequality and poverty, which have become a more or less stable feature of the region. It was precisely in the late 1980s that Latin America became the focus of thought-provoking research concerning (and later a testing ground for) an internally coherent package of economic policy initiatives and structural reforms. These measures were intended to put an end to macroeconomic imbalances and to boost the countries' growth rates. The key components of these measures – trade and capital-account liberalization, labor-market reform, privatizations, and financial and fiscal reform – were the main pillars of what came to be known as the "Washington consensus."[8]

Distributive measures were conspicuously absent from the package of policy recommendations that emerged from the "consensus." The implicit assumption was that the bottom sectors in the income-distribution structure were certain to see an improvement in their situation as a by-product of the upturn in growth and reduction in inflation that the proposed economic reforms would bring about. This view was based on the "trickle down" theory, according to which – in a stable, growing economy – the poorest sectors were bound to benefit, sooner or later.[9]

The first part of the 1990s saw, for the most part, a recovery in economic growth and a decline in inflation, which helped to lower poverty levels. This outcome was supported by additional public expenditure on health and education, which was increasingly being targeted on the poorest sectors of society (Morley, 1998).

Nonetheless, the limitations of this approach were soon revealed. Although most countries saw a reduction in poverty in the 1990s, there was no clear correlation between growth and inequality. In fact, inequality increased in most cases, as shown in Figure 1.2. As income distribution acts as a filter that increases or reduces the "trickle-down" effect, the more unequal a society is, the higher the growth rate required to reach any given poverty-reduction target.[10]

---

[8]See Williamson (1990 and 2003), who shows how recommendations made by international organizations concerning financial openness went much further than the "consensus" itself.

[9]The World Bank, which had been one of the main promoters of the trickle-down hypothesis, recently acknowledged the limitations of this approach. See Perry *et al.* (2006).

[10]This point has been discussed in a number of ECLAC, documents that underscore the difficulty of improving equity and growth in highly heterogeneous societies (see for example, ECLAC, 1990 and 2004). According to a recent World Bank study (2005), in countries with low levels of inequality, each percentage point of growth allows a reduction of roughly four percentage points in poverty, measured as the number of people living on less than one dollar a day; the impact falls to almost zero in countries with high levels of inequality, however.

Figure 1.2 Growth and inequality

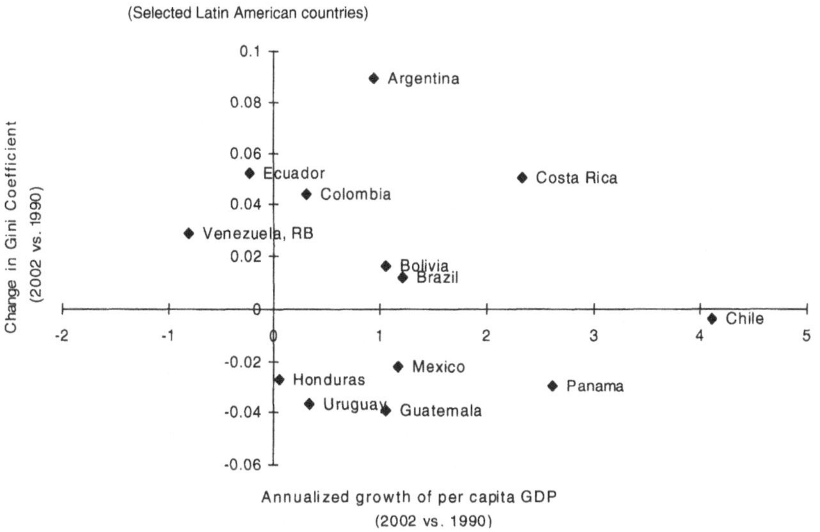

Source: Prepared by the authors.

Partly as a reaction to the poor results of this view of growth as a homoeopathic cure of poverty and partly because of the empirical evidence amassed by more recent research, a new line of thinking has been gaining ground within economic development theory. This line of thought sees poverty and inequality as constraints on economic development and seeks to design policies that will both improve the distribution of wealth and income and raise the productivity of the resources that are in the hands of the poor – and hence the economy's overall growth rate.[11]

Following a line of argument that tends to focus on *ex-ante* inequality (i.e., inequality of opportunities rather than of income), the analysis by Bourguignon and Walton that appears in Chapter 5 of this volume contends, in keeping with this new line of thought, that equity and growth are complementary. In this view, the main challenge for the countries in the region is to fully understand how the link between equity (defined as equal economic, social, and political opportunities) and the growth process operates in those societies. These authors conclude that a characteristic feature of Latin America is the prevalence of institutions that tend to restrict the opportunities open to low- and middle-income groups and to perpetuate the privileges of elites and corporations. The failure to grasp the scope

[11]Studies such as those of Birdsall and Székely (2003) and Lustig *et al.* (2002) are pioneers in this line of thought.

of these inequalities negatively affects investment and innovation and constitutes a factor that hinders economic growth.

Initial differences in opportunities are perpetuated down through the generations in a vicious circle that reproduces inequality and undermines growth. Once we begin to think of inequality as an obstacle to growth, the trade-off between purely macroeconomic policies and social policies disappears; spending on health and education then ceases to be the nightmare of finance ministers concerned with balancing the budget and instead takes its rightful place as a core component of development strategy.

An initial point that emerges naturally from this new approach concerns the need to redistribute assets. The poor need to have greater access to education, land, and markets for services such as credit and insurance. Of course, these broad guidelines do not translate into straightforward, readily applicable policy recommendations, although some policy options for breaking this vicious cycle are discussed in Machinea and Hopenhayn (2005) and in Chapter 6 of this volume, where Székely analyses the specific case of conditional transfer programmes in Mexico.

The poor are poor because they have incomes that are far below the average and possess little or no stock of wealth (wealth, ultimately, is accumulated saving, and saving is a positive function of income). Of course, sufficient investment levels would enable low-income sectors to increase their productivity and thereby gain access to returns that would improve their living standards. However, in addition to lacking sufficient collateral to secure the loans they would need in order to make an investment, lower-income sectors also face the problem of indivisibilities.

Many investments require a minimum fixed outlay before they can be implemented or start to generate a positive rate of return. Moreover, a certain minimum number of years may have to be invested in education in order to amass the necessary human capital to achieve an appreciable jump in income levels. The development of tailor-made financial institutions to cater to the lowest-income deciles, the necessary regulatory adjustments, and subsidies for purchasing machinery and investing in human capital are all policy measures that could improve the situation of the poorest members of society by increasing their access to economic opportunities and making their resources more productive.

This kind of initiative, in turn, would be more effective if adopted in an environment that promotes a more equitable access to production assets. In the case of land, the provision of land deeds, leases or sharecropping contracts would endow small producers with the collateral they need to gain access to credit and insurance markets. Because no insurance market exists for the poorest sectors of society, downswings in the business cycle force these sectors to resort to expedients that exact a dramatic toll in personal terms and reduce society's overall long-term growth rate. These measures may include selling off such farmers' meagre herds of livestock or the withdrawal of their children from school so that they can earn an income in the informal sector which, albeit meagre, nonetheless contributes to their families' subsistence.

An important point to bear in mind in terms of poverty alleviation policies, particularly with respect to extreme poverty, is the urgency of such measures. Children who are victims of undernutrition in the early years of life not only have a higher mortality risk, but also tend to suffer from diminished learning abilities, which negatively affect their performance as citizens and workers when they are adults. Neglect in this area has irreversible consequences over time.

Growth and equity. What can we learn from certain countries' success stories in recent decades?

As Rodrik points out in Chapter 2, we are witnessing the emergence of a new consensus on growth. The basic precept of this consensus is that policy outcomes depend on the context in which policy measures are applied and, therefore, vary from country to country. Hence, the lessons learned from other countries' experiences do not translate into an uncritical transposition of other countries' policy initiatives or institutional arrangements to the region. Experiences cannot be copied without taking account of history, social structure, external settings, political dynamics, and institutions, i.e., the specific characteristics of each country. Clearly, this approach is not a new one for ECLAC, the home of Latin American structuralism, which has placed special emphasis on this view throughout its history.

The notion that a development strategy should be founded on each country's realities warns us against one-size-fits-all recipes such as those proposed by the Washington consensus and by some international organizations during the 1990s. Nonetheless, this should not lead us to the opposite extreme of arguing we cannot learn from other experiences. To do so would be to deny the usefulness of comparative analysis or abstract thought and would, therefore, be tantamount to negating the analytical foundations of our profession, thus bringing us to the brink of a lapse into nihilism (Hausmann, *et al.*, 2004).

As noted by Rodrik in Chapter 2, while it is possible to find a set of principles that are common to all successful growth strategies, there are many different ways in which these principles can be applied, depending on the characteristics of each country. Reasoning along these same lines, in Chapter 3 Easterly calls for humility on the part of economists in international organizations or other centres who issue general policy recommendations based on proclaimed "truths" that, as our own recent history clearly shows are by no means certain.

Economic development is a complex process that reaches far beyond mere quantitative changes and increases in scale. This is attested to by the differing emphases that, over time, economists have placed on the various determinants of growth.[12] Today we can state that growth should be viewed as an ongoing process of change in production structures whereby sectors, product and process technologies, ways of organizing the work process, and business enterprises are created, mutate, and disappear on a cyclical basis.

As Ocampo and Parra state in Chapter 4, the ability to generate new dynamic activities within the framework of this process of structural change is one of the main determinants of growth. The developing world's difficulties in this respect stem from the absence of certain markets (e.g., long-term local-currency credit), imperfect competition in others, information asymmetries (in credit and technology markets and in investment opportunities, for example), and coordination failures. This explains why, in most successful cases, the State has played a decisive, or at least important, role in providing incentives for the emergence of certain types of activities.

Although this leaves us in a better position, when compared with the idea of the "absent State" advocated in the early 1990s, it also raises new questions as to how the State should act and what its capacities and limitations are in the Latin American and Caribbean region of today. The need to ensure high and equitable growth, requires State policies aimed at reducing the structural heterogeneity in the region – not because we are not aware that the dynamics of growth generates heterogeneity, but because we believe that, if that heterogeneity is to constitute a creative phenomenon, then it must not leave roughly 50 percent of the population on the sidelines of the region's modernization process.

Economic history shows us that the variability of growth rates is largely caused by the shocks that economies suffer as a result of sudden fluctuations in the terms of trade, financial crises, and so forth.[13] In Chapter 4 of this volume, Ocampo and Parra provide additional evidence of the importance of external shocks as an explanatory factor for success and failure in terms of economic growth over the past few decades. Latin America which is far from an exception to this rule, has been buffeted by numerous external shocks over the past 25 years. In the 1980s, these shocks took the form of unfavourable terms of trade and a shortage of external financing, while in the 1990s, the volatility of capital movements was the culprit.[14]

Unlike those periods, today much of the region is enjoying favourable external conditions, particularly in relation to the terms of trade, and, to a lesser extent, relatively low international interest rates and lower country-

---

12 See, for example, Easterly (2003).

13 See for example, Easterly *et al.* (1993).

14 See for example, Machinea and López Monti (2005) and Ffrench-Davis (2006).

Figure 1.3 Terms of trade in Latin America

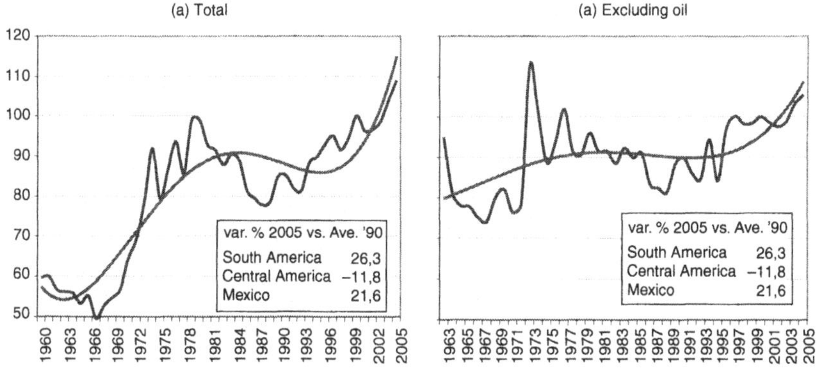

risk premiums.[15] The improvement in the terms of trade is partly the result of stronger commodity prices, but it is also attributable to lower prices for many of the manufactured products which the region imports. It is precisely these lower prices for certain manufactures that prevent the positive aspects of the process from radiating out to the entire region, since some countries, particularly in Central America, have to compete with some of these cheaper manufactures and, therefore, see a deterioration in their own terms of trade (see Figure 1.3).

On this point, it has been claimed, with some justification, that specialization in commodities or commodity-based manufactures is unlikely to lead to sustained growth. The paradox represented by the "curse" of an ample endowment of natural resources is based on the associated deterioration of the terms of trade caused by protectionism in developed countries, the volatility of international prices and a lack of dynamism (slow technological progress, absence of economies of scale, and few externalities).

Nonetheless, there may be reason to be less pessimistic about some of these factors in the future. First of all, the emergence of China and India as major global buyers may provide an underpinning for the region's terms of trade that could keep them well above their average level of the past 30 years. Second, with few exceptions, the region has diversified its exports over the past few decades, thereby making it less vulnerable to real external shocks. Higher exports earnings, in addition to the remittances being received by various countries in the region, are enabling Latin America to grow while at the same time generating a surplus on its balance-

[15]Whereas more favorable terms of trade could be the result of structural factors, as discussed below, better international financial conditions are subject to sudden shifts, as we know from our experience over the past 30 years.

of-payments current account.[16] This unprecedented event in the economic history of the region is also helping to reduce its external vulnerability. Even assuming that the international environment remains largely unchanged (which, of course, is by no means guaranteed while the imbalances in the United States current account persist) and if the developed world moves to reduce agricultural protection, there is still a question regarding the capacity of a natural-resource-based growth strategy in terms of incorporating technology and generating linkages and externalities.

This topic is addressed in greater detail in the next section. Nonetheless, a quick historical review shows that nations such as Australia, Canada, New Zealand and the Nordic countries have made the transition from the extraction of rents from natural resources to the quasi-rents generated by technological innovation.[17] Of course, there are political-economy issues associated with this type of development. Generally speaking, access to land has been more equal in those countries than in nations that have failed to develop value chains. This has resulted in lower poverty indices, a greater accumulation of human capital and the early development of more diversified domestic markets with greater purchasing power.

Another important factor in the establishment of natural-resource-based value chains has been the development of national technological capacities. This type of capacity-building encompasses everything from literacy training to the delivery of a wide-ranging supply of technological services and the presence of a network of universities engaging in applied research.

Can resource-rich countries in the region play a creative role in implementing a scheme of this type? Can the density of the production structure be increased through the incorporation of new activities or sectors based on natural resources? The answer, as evidenced by other countries, is yes; but doing so presupposes the design of a growth strategy in which the State, working in coordination with the private sector, plays a major role (Rodrik, 2004).

In more general terms, ECLAC has described the region's position in the international economy in terms of three models: the maquila model, which involves low levels of value added and technological progress; a resource-intensive commodities model; and the tourism and financial-services export model pursued by a number of Caribbean countries and

---

[16]Although, in the short run, countries that receive migrant remittances may benefit from the large inflows of such funds, which in some countries amount to as much as 15–20% of GDP, this is an issue that warrants more careful analysis: first, because it is largely a symptom of a lack of employment opportunities that is forcing the citizens of a country to emigrate; and, second, because it has a very significant impact on foreign exchange markets in the recipient countries, which gives rise to complex problems in terms of competitiveness.

[17]See, for example, De Ferranti *et al.* (2002).

Panama. None of these models plots out a certain path towards progress in the light of distributive issues or technological externalities. Be this as it may, these models are the pillars of the region's competitiveness, and it makes more sense to explore possible development paths based on what already exists than to return to the starting point and conjure up completely different growth models.

From the standpoint of equity, however, a pattern of specialization based on natural resources does not seem to hold out much promise in terms of improving income distribution, mainly because, in much of the region, the production of commodities tends to be a highly concentrated activity that generates a quite limited demand for labor and few incentives for human capital formation. This is particularly true of traditional agriculture and mining. The rapid integration of China and India (which, together with Pakistan, Indonesia and Bangladesh make up 50 percent of the world's population) into international trade flows, as noted earlier, signals the emergence of an infinitely elastic supply of low-paid labor. Given this situation, in combination with the bias towards skill-intensive technologies witnessed in recent years, it is hardly surprising that skills-based wage gaps widened during the liberalization process or that there appear to be few grounds for expectations of improvements in income distribution, at least by way of the labor market, for the region.

This having been said, in principle the higher incomes arising from the region's improved terms of trade ought to imply an increase in national income, which could, in theory, resolve the issue of distribution. Lump-sum taxes exist only in theory, however, so the operational challenge for public policy is a particularly demanding one. This is especially true in terms of the State's ability to generate sufficient revenues to finance increased social spending aimed at building up human capital in coordination with productive development policies – a point that will be discussed in the following section.

Towards growth with greater equity

Since the region's poor income distribution is also a consequence of an unequal distribution of real and financial assets, we need to think about what kinds of public policies can be most effective in changing the distribution of those assets (capital, knowledge and technology). As we have seen, inequality not only hinders poverty reduction; it also interferes with growth. Thus, it is no longer a question of viewing inequality as the price to be paid for an increase in per capita GDP or regarding its reduction as a potential by-product of development. Instead, it must be rightfully seen as a constraint on the growth process as such.

As ECLAC contends in a recent study (2004), if Latin America is to achieve sustained economic growth in conjunction with gains in productivity and equity, public policies have to be focused on reducing the structural heterogeneity characteristic of its economies. This heterogeneity increased considerably in the 1990s because, since the various economic agents were in widely differing positions to face the far-reaching changes (particularly economic liberalization) that occurred during that period, their ability to adapt to them was also markedly unequal.

Productive development strategies in the region therefore need to "level the playing field" by eliminating obstacles that have a differential effect on the various types of business enterprises (large firms, medium-sized and small formal businesses, and informal microenterprises) that operate on the basis of clearly differing productivity dynamics. Although growth dynamics as such generate heterogeneity, when this phenomenon reaches the levels and the "durability" seen in the region, it clearly is undermining not only equity but also growth itself. Hence the need for policies specifically designed to integrate excluded groups into the growth process and to provide small and medium-sized enterprises with access to credit, technology, markets, and knowledge and to enable them to develop linkages with the wider production structure. Such policies need to be articulated around three broad strategies: inclusion, modernization, and densification of the production structure. This question is discussed in depth by ECLAC (2004) and by Machinea and Vera (2005). Here we will confine our discussion to three topics that we consider to be of strategic importance: international trade, innovation and financing.

The selection of these three topics is not intended to overlook the importance of other issues such as saving and investment, human capital formation, infrastructure or institutions – areas in which the region displays considerable shortcomings, albeit of differing degrees and natures depending on the country. On the contrary, all of these issues are not only of prime importance but are also very closely related to the topics that we will be talking about in greater depth here. Trade promotes growth by generating new investment opportunities. The same can be said of innovation, broadly defined. It is also difficult to foster investment in the absence of financing. By the same token, innovation is contingent upon the presence of human resources that are capable of adopting, adapting, and creating. And all of these factors require an appropriate institutional framework that, of course, encompasses property rights, but which also embraces a great deal more.

The role of foreign trade within a productive development strategy is intertwined with a number of issues of strategic importance for the region's economic performance. Let us take two examples. First, external constraints have always been a key and recurrent issue in the analysis of the region's countries' boom and bust cycles, particularly for Latin American structuralists and their intellectual descendants. Second, on a more contemporary level, the feverish rush to sign bilateral agreements attests to the importance that policymakers attach to gaining access to industrialized markets and to building institutions under the terms of those agreements.

Bilateral agreements are certainly important for various reasons, one of the most important being the generation of new markets, but in no way do they guarantee a simple solution for the complex process of growth. Nor did the structural reforms of the 1990s, particularly economic liberalization – possibly one of the most overblown (and overacted) components of the package of recommendations to have emerged from the Washington consensus.[18]

We should also bear in mind that exports may be the solution to the growth problem only in very small economies where integration into world markets is enough to ensure full employment resources. In larger economies, growth depends, to a great extent, on the performance of activities that produce goods and services for the domestic market. Thus, in these economies, development cannot be seen solely as a function of export activities (Ffrench-Davis, 2005).

While there are considerable doubts surrounding the impact of liberalization on the growth process, there does indeed appear to be a positive link between exports and growth, as demonstrated by Manuel R. Agosin in Chapter 9 of this volume. And this linkage is more influential today than it was in the past. In other words, in these times of globalization, a development strategy that seeks to promote growth in the absence of an increase in exports would hardly seem to be viable. Furthermore, as Agosin also notes, it is easier to find economic success stories among countries with a diversified export structure than among those whose exports are concentrated in just a few products.

The empirical evidence also seems to show that the most successful economies in terms of growth are those that export high- and intermediate-technology manufactures. The studies conducted by Ocampo and Parra (Chapter 4) and Rodrik (2006) both provide some evidence on this point.

Nonetheless, although an export basket concentrated in primary commodities (or products based on them) would appear to have a less dynamic effect on growth than exports of manufactures, particularly high-tech ones, the region's experiences show that exports of manufactures do not necessarily entail a qualitative leap to more complex, technology-intensive goods. Mexico and Central America, for example, export manufactured products of differing technological contents (greater in the case of Mexico), but their exports do not seem to have had a major impact in terms of boosting growth in those countries. This is because exporting manufactures

[18]Bilateral agreements, and particularly North–South accords, have certain types of costs that we have discussed extensively over the last two years. See, for example, ECLAC (2004).

Figure 1.4 Structure of exports by degree of technological intensity

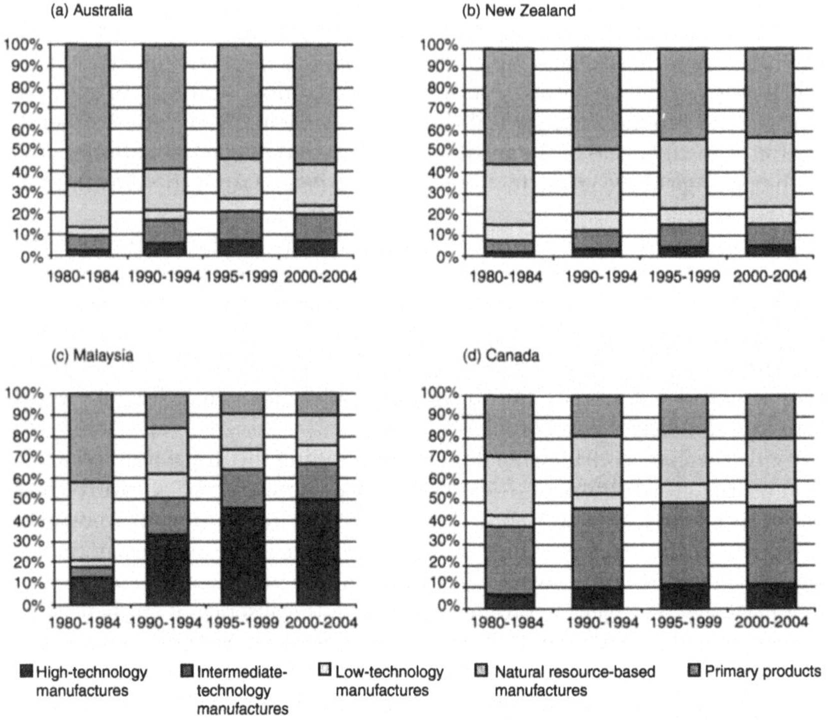

does not necessarily have dynamic spillover effects on the rest of the production structure, nor does it ensure the existence of significant externalities. In other words, we need to do more than simply export medium- and high-technology manufactures in order to boost economic growth. A country also needs to have the knowledge to produce such goods – not simply to assemble them in the final stage of the production process – and the capacity to generate backward linkages that will increase the density of the production process.

As noted earlier, some countries have succeeded in moving from a production structure based on natural resources to a more diversified and more knowledge-intensive structure. In some cases, this transition has resulted in exports having a greater technological content, as in the case of the Nordic countries, Malaysia, and, to a lesser extent, Canada. In other cases, the export structure has continued to be based on natural resources (e.g., Australia and New Zealand) (see Figure 1.4). In all of these examples, however, it is clear that knowledge is being incorporated into the production process, that technology transfers are taking place, and that linkages with other production sectors are being forged.

The importance of export diversification as a positive factor for economic growth poses a major issue for the countries of the region. The high prices currently being commanded by South America's commodity exports and the voluminous remittances being received by Mexico, Central America, and the Caribbean countries could potentially generate a Dutch-disease effect that could undermine our ability to create new activities or, in particular, new exports. What can be done to prevent this? Countries where improvements in the terms of trade are concentrated in activities where the main producer is the public sector have the option of withdrawing resources from those activities and using them to promote emerging ones, which may be independent from the original activity or related to it (linkages of one type or another). In the case of private-sector exports, the issue is more complex, at least from a political economy standpoint. Nonetheless, it should be remembered that the region's first stabilization fund was for coffee – a good produced entirely by the private sector.[19]

Nonetheless, the possibility of increasing and diversifying exports, and the impact this can have on the rest of the production structure, do not depend solely on having greater market access or the maintenance of a high real exchange rate. As aptly pointed out by de Paiva Abreu in Chapter 10, even though these factors are important, and indeed necessary, a great deal can also be achieved through domestic policies targeting the production sector. Although the constraints imposed in this regard by the World Trade Organization (WTO) need to be taken into account, de Paiva Abreu rightly points out that there is still substantial manoeuvring room for designing horizontal and vertical policies to promote production. In particular, this author highlights the need for policies to leverage and mobilize national innovation systems, including science and technology institutions, universities, certification institutes, business associations and private enterprises.

This brings the issue of innovation to the fore. The importance of innovation in the design of a growth strategy has not only been increasingly recognized in the economic literature, but has also occupied a progressively more important place on the public agendas of the region's governments. This may be accounted for by the region's disappointing record in terms of factor productivity growth,[20] as well as by the widespread perception that natural resources' very limited contribution to growth is attributable to a lack of innovation in that area.

It is also clear that market failures in this area make some form of State intervention necessary. As pointed out by Katz (2005), even where production structures are specialized in natural resources, the State has an important role to play in helping to generate and expand the available

[19]See Jiménez and Tromben (2006) on the integration of compensation funds.
[20]On this issue see Solimano and Soto (2005).

knowledge infrastructure in areas such as medical technology, computer sciences, biotechnology, and others.

The evidence shows that in the specific form of innovation known as "creation" (i.e., local knowledge generation through R&D activities), the region is lagging far behind other economies. As noted by Machinea and Vera (2005), the region's countries not only spend quite little on R&D, but what they do spend is inefficient as measured by expenditure per patent obtained. These authors suggest that one likely reason for this inefficiency may be that the private sector accounts for a smaller share of total R&D expenditure than it does in other more successful countries such as Canada, the Republic of Korea or New Zealand. This raises the issue of what kinds of incentives should be offered for activities whose social benefits exceed their private profitability.

R&D is not the only type of innovation required by developing countries, however. The pioneering work of Jorge Katz[21] on Latin American industrialization draws attention to the important role played by the incremental innovations needed to adopt and adapt technologies. Thus, if innovation is to be interpreted broadly, beyond R&D activities as such, we might well ask ourselves whether adoption and adaptation are not equally or even more important in the initial phases of development. If this is the case, then focusing exclusively on R&D expenditure would lead to an underestimation of the region's efforts in this area.

Arguing along similar lines, Maloney and Perry (2005) show that several successful countries, which today have high levels of R&D expenditure, also went through a stage in which such expenditure was much lower and innovation activity basically involved copying and adapting. Over the years, the incorporation of innovations in these countries has relied much more heavily on the acquisition of licenses than in Latin America, where foreign investment has been a much more important factor. Here again, the region's weaker performance reflects the low rates of technology transfer associated with the direct investment it receives (Mortimore *et al.*, 2001).

Be that as it may, once a certain phase of the development process has been reached, it would seem that sustained growth requires an increase in expenditure on R&D. In view of the levels of R&D expenditure seen in the rest of the world, the use of the region's scarce resources must be focalized if we expect to be relevant players in any activity. Nonetheless, the question remains as to how to choose given sectors or activities and how to design an incentive system that will maximize efficiency.[22]

---

[21]See, for example, Katz (1986).

[22]For a discussion of appropriate incentives, see Maloney and Perry (2005).

Finally, the lack of sufficient financing on appropriate terms has been an ongoing problem for growth and equity in the region. The following stylized facts appear in virtually all the countries' experiences:

- Intermediation spreads are wide, and as a result of capital markets' lack of depth, financing tends to be channelled into consumption rather than into productive ventures;
- Long-term financing denominated in local currency is very scarce;
- External financing is generally available only to large corporations, and many small and medium-sized enterprises are, therefore, unable to implement potentially profitable projects;
- The preponderance of dollar-denominated financing increases the countries' vulnerability to external shocks; and
- Financing for "innovative" projects is unavailable.

As Castelar and Bonelli point out in Chapter 7, although the financial system was one of the sectors in which economic reforms were implemented most intensively throughout the 1990s, these reforms contributed very little to sustained growth and even less to the promotion of equity. As outlined by Ffrench-Davis in Chapter 8, instead of strengthening the process of capital accumulation and thereby promoting economic growth, the opening up of domestic economies to capital movements has been associated with increased external vulnerability and the emergence of successive financial crises.

Castelar and Bonelli also show how the combination of instability in financial markets, high real interest rates, high reserve requirements on bank deposits, deficient analysis of debtors and insufficient protection for creditors lead to financial disintermediation and heighten the preference for liquidity and for very short-term financial assets.

This state of affairs results in a virtual absence of long-term financing, which generates a bias against long-term assets and, hence, against investment. The fact that the smallest enterprises and the poorest citizens have no collateral generally blocks their access to formal credit channels (thereby compounding the problem posed by the fact that an investment must reach a certain minimum threshold amount in order for it to generate a positive return). The denomination of loans in foreign currency increases borrowers' exchange-rate risk, especially for businesses whose small size and lack of access to technology exclude them from international markets and whose revenues are, therefore, exclusively in local currency. Similarly, the absence of insurance markets for poor clients forces underprivileged sectors to sell off their scarce assets at a loss in the downswings of the business cycle or to suspend investment activities of strategic importance, as human capital formation, which are cut short when parents take their children out of school in order to put them to work.

Although our analysis has been concerned with long-term issues, before concluding we would like to devote a few paragraphs to short-term macroeconomic policy. Latin America's recent performance has amply reflected the high economic and social costs of instability in the real sector of the economy. The traditional goal of maintaining a macroeconomic framework that reduces nominal volatility (by keeping inflation low), therefore, needs to be complemented by countercyclical policy actions aimed at making growth processes less volatile. These policy measures should address fiscal, monetary, exchange-rate, and financial variables.

Fiscal policy must be designed to cope with fluctuations in the business cycle. In order to avert sharp fluctuations both in the provision of public services and in the real exchange rate and interest rate, the obvious recommendation is to save resources during economic booms for use in subsequent recessions.[23] This kind of policy effort is subject to a number of tensions and conflicts, however, including the difficulty of separating out trend variables from cyclical variables in economic fluctuations.

Monetary policy should provide for countercyclical reserve requirements and a flexible exchange rate that is compatible with the targeted inflation rate and external balance. It is important, however, to avoid being overly ambitious in terms of inflation targets, at least when inflation rates are already at single-digit levels, and to bear in mind that the "inflation band" is designed for use in the event of supply shocks. It should also be remembered that real volatility is in part a reflection of the real exchange rate's excessive divergence from its medium-term trend, which has a negative impact on trade and particularly investment, especially in tradable goods.

The difficulties involved in reducing exchange-rate volatility in a region exposed to powerful external shocks are not to be underestimated, but it is clear that an excessive appreciation (as experienced by several of the region's economies in the 1990s) works against the countries' position within the global economy and particularly against their export diversification. Therefore, economic policymakers, and especially central bankers, should pursue a secondary goal of maintaining a competitive exchange rate. The tools they could use for this purpose could range from direct interventions and deterrent actions by the central bank to controls on short-term capital inflows, where appropriate.[24] More active monetary pol-

[23]Fiscal policies, particularly in developing countries, usually tend to be procyclical due to a shortage of resources in the downswing of the cycle or to the accumulation of pending demands, compounded by an erroneous perception of the durability of fiscal strength, in the expansionary phase. See Gavin *et al.* (1996).

[24]For a further discussion of this issue, see ECLAC (2004), or the chapters by Ocampo and Parra and by Ffrench-Davis in this volume.

icies aimed at underpinning the real exchange rate clearly need to be matched by greater fiscal discipline.

It is also clear, however, that the exchange rate cannot be maintained "at any cost," among other reasons because it is difficult to define an equilibrium exchange rate. In addition, under certain circumstances, maintaining a given rate can fuel excessive inflationary pressures. The point that we wish to emphasize is that excessive fluctuations in the real exchange rate, particularly sharp appreciations, have a negative effect on an economy's export-based position in external markets and exacerbates the real sector's volatility. This is why the real exchange rate should not be treated as a "residual" variable of economic policy.

Finally, financial policy should aim to reduce vulnerability and ensure access to credit at reasonable rates and maturities. This, in turn, calls for improvements in prudential regulation, a deepening of the financial system and an effort to discourage dollarization, while also reducing currency and maturity mismatches. In the medium term, instruments need to be designed to help democratize access to credit.

Concluding observations

Ethical considerations and the principle of solidarity are not the only reasons why we should strive to reduce inequality and poverty. There are also other powerful reasons having to do with economic development and a concern for harmonious coexistence among citizens in democratic, civilized societies. The existence of vast sectors of the population who are unable to lead a decent life is not only morally repugnant but also paves the way for political instability, racial and religious hatred, and social conflict.

This is a domain in which economists have an important role to play. Ultimately, it is a matter of carrying on a long and honourable tradition. And we will succeed in doing so if we continue to search for new answers to the questions that, at the dawn of modern economic thought, Adam Smith asked regarding the origin of the wealth of nations and David Ricardo rose concerning the laws that govern its distribution.

References

Agosin, M. (2001) "Korea and Taiwan in the financial crisis," in R. Ffrench-Davis (ed.), *Financial Crises in "Successful" Emerging Economies*, ECLAC/Brookings Institution, Washington, DC.

Birdsall, N. and M. Székely (2003) "Bootstraps not band-aids: poverty, equity and social policy," in P.P. Kuczynski and J. Williamson (eds), *After the Washington Consensus: Restarting Growth and Reform in Latin America*, Institute for International Economics (IIE), March.

De Ferranti, D., G.E. Perry, D. Lederman and W.F. Maloney (2002) *From Natural Resources to the Knowledge Economy*, World Bank ,Washington, DC.

Easterly, W. (2003) *En busca del crecimiento. Andanzas y tribulaciones de los economistas del desarrollo*, Antoni Bosch (ed.), Barcelona.

Easterly, W., M. Kremer, L. Pritchett and L. Summers (1993) "Good policies or good luck? Country growth performance and temporary shocks," Working Paper No. 4474, NBER.

ECLAC (Economic Commission for Latin America and the Caribbean) (2006) *Shaping the Future of Social Protection: Access, Financing and Solidarity*, Santiago, Chile.

ECLAC (2004) *Productive Development in Open Economies*, Santiago, Chile.

ECLAC (1990) *Changing Production Patterns with Social Equity. The Prime Task of Latin American and Caribbean Development in the 1990s*, ECLAC Books, No. 25, Santiago, Chile.

Engermann, S. and K. Sokoloff (2002) "Inequality before and under the law paths of long-run development in the Americas," Annual Bank Conference on Development Economics, Oslo, Norway, June.

Fajnzylber, F. (1992) "Industrialización en América Latina: de la 'caja negra' al 'casillero vacío,'" *Cuadernos de la CEPAL*, No. 60, Santiago, Chile.

Ffrench-Davis, R. (2006) "Macroeconomics-for-growth under financial globalization: four strategic issues for emerging economies," in R. Ffrench-Davis (ed.), *Seeking Growth under Financial Volatility*, ECLAC, Palgrave Macmillan, New York.

Ffrench-Davis, R. (2005) *Reforming Latin America's Economies after Market Fundamentalism*, Palgrave/Macmillan, London.

Ffrench-Davis, R. and J.A. Ocampo (2001) "The globalization of financial volatility: challenges for emerging economies", in R. Ffrench-Davis (ed.), *Financial Crises in "Successful" Emerging Economies*, ECLAC/Brookings Institution, Washington, DC.

Fields, G.S. (2005) "A guide to multizector labor market models," *Social Protection Discussion Papers*, World Bank, Washington, DC, April.

Gavin, M., R. Hausmann, R. Perotti and E. Talvi (1996) "Managing fiscal policy in Latin America and the Caribbean: volatility, procyclicality, and limited creditworthiness," *Working Paper Series*, No. 326, IDB, Washington, DC.

Hausmann, R., D. Rodrik and A. Velasco (2004) "Growth diagnostics," Initiative for Policy Dialogue (IPD), Columbia University.

Jiménez, J.P. and V. Tromben (2006) *Política fiscal en países especializados en productos no renovables en América Latina*, ECLAC, Santiago, Chile.

Katz, J. (2005) "Market-oriented reforms, cycles of destruction and creation of production capacity and the building up of domestic technological capabilities," paper presented at the Seminar on Economic Growth with Equity: Challenges for Latin America", ECLAC, Santiago, Chile, September.

Katz, J. (ed.) (1986) *Desarrollo y crisis de la capacidad tecnológica latinoamericana: el caso de la industria metalmecánica*, ECLAC/IDB/IDRC, Buenos Aires.

Kuznets, S. (1955) "Economic growth and income inequality," *American Economic Review*, 45(1).

Lewis, W.A. (1954) "Economic development with unlimited supplies of labor," *Manchester School of Economics and Social Studies*, 22 May.

Lustig, N., O. Arias and J. Rigolini (2002), "Reducción de la pobreza y crecimiento económico: la doble causalidad," *Serie de informes técnicos del Departamento de Desarrollo Sostenible*, IDB, Washington, DC.

Machinea, J.L. and M. Hopenhayn (2005) "La esquiva equidad en el desarrollo latinamericano. Una visión estructural, una aproximación multifacética," *Serie informes y estudios especiales*, No. 14, ECLAC, Santiago, Chile, November.

Machinea, J.L. and R. López Monti (2005) "Un análisis comparativo de los movimientos de capitales y términos de intercambio en América Latina y el Caribe: 1970–2004", ECLAC, Santiago, Chile.
Machinea, J.L. and C. Vera (2005) "Comercio, inversión directa y políticas productivas," *Serie informes y estudios especiales*, no. 16, ECLAC, Santiago, Chile.
Maloney, W. and G.E. Perry (2005) "Hacia una política de innovación eficiente en América Latina," *Revista de la CEPAL*, no. 87, December.
Morley, S.A. (1998) "La pobreza en tiempos de recuperación económica y reformas en América Latina: 1985–1995", in E. Ganuza, L. Taylor y S. Morley (eds), *Política Macroeconómica y Pobreza: América Latina y el Caribe*, Grupo Mundi Prensa.
Mortimore, M., S. Vergara and J. Katz (2001) "La competitividad internacional y el desarrollo nacional: implicancias para la política de Inversión Extranjera Directa (IED) en América Latina," *Desarrollo Productivo Series*, no. 107, ECLAC, Santiago, Chile.
Perry, G.E., O. Arias, J.H. López, W. Maloney and L. Servén (2006) "Poverty reduction and growth: virtuous and vicious circles," *The World Bank*, Washington, DC.
Rodrik, D. (2006) "Políticas de diversificación económica," *Revista de la CEPAL*, No. 87, December.
Rodrik, D. (2004) "Industrial policy for the twenty-first century," UNIDO, September.
Rodrik, D. (1997) *Has Globalization Gone Too Far?*, Institute for International Economics, Washington, DC.
Ros, J. (2001) *Development Theory and the Economics of Growth*, The University of Michigan Press.
Solimano, A. and R. Soto (2005) "Economic growth in Latin America in the late 20th century: evidence and interpretation," *Serie Macroeconomía del Desarrollo*, No. 33, ECLAC, Santiago, Chile.
Williamson, J. (2003) "Overview: an agenda for restarting growth and reform", in P.P. Kuczynski and J. Williamson (eds.), *After the Washington Consensus: Restarting Growth and Reform in Latin America*, Institute for International Economics, Washington D.C.
Williamson, J. (1990) "What Washington means by policy reform", in J. Williamson (ed.), *Latin America Adjustment: How Much Has Happened*, Institute for International Economics, Washington, D.C.
Wood, A. (1997) "Openness and wage inequality in developing countries: The Latin American challenge to East Asian conventional wisdom", *The World Bank Economic Review*, 11(1).
World Bank (2005) *World Development Report 2006, Equity and Development*, Washington, DC.

Part I

Recent Successful Experiences on Economic Development

2

What Produces Economic Success?

Dani Rodrik[1]

Introduction

Some 20 years ago, it would have been relatively easy to come up with an answer to the question posed by this chapter's title. Economic success, it was thought, could be achieved by loosening the governmental controls that held markets in poor countries in their grip, and by freeing up private economic activity. The strategy was clear: reduce barriers to imports, remove price controls and other market impediments, bring public spending under tight rein, and sell off public enterprises. Such was the nature of the consensus around these policy solutions that researchers that came of age around this time (like me) found themselves driven to do political economy analysis rather than normative economic analysis. After all, it seemed like all the important policy questions had already been answered. We knew what governments needed to do; what was needed was to understand why they failed to do it.[2]

Interestingly, this policy agenda (which came to be known as the Washington Consensus thanks to John Williamson's infelicitous naming) was not derived from the actual experience of any real countries.[3] It was partly a negation of the policies in place – and which, therefore, had become associated with economic failure. Since so many of the countries caught up in crisis and stagnation employed import-substitution

[1]I am grateful to Ricardo Ffrench-Davis, José Luis Machinea, Jaime Ros, and Andrés Solimano for helpful comments. I remain solely responsible for errors.

[2]My 1996 paper "Understanding economic policy reform" captures that general mood quite well, although I did emphasize in that paper that the policy choices made in actual success cases (such as those in East Asia) differed substantially from the agenda on offer at the time.

[3]Chile, an early success, was often portrayed as an instance where policies of the Washington Consensus type had paid off handsomely. But the reality was quite different (Ffrench-Davis, 2005).

policies, had high barriers to trade, and ran large fiscal imbalances, it seemed to follow that the removal of these would unlock their growth potential. It took some stretching for the experience of East Asian countries to fit into this picture, but that too was done. It was also partly a reflection of economists' implicit ideological preference for markets over governments. Economists tend to think that even advanced countries would be richer if they had fewer government controls in place. When the crises of the 1980s created temporary space for technocrats to substitute for politicians, these predilections shaped the reform agendas that emerged.

The past two decades have led to considerable rethinking and soul-searching. This is not the place to revisit the dissatisfactions with the Washington Consensus, but it is enough to say that things have not worked out as it was hoped. Given the list of policy reforms around the world since 1980, a disinterested observer would have guessed that the countries that most rapidly improved their economic performance would have been Latin America and Sub-Saharan Africa, in that order. The observer would hold little hope for China, India, or Vietnam, economies that still remained mired in state ownership and government controls into the new century. That the outcomes have been so different leaves us with an interesting paradox: the last quarter century has been a great time for economic development (as large populous countries like China, India, and Vietnam have made important strides forward), but a bad time for economic development *policy* as conceived in Cambridge, MA, or Washington, DC. Luckily for the world, Beijing, Delhi, and Hanoi had domestic drummers they listened to.

Today there are few who want to take credit for the policies of the 1990s in Latin America. Even John Williamson, with justification, says that what ended up being implemented was not quite the moderate market-oriented agenda he had in mind, but one that went considerably beyond (especially in the financial arena) in the direction of market fundamentalism. And those who had a hand in running the economies say, also with justification, that the reform agenda they embarked on is one that requires much deeper political and institutional underpinnings than they realized at the time.

But what are the real lessons of the last quarter century? Where do we go from here? I begin by providing an overview of the range of views that exist at present. These views point to an emergent "consensus" that is significantly less self-assured about the ability of economists to proscribe potent treatment, views reform as heavily dependent on context and therefore varying from country to country, and looks at institutions as the ultimate arbiter of how things will go. I am in agreement with much of this. But I also emphasize two potential downsides with this emergent approach, which I will argue need to be confronted head-on. First, the idea that institutional quality is the ultimate determinant of economic convergence should not detract us from the myriad small things that countries can do – and which fall far short of institutional change – to get economic growth started. Second, the idea that growth policies are context-specific does not mean "anything goes," or that we lack a universal approach to designing growth strategies. These ideas are developed in the penultimate sections of the paper.

Current thinking: Where we are

Throughout the 1990s, ECLAC has advocated a more structuralist, more market-skeptic agenda that has held quite well over time, and which I think points us in the right direction as we look into the future (see for example ECLAC, 2002, 2004; Ffrench-Davis, 2005). ECLAC has always had a "productivist" approach to economic policy – one that emphasizes the needs of the real economy and of the more advanced sectors within it. It has not been shy in pushing for activist public policies to facilitate economic restructuring. This gives ECLAC its distinctive outlook among international institutions.[4] ECLAC has also led the way with its proposals on reforming global economic governance – for example by calling for greater acceptance of national economic diversity and by advocating the symmetric treatment of labor and capital mobility.

Other institutions, often having played the role of cheerleader for the reforms of the 1980s, and 1990s have had to adjust their views. It is interesting to see the result. Most noteworthy in this respect is the World Bank's recent report on "Lessons of the 1990s" (World Bank, 2005). This document is upfront about several myths that need to be cleared away before progress can be made on growth policies. It acknowledges that economic performance in the 1990s cannot be easily explained by the prevailing views on reform; that reforms that went aggressively after efficiency triangles often overlooked large growth rectangles; that financial liberalization was often oversold; that there are many different ways to implement first-order principles such as openness to trade and macroeconomic stability (other than import liberalization and reduction in government spending); that successful countries were those that used their policy autonomy to devise creative strategies to target their specific binding constraints to growth; that institutional reform is a lot more complicated than simply substituting rules for discretion; that pragmatic, incremental reforms may dominate ambitious efforts; and so on. Many of these are quite radical ideas, at least by the standards of the 1990s, and it is not surprising that they remain controversial within the World Bank itself. Yet, it looks from the outside as if (at least some of) the operational staff of the Bank are

[4]This tradition extends of course all the way back to the institution's first leader, Raul Prebisch.

genuinely looking for ways to turn these findings into concrete growth strategies for their clients.[5]

A new report from the Inter-American Development Bank (2005) represents a breakthrough of a different kind. First, it takes it as a starting point that there are no given set of policies that can be relied on to generate economic growth, and that similar policies work very differently in different settings. Hence the maintained assumption itself is an important break with established precedent – and shows the extent to which the arguments that the World Bank's (2005) aforementioned report takes pains to establish are already being internalized. The core of the IDB's report is an analysis of the *political process* through which policies get on the agenda, get adopted, and are implemented. By way of analysis, we get not cross-country growth regressions, but choice-theoretic models that trace out the incentive effects of political and institutional arrangements. In this treatment, economic policies are entirely the endogenous outcome of political equilibria. The action lies in institutional arrangements and rules, not in policies per se. In effect, the message to policy makers is this: the process by which policies get determined is more important than the nature of the policies themselves. So don't worry about trade liberalization, say, or about the size of the deficit. Worry instead about the nature of political/institutional arrangements that generate your trade and fiscal policies.

Contrast all this with the line taken by the IMF, as exhibited in a recent report on Latin America (Singh *et al.*, 2005). The basic argument here is that Latin American countries did basically the right things, but that their efforts did not go deep enough. Using the report's own words, "reforms were uneven and remained incomplete" (p. xiv). "More progress was made," the report claims, "with measures that had low up-front costs, such as privatization, relative to reforms that promised greater long-term benefits, such as improving macroeconomic and labor market institutions, and strengthening legal and judicial systems" (p. xiv). The same diagnosis is expressed, using less diplomatic language, in the title of one of Anne Krueger's speeches on policy reform: "Meant well, tried little, failed much" (Krueger, 2004). Hence the uneven and disappointing growth performance of the region. The policy implication of this diagnosis is basically simple: do more of the same.

At some level, the analyzes of the World Bank, the IDB, and the IMF are quite similar: Latin American policy makers stopped at fixing the policies (and the "easy" ones at that), whereas the main problem was getting the

[5]Roberto Zagha of the World Bank was the key individual behind the "Lessons of the 1990s" report. Ricardo Hausmann and I have been collaborating with him and other Bank staff in an effort to employ a "Growth Diagnostics" framework to generate tailor-made programs for specific countries.

institutions right. Such analyzes exhibit an increasingly common habit of thought which we might call "institutions fundamentalism," to relate to and distinguish from the earlier obsession with "market fundamentalism."[6] Unfortunately, too little effort goes typically to trying to understand what "getting institutions right" means in this context and how one gets the needed institutions up and running. These questions are of course truly hard, and I am not even sure that economists are the best placed to answer them. The IDB report referred to earlier does a good job of drawing on the relevant academic literature and linking it up with Latin American realities.

With few exceptions, academics have had relatively little engagement with this debate. One of the exceptions is William Easterly, whose survey for the forthcoming *Handbook on Economic Growth* tries to come to grips with the reality of unfulfilled reform potential (Easterly, 2004). His detailed work shows that what we once thought we had – systematic, predictable, robust relationships between policy variables on the right hand side of a regression and growth outcomes on the left – was simply a mirage. Change your sample a bit, try a different time period, use an alternative estimation technique, or alter the proxy for the policy in question, and the original result is likely to disappear before you can say "robustness test." Easterly's take from this is in line with the emergent consensus: what matters are not "policies" but "institutions." It is good institutions that make the difference between wealth and poverty. Trying to implement good policies does not buy you much unless you are able to put in place appropriate institutions of property right protection, rule of law, and governance.

Philippe Aghion (in work that is mostly joint with Peter Howitt) takes a different approach (Aghion and Howitt, 2005). In his work, the key feature of countries that determines the suitability of different policies is their distance from the world technology frontier. The challenge for countries that are at or near the frontier is to innovate – develop new technologies and products. The challenge for countries that are far from the frontier (most poor countries) is to imitate – that is, adopt technologies and products that have already been developed elsewhere. In a series of models, Aghion and his co-authors show that what works in the former set of countries may not work in the latter. Subject a firm in the latter kind of country to greater competition from a firm in a frontier country, and the firm will simply drop out (since it has no hope of catching up). Policies of protection and regulation may therefore be appropriate – at least for a while – during the process of technological catch-up. Aghion argues that this kind of model

[6] I have contributed to institutions fundamentalism with Rodrik *et al.* (2004). One serious challenge to institutions fundamentalism has been launched by Glaeser *et al.* (2004) who find the empirical approach in the institutions-cause-income literature flawed and think it is human capital (and dictators) that cause growth.

has the potential to explain why reforms in a wide range of areas have produced disappointing results in poorer countries.

Even this brief overview of the recent literature shows how far we have come from the early days of the Washington Consensus. The confidence in economists' ability to prescribe growth-promoting policies has taken a heavy battering. "Quick fixes" (i.e., simple policy reforms and market liberalization) have been replaced with "deep fixes" (i.e., institutional change). "Different strokes for different folks" has been transformed from a heretical notion to a near-mainstream idea.

As useful as much of this correction is, it also has potentially debilitating side effects. Institutions are by their very nature deeply embedded in society. If growth indeed requires major institutional transformation – in the areas of rule of law, property rights protection, governance, and so on – we necessarily need to be pessimistic about the prospects for growth in poor countries. After all, such institutional change typically happens very rarely – perhaps in the aftermath of war, civil wars, revolutions, and other major political upheavals. The cleanest cases that link institutional change to growth performance occur indeed at such historical junctures: consider for example the split between East and West Germany, or of North and South Korea. But, what are poor countries that do not want to go through such upheavals to do?

Second, the conclusion that policies work differently in different settings and the recommendation that countries need to develop their own specific fixes can generate undesirable consequences. They can easily turn into policy nihilism ("nothing really works"), lack of policy discipline ("anything goes"), or evasion of responsibility by outsiders ("they need to work out their own problems").

Luckily, as I will demonstrate in the rest of the chapter, neither set of implications is warranted. Growth can be generated without major institutional reform, and there are common diagnostic tools that countries can use to design their own, context-specific growth policies.

Igniting growth: What do the data say?

If deep and wide-ranging institutional change were a prerequisite for economic growth, high-growth episodes would be rare and they would be accompanied by these tumultuous transformations. In fact, growth accelerations tend to be quite common, and they are accompanied by significant institutional changes only infrequently.

We know this from some work I have done with my colleagues Ricardo Hausmann and Lant Pritchett and reported in Hausmann *et al.* (2005). We defined a "growth acceleration" as an instance in which an economy increased its growth rate by at least 2 percentage points per annum, and maintained high growth for a period of at least 8 years. We excluded extremely small countries from the analysis (since they have highly volatile

Table 2.1 Frequency of growth episodes (%)
Number of growth episodes divided by number of datapoints in that decade and region

	Region								
Decade	*Asia*	*Africa*	*Middle East*	*Europe*	*Latin America*	*Other*	*Total*	*Episodes*	*Observations*
1950s	11.11%	5.26%	22.22%	12.82%	3.77%	10.00%	8.78%	13	148
1960s	6.12%	3.49%	5.26%	0.76%	2.78%	6.90%	3.44%	23	668
1970s	3.36%	2.46%	6.06%	0.00%	2.81%	1.89%	2.49%	23	922
1980s	5.30%	0.56%	1.12%	2.78%	0.97%	0.00%	1.62%	16	990
1990s	3.13%	1.10%	0.00%	4.26%	5.45%	4.76%	2.96%	8	270
Total	4.90%	1.87%	4.08%	2.34%	2.53%	2.89%	2.77%	83	2,998
Episodes	18	20	10	12	17	6	83		
Observations	429	965	245	513	673	173	2,998		

Source: Hausmann *et al.* (2005).

Table 2.2 Acceleration probabilities: income quartiles against decade and region

	Income Quartile (4 is the highest)					
Decade	*1*	*2*	*3*	*4*	*Total*	*Episodes*
1950s	8.33%	5.41%	10.81%	10.53%	8.78%	13
1960s	5.52%	2.94%	1.83%	3.51%	3.44%	23
1970s	3.96%	3.45%	2.63%	0.00%	2.49%	23
1980s	1.23%	1.60%	2.02%	1.60%	1.62%	16
1990s	3.03%	2.94%	2.99%	2.90%	2.96%	8
Total	3.54%	2.77%	2.69%	2.10%	2.77%	83
Episodes	26	21	20	16	83	

Source: Hausmann *et al.* (2005).

Table 2.3 Predictability of growth accelerations

(a) *All growth episodes*	
Percentage proportion of growth accelerations that are preceded or accompanied by:	
Economic liberalization	14.5
Political regime change	49.4
External shock	27.5
Percentage proportion of occurrences of column variable that is accompanied or followed by growth accelerations:	
Economic liberalization	18.8
Political regime change	13.9
External shock	5.2
(b) *Sustained growth episodes only*	
Percentage proportion of sustained growth accelerations that are preceded or accompanied by:	
Economic liberalization	18.8
Political regime change	53.1
External shock	33.3
Percentage proportion of occurrences of column variable that is accompanied or followed by sustained growth accelerations:	
Economic liberalization	22.2
Political regime change	8.5
External shock	2.1

Source: Hausmann *et al.* (2005).

Notes: We allow for a five-year lag between a change in the underlying determinant and a growth acceleration. The timing of the growth acceleration is the three year window centered on the initiation dates.

economies) and also ruled out cases of recovery from extended crises (by requiring that the pre-acceleration level of income be exceeded during the episode). Data limitations meant that we could search for such accelerations during the 1957–92 time span and for 106 countries. We were surprised by the large number of growth episodes that our filter identified: 83 cases in all. Summary statistics on these cases are presented in Tables 2.1 and 2.2.

While many of these growth take-offs are well known (e.g., China 1978, Argentina 1990, Mauritius 1971, Korea 1962, Indonesia 1967, Brazil 1967, Chile 1986, Uganda 1989), many others are not. Aside from the sheer *number* of accelerations, the *magnitude* of the typical acceleration is also striking. Conditional on a growth acceleration of at least 2 percentage points, the average (median) acceleration was 4.7 (4.0) percentage points. In other words, in the typical episode output reached almost 40 percent higher at the end of the episode than it would have been in the absence of an acceleration. Of the 106 countries in the sample, 60 (or 54.5 percent) have experienced at least one growth acceleration and 23 (or 20.9 percent) have experienced two (or more) accelerations. The average probability that a country would experience an acceleration in any given decade was about 1 in 4. Moreover, accelerations were common in all regions of the world. It is not surprising to learn of course that East Asia had the highest incidence of growth accelerations. But while Sub-Saharan Africa had the lowest incidence, we still identified 20 instances of growth take-offs there.

Note from Table 2.2 that growth accelerations were most frequent in the lowest income quartile and least frequent in the highest quartile, indicating that the forces of economic convergence are (at least weakly) in play. This is largely inconsistent with the view that poverty traps are a dominant feature of the low-income world. The poor countries in our sample have, if anything, a higher probability that they will experience growth take-offs.

Since the institutional indicators that most research focuses on vary very little over time, it is a foregone conclusion that they cannot explain this growth pattern. To probe this issue deeper, we next asked whether standard explanators could help explain these growth take-offs. We categorized explanatory variables under three headings: (i) economic reform (captured by the Wacziarg–Welch [2003] index); (ii) political change (captured by a three-point or larger move in country's Polity score); and (iii) external shock (captured by exceptionally favorable movements in the terms of trade). The question is the extent to which these variables are able to predict the growth take-offs in our sample. To give them the maximum chance to have an effect, we allowed up to a 5-year lag, and placed the growth acceleration date in a 3-year window centered on the date that our exercise had identified. The core of the exercise consists of a series of probit regressions, but Table 2.3 below summarizes the results quite well.

Table 2.3 shows the answers to two types of questions: (a) what proportion of growth accelerations are preceded or accompanied by changes in our list of determinants; and conversely, (b) what proportion of changes in the determinants are accompanied or followed by growth accelerations. With regard to economic reform, the table shows that only 14.5 percent of accelerations are associated with major economic liberalization – or, equivalently, that 85.5 percent of growth accelerations are not preceded or accompanied by liberalizations. Moreover, fewer than one in five episodes (18.8 percent) of economic liberalization are followed by growth take-offs. With regard to political changes, we find that around half of growth accelerations are preceded by political-regime changes. This may seem high, but on the other hand only a tiny proportion of political-regime changes (13.9 percent) are followed by growth accelerations. So it appears that political regime changes result in a lot of false-positives. Finally, the relationship between growth accelerations and positive terms-of-trade shocks is quite weak. Somewhat more than a quarter of growth accelerations are preceded by such shocks, but only 5 percent of positive terms-of-trade shocks are followed by growth accelerations.

Would the analysis lead to different results if we were to restrict attention to growth accelerations that are *sustained* beyond our 8-year horizon? Would the determinants do better if we were to focus solely on cases of *sustained* growth accelerations? The short answer is no. The bottom panel of Table 2.3 shows the relevant numbers. Only 18.8 percent of sustained growth episodes are preceded or accompanied by major economic liberalization, while only 22.2 percent of economic liberalizations are followed by sustained growth take-offs. Once again, around half of all growth take-offs are preceded by political changes, but the vast majority of political changes do not produce economic booms. The bottom line is clear: growth accelerations seem to be driven largely by idiosyncratic causes.

To sum up the results, far from being a rare event, growth take-offs (that last for the better part of a decade) are quite a common occurrence. There is a poor match between occurrences of growth takeoffs and favorable external, economic, or political circumstances. In particular, there is scant evidence that major institutional reform – of the economic or political kind – is the *sine qua non* of growth take-offs.

How do we reconcile this with the view that emphasizes the centrality of institutions? Very simply, by distinguishing between what it takes to *ignite* growth and what it takes to *sustain* growth. The empirical analysis I reported on above deals with the first challenge only. It addresses the question of stimulating growth, and suggests strongly that deep-seated institutional reforms are not required. But sustaining economic growth is a somewhat different matter. As countries grow, they need to develop institutional capabilities across the board in order to withstand the inevitable shocks along the way and to maintain continued productive dynamism. So ultimately convergence does matter on institutions, but only in the long term. Conversely, institutional reform does not guarantee growth take-offs because it does not necessarily target the immediate constraints on economic growth (as I will elaborate in the next section). So the distinction between igniting and sustaining growth – and the possibility that they may have different prerequisites – has immense practical implications. It suggests that addressing the problem of low growth with a large institutional reform agenda is neither necessary nor effective. This is where I think the new institutions fundamentalism goes wrong.

In support of this line of argument, note that the empirical literature that underpins institutions fundamentalism (Acemoglu *et al.*, 2001; Easterly and Levine, 2002; Hall and Jones, 1999; Rodrik *et al.*, 2004) is all based on regressing *income* on some measure of institutional quality. The dependent variable is income, not growth. Therefore, the appropriate interpretation of this literature is that it demonstrates a long-term relationship between these two variables. Measures of institutions enter *growth* regressions in a much less strong way. Their statistical and quantitative significance depends on the sample of countries, time period considered, and the nature of the covariates. Therefore, the finding that income convergence is strongly dependent on institutions in the long-run is not inconsistent with the finding that growth episodes do not correlate strongly with institutional causes.

So what are the implications for growth policies?

The preceding discussion suggests that the focus of growth strategies should differ depending on where an economy is in the growth process. If the economy is already growing, policy makers need to focus on the institutional underpinnings of a modern market economy to ensure that growth does not run out of steam and that full convergence is achieved. This means enhancing the legal and judicial system, public administration, regulatory, fiscal, and monetary institutions, and so on; it also means deepening (or establishing) democratic rule and participatory politics. Without such reforms, growth will either peter out or stop in its tracks when the economy is hit with an external shock.[7] But when the economy is not growing, which is the more typical situation, the focus has to be igniting growth in the short run. The

[7]The inability to respond to negative external shocks can be traced ultimately to poor institutions of conflict management (Rodrik, 1999). See Solimano and Soto (2004) for a recent analysis of growth cycles in Latin America, including growth crises.

just-mentioned institutional reforms are surely good for an economy;[8] but they will not necessarily ignite growth because they do not necessarily address the most binding constraints on growth. Policy makers need to engage in a diagnostic process to uncover what these binding constraints are, and target them directly. In this section, I develop this last point drawing on Hausmann *et al.* (2004) and Rodrik (2004).

In a world where technology allows advanced countries to produce tens of thousands of dollars worth of output per year per worker and where markets are global, poor countries must remain poor because their economies malfunction in some way. Typically, of course, there is not a single source of malfunction. There is a wide range of syndromes associated with poverty and low growth: entrepreneurs do not want to invest, schooling is low, public health is poor, infrastructure is weak, credit is highly rationed, markets are small and segmented, the tax and regulatory burden is too high in the formal sectors, and government officials are often corrupt. While this may suggest that we need to work on all these fronts simultaneously to create the conditions for growth, the strategy that this implies is in fact a non-strategy. It essentially amounts to eliminating poverty by removing all the symptoms associated with it. Yes, Sierra Leone will indeed look like Sweden once its markets and institutions work like those of Sweden – but that does not much help policy makers in Sierra Leone.

A genuine growth strategy requires the identification of priorities, areas that we need to tackle first before we move on to the others. Amazingly, operational country work in multilateral and bilateral lending agencies is rarely based on an explicit methodology for generating these priorities. To the extent that a prioritization strategy can be discerned, it usually consists of some kind of benchmarking exercise: indicators are compared in a cross-country setting, and the dimensions on which the country looks furthest behind are selected as areas which require the most immediate attention. So if a country looks bad in terms of its ICT indicators – relative to other countries at similar income levels – this is taken as an indication that improving information technology is a priority. Or if a country's trade policies look less liberal than those of its peer group, this is taken as an indication that trade liberalization needs to be on the agenda. This kind of exercise can be done at various levels of sophistication, but it is rarely based on an actual analysis of what is holding a country back. The implicit assumption is that reform will have the largest growth payoff when it tackles the "distortions" that look the largest by cross-national standards. That is obviously false, since the partial derivative of economic perfor-

[8]Some standard institutional reforms can backfire if undertaken too early in the development process. An IPR regime or an independent central bank are some possible examples.

Figure 2.1 Growth diagnostics

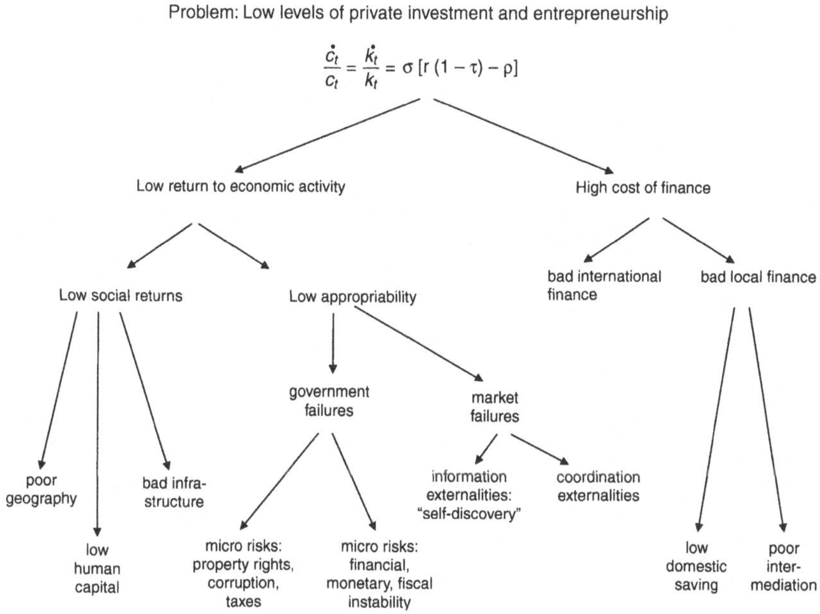

Source: Hausmann *et al.* (2004).

mance with respect to any particular distortion depends on a whole host of structural characteristics, only a few of which are directly observable to the policy analyst.

The obvious alternative is to ask directly what is holding back private investment and economic activity. This can be done with the assistance of the decision tree we developed and used in Hausmann *et al.* (2004), reproduced here (Figure 2.1). The analysis follows a sequential logic. We first ask whether investment (broadly construed) is constrained on the demand or the supply side. In other words, is private investment low because firms and entrepreneurs do not want to invest (low investment demand) or because they do not have adequate access to investment funds (low investment supply). Depending on the answer, we next ask a different set of questions. If the problem is low investment demand, is the problem with low social returns or with low private appropriability? If it is low social returns, is that due to poor infrastructure, poor geography, or low levels of human capital? If it is low appropriability, is it due to market failures such as externalities or to government failures such as high taxes or corruption. If, on the other hand, the problem lies with inadequate investible funds, is that due to problems with domestic finance or problems with external finance? And so on.

This kind of analysis may seem impossible to carry out, but actually it is merely difficult. The central idea that we use in implementing it is to check for diagnostic signals that each one of these problems generates. For example, an economy where investment is constrained by the low investment demand is one where real interest rates will be low or moderate, banks will have plenty of liquidity, creditors will be running after debtors (rather than the other way around), and the current account balance will be positive. An exogenous increase in the availability of foreign resources (an increase in remittances or an improvement in the terms of trade) will lead to a reduction in the domestic saving effort rather than an increase in investment. These kinds of diagnostic tests can be used to distinguish cases like El Salvador and Brazil from each other. Both of these countries have low investment–GDP ratios, but the evidence points to El Salvador being constrained on the investment demand side while Brazil is constrained on the financing side.

Similar diagnostic tests can be performed for other nodes of the decision tree as well. For example, suppose we have identified a case where we think the problem is low investment demand (low private returns to economic activity). We next need to decide whether this is due to low social returns or low private appropriability. To check on the former possibility, we ask whether the tell-tale signs are in place. Hence, if the returns to investment are being held back due to low levels of human capital, we would observe high returns to schooling (a large skill premium). If the constraint is infrastructure, we would observe transport bottlenecks, a high demand for private sources of energy, and so on.

Obviously, much of this is more art than science. But the diagnostic approach offers a systematic way in which binding constraints can be identified, or at least categorized as a prelude to designing growth strategies. It has the virtue that it is a universal tool that can generate country-specific approaches. Putting the framework to work, we can understand why some countries need their financial systems fixed first, others need more schools and clinics, and yet others will only respond to industrial policies that address market failures.

Hence the diagnostic approach embeds all existing approaches to economic development. Indeed it clarifies the maintained assumptions in each of these schools of thoughts. So those who argue for increased foreign aid must be thinking that the binding constraint is lack of domestic saving. Those who want to invest in health and school must think the problem is with low social returns to private investment. Those who want to improve governance must think the problem lies with poor private appropriability of otherwise high social returns. Those who want to implement industrial policies must think that the source of the low private appropriability is coordination and information externalities. This kind of framework helps us carry out a more intelligent discussion about these alternatives, even if it does not definitively resolve who is right.

Diagnostic analysis is only the first step in designing effective growth strategies. The second step is policy design, that is the formulation of policies that best tackle the problems identified in the diagnostic stage. In principle, welfare economics provides the needed tools here: each wedge between market prices and social valuations is best removed by applying the appropriate Pigovian tax or subsidy. In practice, though, second-best issues greatly complicate matters and necessitate imagination and willingness to experiment (Rodrik, 2004).

And finally, there is the need to undertake the diagnosis/policy design analysis on an ongoing basis. It is in the very nature of the diagnostic approach that *a constraint that did not bind initially will eventually become binding as growth picks up*. Building good institutions in the legal, fiscal, regulatory, and governance spheres is in fact nothing other than putting in place the mechanisms that automate the process of diagnosing constraints and generating solutions. Rich countries are those that have managed to put those mechanisms in place. On their way to riches, poor countries need a bit more help from a self-conscious diagnostic exercise of the type sketched out above.

Concluding remarks

I have argued in this chapter that we are seeing the emergence of a new consensus on growth policies. This consensus, correctly in my view, stays away from recommending specific policy reforms. In fact, it is explicitly cautious about our ability to generate systematic policy recommendations. It stresses instead the primacy of institutions, the "rules of the game" in society. It argues, again correctly in my view, that getting these rules to generate the right incentives is much more important in the long run than any specific policy action (such as reducing import barriers or cutting the fiscal deficit). The new consensus is also explicit about the contingent nature of any policy advice: there are no "ten commandments," no quick fixes independent of context. Policies need to be tailored to local circumstances.

The experience with economic growth in the last 60 years does allow us to make some key generalizations. For example, all high-growth countries have pursued *"responsible" monetary and fiscal policies* that prevent high inflation and the buildup of unsustainable debt levels. All successful countries have sought to *integrate with the world economy*. All have provided their investors with *effective property rights and contract enforcement*. All have maintained a certain degree of *social cohesion, solidarity, and political stability*. And the list can be extended to include a few more of these higher-order principles – such as an appropriate environment for productive diversification and innovation, social insurance and safety nets, prudential regulation of financial intermediaries, appropriate management of the exchange rate and of the capital account, and so on.

However, what we have also learned is that these higher-order principles do not map into clear policy recommendations. It is impossible to have observed the patterns of development around the world during the past two decades and not realized that protection of property rights, contract enforcement, macroeconomic stability, integration into the world economy, and so on can be achieved in a number of different ways (Rodrik, 2004).

The major challenge ahead of us is to turn these ideas into an operational framework. I have provided some ideas here on how this can be done. The growth diagnostics approach has the advantage that it is both general and specific. It is general in the sense that it provides a universal approach to designing growth strategies. It is specific in that it aims to identify bottlenecks that are particularly costly to growth in the setting under analysis. My colleagues and I have found it to be a useful framework for thinking about the problems of countries like El Salvador and Brazil. But it clearly needs to be road-tested in many other settings before its utility can be truly established.

References

Acemoglu, D., S. Johnson, and J.A. Robinson (2001) "The colonial origins of comparative development: an empirical investigation," *American Economic Review*, 91(5), December, pp. 1369–401.

Aghion, Ph., and P. Howitt (2005) "Appropriate growth policy: a unifying framework," Harvard University, August.

Easterly, W. (2004) "National policies and economic growth: a reappraisal", New York University, February.

Easterly, and R. Levine (2002) "Tropics, Germs, and Crops: How Endowments Influence Economic Development", mimeo, Center for Global Development and Institute for International Economics.

ECLAC (Economic Commission for Latin America and the Caribbean) (2004) *Productive Development in Open Economies*, Santiago, Chile, June.

ECLAC (Economic Commission for Latin America and the Caribbean) (2002) *Globalization and Development*, Santiago, Chile, April.

Ffrench-Davis, R. (2005) *Reforming Latin America's Economies after Market Fundamentalism*, Palgrave Macmillan, London.

Glaeser, E., R. La Porta, F. Lopez-de-Silanes, and A. Shleifer (2004) "Do institutions cause growth?" *Journal of Economic Growth*, September.

Hall, R. and Ch.I. Jones (1999) "Why do some countries produce so much more output per worker than others?" *Quarterly Journal of Economics*, 114(1), February, pp. 83–116.

Hausmann, R., L. Pritchett, and D. Rodrik (2005) "Growth accelerations", *Journal of Economic Growth*.

Hausmann, R., D. Rodrik, and A. Velasco (2004) "Growth diagnostics", Harvard University, October.

Inter-American Development Bank (2005) *The Politics of Policies: IPES 2006*, Washington, D.C.

Krueger, A.O. (2004) "Meant well, tried little, failed much: policy reforms in emerging market economies", Remarks at the Roundtable Lecture at the Economic Honors Society, New York University, New York, March 23.
Rodrik, D. (2004) "Rethinking growth policies in the developing world", Harvard University, October.
Rodrik, D., A. Subramanian, and F. Trebbi (2004) "Institutions rule," *Journal of Economic Growth*, No. 2.
Rodrik, D. (1999) "Where did all the growth go? External shocks, social conflict and growth collapses," *Journal of Economic Growth*, December.
Rodrik, D. (1996) "Understanding economic policy reform," *The Journal of Economic Literature*, 34(1), March, pp. 9–41.
Singh, A., A. Belaisch, C. Collyns, P. De Masi, R. Krieger, G. Meredith, and R. Rennhack (2005) *Stabilization and Reform in Latin America: A Macroeconomic Perspective on the Experience since the Early 1990s*, IMF Occasional Paper, February.
Solimano, A. and R. Soto (2004) "Economic growth in Latin America in the late 20th century: evidence and interpretation," ECLAC, May.
Wacziarg, R. and K. Horn Welch (2003) "Trade liberalization and growth: new evidence," Stanford University, November.
World Bank (2005) *Economic Growth in the 1990s: Learning from a Decade of Reform*, World Bank, Washington, DC.

3
Development Success: May History Breed Humility

William Easterly[1]

> The nature of man is intricate; the objects of society are of the greatest complexity: and therefore no simple disposition or direction of power can be suitable either to man's nature or to the quality of his affairs.
>
> Edmund Burke (1790)

> It is not reasonable to assume that a complete reconstruction of our social system would lead at once to a workable system.
>
> Karl Popper (1971)

> The curious task of economics is to demonstrate to men how little they really know about what they imagine they can design.
>
> F.A. Hayek (1988)

Introduction

The past quarter-century (not to mention the past half-century) has been a humbling one for advisors striving to discover the secrets to development success. This chapter argues that there are three facts that should prove particularly humbling: (1) the failure of structural adjustment and shock therapy, (2) the rarity of "miracles", and (3) the homegrown nature of most success stories, with only a limited role for outside advice and foreign aid.[2] This chapter reviews these facts, and concludes with some thoughts for policy advisors.

---

[1]I am grateful for research assistance from Elizabeth Potamites, and for comments received by conference participants, and for separate comments by Ricardo Ffrench-Davis, José Luis Machinea, and Andrés Solimano.

[2]This continues some work presented earlier in Easterly (2001), and some material forthcoming in Easterly (2006). For some related thoughts, see Birdsall *et al.* (2005).

Fact 1: The failure of structural adjustment and shock therapy

Structural adjustment loans (SALs) were the brain-child of World Bank President Robert McNamara and his deputy Ernest Stern, who sketched out the idea on a flight the two took together to the Bank-Fund Annual Meeting in Belgrade in September 1979. Structural adjustment loans were loans given to finance imports, conditional on countries adopting free markets (see Table 3.1). The IMF, who had already been doing conditional

Table 3.1 Structural adjustment loans, growth, and inflation in poor countries with most structural adjustment loans received

	Number of IMF and World Bank adjustment loans 1980–99	*Annual per capita growth rate from the date of first structural adjustment loan (%)*	*Annual inflation rate from first adjustment loan to 1999 (%)*
African countries that were in the world's top 20 of structural adjustment loans received in 1989			
Niger	14	–2.30	2
Zambia	18	–2.10	58
Madagascar	17	–1.80	17
Togo	15	–1.60	5
Cote d'Ivoire	26	–1.40	6
Malawi	18	–0.20	23
Mali	15	–0.10	4
Mauritania	16	0.10	7
Senegal	21	0.10	5
Kenya	19	0.10	14
Ghana	26	1.20	32
Uganda	20	2.30	50
Top ten recipients of structural adjustment loans over 1990–99 among Ex-Communist Countries (growth and inflation measured from first adjustment loan to 1999)			
Ukraine	10	–8.4	215
Russian Federation	13	–5.7	141
Kyrgyz Republic	10	–4.4	25
Kazakhstan	9	–3.1	117
Bulgaria	13	–2.2	124
Romania	11	–1.2	114
Hungary	14	1.0	16
Poland	9	3.4	52
Albania	8	4.4	40
Georgia	7	6.4	37

Source: Easterly (2006).

loans for a long time, signed on to the new idea as well. What was the inspiration for the World Bank financing comprehensive reforms instead of financing piecemeal improvements? The idea was that developing countries needed the big reforms in order for individual projects to be productive.

This reasoning was appealing. I used to believe in shock therapy and structural adjustment myself. We proponents of such comprehensive reforms convinced ourselves at the time that partial reform will not work unless all of the complementary reforms happen quickly and simultaneously. Sometimes we clinched the argument with a metaphor like "you can't cross a chasm in two leaps." It seemed plausible that the returns to small interventions will be low if the whole economic and political system is messed up, hence the attempt to remake the system in one fell swoop. The "Washington Consensus" was a check-list of all the things that had to be done at once.

What we shock therapists didn't realize is that *all* reforms are partial; it is impossible to do everything at once and no policymaker has enough information to even know what "everything" is. The choice is between large-scale partial reforms (which shock therapy mislabels comprehensive reform) and small-scale partial reforms. Either large-scale or small-scale partial reforms could backfire, but it is much easier to correct the small mistakes than the large mistakes. The unintended consequences problem is greater with a large-scale reform than with a smaller one. The attempted changes at the top are out of touch with the complexity at the bottom, as we will see in this chapter. To make a long story short, the shock therapy often ran afoul of poor institutions that failed to prevent public corruption and private looting.

The World Bank and IMF gave Cote d'Ivoire 26 structural adjustment loans in the 1980s and 1990s. Per capita income plunged throughout the period in one of the worst and longest depressions in economic history. Today, Cote d'Ivoire is mired in civil war. Indeed, it's a little unnerving that almost all recent cases of collapses into anarchy in Africa (Somalia, Zaire, Sierra Leone, Liberia, Burundi, Sudan) were preceded by heavy World Bank and IMF involvement. Although I don't think the IMF and World Bank caused the collapse into anarchy, it would be hard to argue their involvement in these cases had a *positive* long-run effect.

I picked out the African countries that were in the top 20 worldwide in number of structural adjustment loans received from the World Bank and IMF. Most African countries that received intensive treatment from structural adjustment have negative or zero growth. I also list the top 10 recipients of structural adjustment loans in the ex-Communist countries. Most ex-Communist countries that received shock therapy and many structural adjustment loans have sharply negative growth and high inflation (see Table 3.1).

On balance, the outcomes associated with frequent structural adjustment lending are poor. There is the usual problem of selection bias: doctors treat people who are already sick. However, there are three features of structural adjustment outcomes that suggest a *non*-positive effect of IMF and World

Bank SALs. First, things were so bad in so many recipients of structural adjustment that it stretches belief that it had a strong *positive* effect. Second, since structural adjustment loans were repeated year after year, one wonders why the patient did not improve after repeated doses of the medicine. Finally, formal statistical methods to control for possible reverse causality from crises to treatment still finds that structural adjustment lending had a zero or negative effect on economic growth (Easterly, 2005). An influential recent study by Adam Przeworski of NYU and James Vreeland of Yale (2000) still finds that the effect of IMF programs on growth is negative, even controlling for the adverse selection effect. A related piece of evidence: African countries (even the "success stories" such as Ghana and Uganda) couldn't pay back zero-interest Structural Adjustment Loans, and the World Bank and IMF had to forgive the debts.

Structural adjustment was also deployed in the ex-Communist countries of Eastern Europe and the former Soviet Union, where it became known as shock therapy. Unfortunately, the attempted leap across the chasm fell a little short of the other side, as shown in Figure 3.1, aside from the Polish success story. It's hard to know how to attribute blame for this disaster, but clearly the high expectations of the Western reformers were not realized.

Another region where there was great hope for comprehensive reform was Latin America, which had followed a regime of state intervention and restrictions on free trade from the 1950s through the 1970s. After the debt crisis of the early 1980s, in which Latin American countries were cut off from access to new loans from international private banks, they started moving towards free markets. As usual, SALs from the World Bank and IMF supported these comprehensive reforms. One widely-used index shows increasing economic freedom from 1985 to 2000 on average in Latin America (Figure 3.2).

Unfortunately, the comprehensive reform in Latin America has not been accompanied by economic growth. Ironically for structural adjustment proponents, the best period for Latin American growth was in the period of state intervention, 1950–80. If that growth had continued, income in Latin America would now be three times higher than in 1950. Instead in 2003, income is barely twice the level of a half century earlier, with little progress made over 1980–2003 (see Figure 3.3). The backlash against free markets is unfortunately now gaining strength in Latin America, with free markets tarnished by the utopian expectations of structural adjustment.

So we have three regions where there were great hopes for structural adjustment and shock therapy: Africa, the former Communist countries, and Latin America – and three regions where these hopes were dashed. What went wrong?

One response to failure was to do more of the same. The IMF and World Bank kept on doing structural adjustment loans (SALs) for over two decades despite the record of failure. They missed the warning signs that SALs were not working (you could understand this for the early days, but for

Figure 3.1 Growth trajectory in 1990s of intensive-AL transition cases

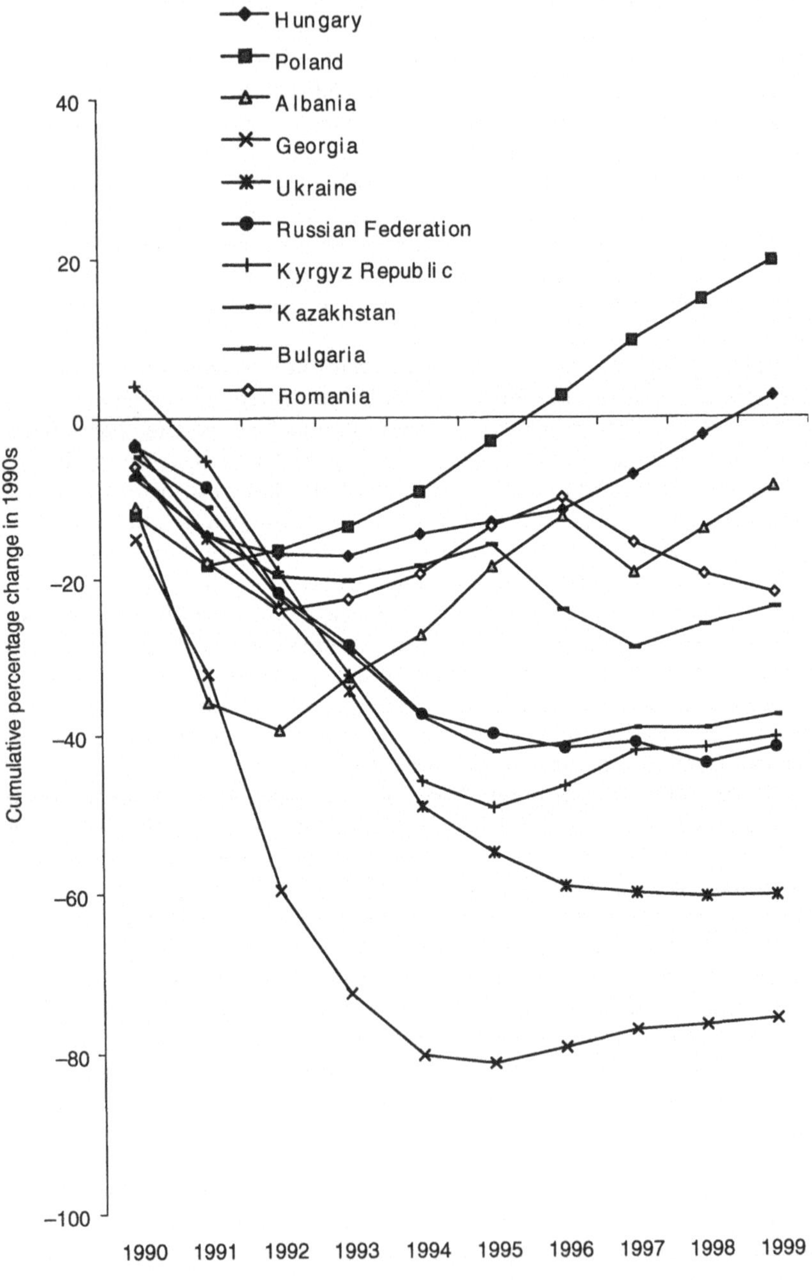

Source: Easterly (2006).

Figure 3.2 Economic freedom index in Latin America

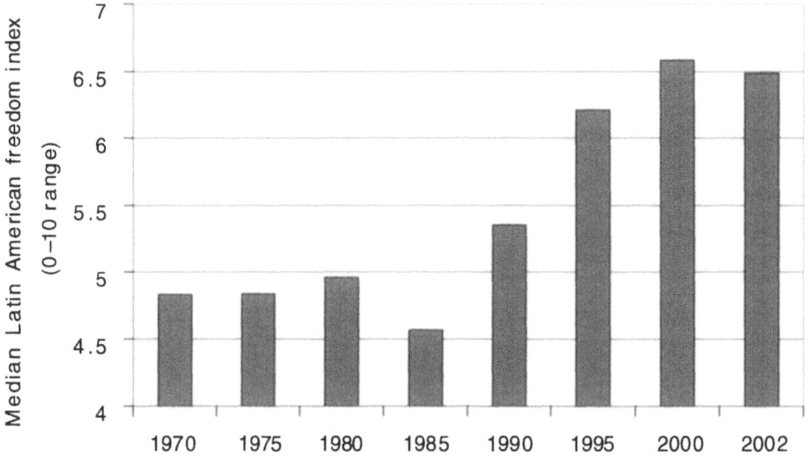

Source: Easterly (2006).

25 years?) Today, they are still doing SALs, they have just changed the name to "Poverty Reduction Support Credits" or "Development Policy Loans" (World Bank) or "Poverty Reduction and Growth Facilities" (IMF).

Why is it so difficult to do successful free market reforms? Economists have realized increasingly in recent years that real and financial market transactions need an awful lot of preconditions to work, such as trust between participants, informal and formal means of contract enforcement, property rights, and security against expropriation by the state, to name just a few. Otherwise, transactions will not take place out of fear of cheating and theft. Where do all these good things come from? Well, they come from a second category of things such as social norms, informal networks of merchants and financiers, formal institutions like courts and police, legal codes, a strong and credible state, and majoritarian democracy with strong protections for minority interests. Where does this second category of things come from? Well, it in turn depends on a third category of things like pre-colonial and colonial history, the disease environment, the agricultural and mineral endowments, other geographic features like climate, luck, location, events elsewhere in the neighborhood, and in general complex bottom-up social and cultural processes that we can barely hope to understand.[3]

[3]I can hardly do justice to the vast literature, which includes Acemoglu *et al.* (2001, 2002, 2004); Dixit (2004); Easterly and Levine (2003); Engerman and Sokoloff (2002); Fafchamps (2004); Glaeser *et al.* (2004); Levine (2005); McMillan (2002); Rauch (2001); Rodrik *et al.* (2004) Seabright (2004); World Bank (2002), as well as earlier classics by Douglass North, Mancur Olson, James Buchanan, Gordon Tullock, and Friedrich Hayek.

Figure 3.3 Per capita income index in Latin America (log base 2 scale, 1950 = 1): actual and trend, 1950–2003

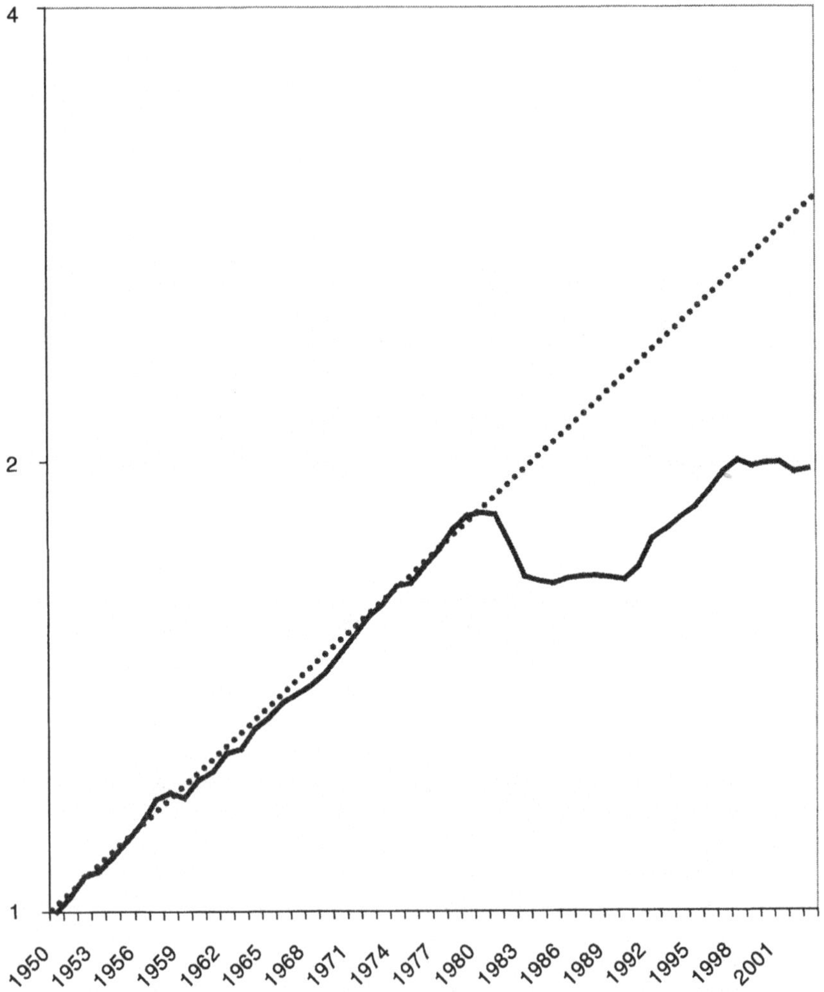

As if all this were not enough, the effects of "free market reforms" reflects not only social and institutional conditions, but expectations about future reforms and social and institutional conditions. As Pritchett (2005) argues: The total output impact of a policy action or an announced policy reform depends on how these change economic agents' beliefs about the future sequence of policy actions (conditional on realizations of states of the world) and how these in turn affect economic agents' choices (investment, reallocation, innovation) and the growth impact of an output impact of any given magnitude is determined by the speed of adjustment to the output impact.

So nobody can design a comprehensive reform for a poor country that creates benevolent laws and good institutions to make markets work. The rules that make markets work reflect a complex bottom-up search for the social norms, networks of relationships, and formal laws and institutions that have the most payoff (see Hausmann *et al.*, 2004). To make things worse, these norms, networks, and institutions change in response to changed circumstances and their own past history. Political philosophers like Burke, Popper, and Hayek had the key insight that this social interplay was so complex that a top-down reform that tries to change all the rules at once can make things worse rather than better.

Avinash Dixit has a more recent example of why top-down reform may have unintended consequences. Suppose a society is facilitating market transactions mainly through informal networks. Such networks are self-enforcing in that any cheater can be expelled from the network and thus lose all future business opportunities. Now suppose that the World Bank twists the arm of the government to set up a system with formal rules overseen by courts. Suppose such a parallel system is at least partially effective, making some business opportunities possible through the formal rules. Now some of the participants in the informal networks can cheat their partners, exit the network, and begin operating in the formal system. A society could get caught in a disastrous in-between situation in which the networks are breaking down, disrupting the previous trades, but the formal system is still operating imperfectly, limiting the scope for new trades. Having two sets of rules is often worse than having one. A reform where the gradual introduction of formal rules *reinforced* the existing networks would have worked better than one that tried to replace them. A plausible story for the evolution of institutions in the West is that that informal relationships and norms in networks gradually hardened into formal rules (which are still supported by informal relationships and norms) (see Hayek, 1973; and Cooter, 1996).

This is armchair speculation, but Dixit's story may help explain why the transition from communism to capitalism was such a disaster, as well as why market reforms in Latin America and Africa were disappointing. Even with severely distorted markets, the participants had formed networks of mutual trades and obligations that made the system functional at some level. Trying to change the rules all at once with the rapid introduction of free markets disrupted the old ties, while the new formal institutions were still too weak to make free markets work well. Gradual movement to freer markets would have given more time for the participants to adjust their relationships and trades.

The main moral of the story is that free market opportunity depends on bottom-up social choices that planners usually don't begin (or try) to understand. When researchers try a little harder (as did many of the

Figure 3.4 Power law of per capita income in pooled sample for 137 countries, 1820, 1870, 1913, 1950, 2001

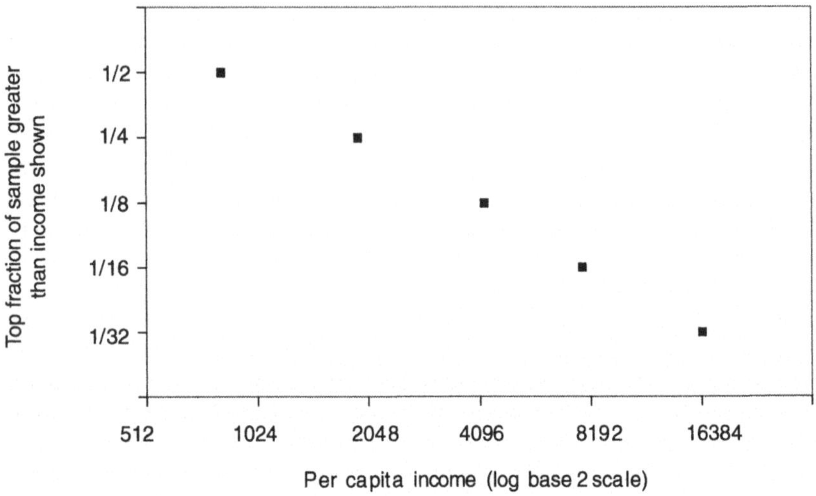

Source: Author's calculations using Maddison (2003) dataset.

hard-working researchers cited here), there is hope for gradual, piecemeal reform and spontaneous efforts by poor people themselves.

Fact 2: Miracles are rare

There is another fact that is so obvious that I am embarrassed to mention it, except that many of the writings on success stories omit to mention it. This is that success stories make up a small minority of cases both in recent experience and in economic history. Figure 3.4 shows this in the form of a power law in which the magnitude of success is inversely and tightly related to the probability of that magnitude being achieved. A power law is when this relationship is linear in logs of both probabilities and outcome magnitudes. Figure 3.4 shows both axes in log base 2 scale, so that a unit increase means a doubling of either income (on the x-axis) or the probability of that income being realized (on the y-axis). The data underlying the graph are the pooled sample of 137 countries with income measured roughly every 50 years. The relationship in the graph shows that every time the magnitude of per capita income is doubled, the probability of attaining that income is roughly halved. What the graph shows is that high income is rare in both time and space: it did not occur until recently in rich countries, and it has not occurred at all for most countries. So the historical experience of 1820–2001 says that for any given country in any given year, there is a probability of $^1/_2$ that per capita income will be higher than \$817,

Table 3.2 Income increases and likelihood from 1950 to 2001

Probability:	*Ratio of 2001 income to 1950 income greater than:*	*Country examples:*
1 out of 32	10.8	South Korea, Taiwan, Botswana, Japan
1 out of 16	7.8	Hong Kong, Singapore, China, Thailand
1 out of 8	5.4	Spain, Portugal, Puerto Rico, Ireland
1 out of 4	3.6	Turkey, Netherlands, Swaziland, Dominican Republic
1 out of 2	2.4	Chile, Switzerland, Jordan, Colombia

Source: Author's own calculation from Maddison (2003) dataset.

while there is only a probability of 1/32 that income will be 16 times higher than that.

Of course, per capita incomes in every country could increase together at the same rate from now on, but since we know there is *no* tendency towards absolute convergence and even some evidence for absolute divergence (Pritchett, 1997), there is no reason to expect the basic power law to change. Moreover, a power law also seems to hold for economic growth magnitudes, as measured by the ratio increase over half centuries from the Maddison data 1820–2001. Large six-fold increases over half a century, like the East Asian miracles, are a rarity.[4]

There is a huge literature on power laws across all the sciences. They show up in such diverse places as earthquakes, avalanches, phase transitions in physics, visits to blogs on the Internet, city populations, war casualties, citations of scientific articles, and firm sizes (Buchanan, 2001). Income and wealth distribution within countries is well known to follow a power law at the higher income and wealth levels.[5] A lot of the writing about power laws gets fairly breathless and seeks to uncover some deep principle of the universe underlying them. More prosaically, they seem to arise when the magnitude of an outcome depends on a lot of complementary factors. There is only a small probability that all of the complementary factors will be aligned for huge success. Mediocre success or even failure happens if any of the complementary factors are askew.

[4]This may seem to contradict a finding by Hausmann *et al.* (2005) that large growth accelerations are common. However, they also find that large growth accelerations are typically not sustained, which is why a large ratio increase over half a century is rare.

[5]Some random references: Brock (1999); Di Guilmi *et al.* (2003); Quadrini and Ríos-Rull (1997).

For those who are interested in history more recent than 1820, Table 3.2 lists the probabilities and income ratio increases for 1950 to 2001, out of a sample of 130 countries (again from Maddison). Large income increases get rare as we approach the stratosphere of very large increases in income (10-fold) over the past half century.

This chapter is not as concerned as the rest of the power law literature as to whether income increases or per capita income levels exactly follow a power law. My much more modest point here is that economic miracles are rare. An awful lot of things have to go right for miracles to occur, like all the complex factors described in the previous section. It is unrealistic to

Table 3.3 Ten best and worst per capita growth rates, 1980–2002

Country name	*Per capita growth (%), 1980–2002*	*Aid/ GDP (%) 1980–2002*	*Percent of time under IMF programs (%), 1980–2002*
Ten best per capita growth rates, 1980–2002			
South Korea	5.9	0.03	36
China	5.6	0.38	8
Taiwan	4.5	0.00	0
Singapore	4.5	0.07	0
Thailand	3.9	0.81	30
India	3.7	0.66	19
Japan	3.6	0.00	0
Hong Kong	3.5	0.02	0
Mauritius	3.2	2.17	23
Malaysia	3.1	0.40	0
median	*3.8*	*0.23*	*4*
Ten worst per capita growth rates, 1980–2002			
Nigeria	−1.6	0.59	20
Niger	−1.7	13.15	63
Togo	−1.8	11.18	72
Zambia	−1.8	19.98	53
Madagascar	−1.9	10.78	71
Cote d'Ivoire	−1.9	5.60	74
Haiti	−2.6	9.41	55
Liberia	−3.9	11.94	22
Congo, Dem. Rep.	−5.0	4.69	39
Sierra Leone	−5.8	15.37	50
median	*−1.9*	*10.98*	*54*

Source: Easterly (2006).

expect to replicate the success of the East Asian (+ Botswana) success stories in a large number of other developing countries, because history speaks loudly that such rapid development is rare.

Fact 3: Most recent success stories are home-grown

Most of the recent success stories are countries that did *not* get a lot of foreign aid and did *not* spend a lot of time in IMF programs, two of the indicators of what outsiders do for a country (Table 3.3). Most of the recent disasters are just the opposite – tons of foreign aid and much time spent in IMF constraints. This of course involves a lot of reverse causality, as the disasters were getting IMF assistance and foreign aid *because* they were disasters, while the IMF and the donors bypassed success stories because they didn't need the help. It thus does not prove that foreign assistance causes disaster. But it does show that outlandish success is very much possible without outside tutelage, while repeated treatments don't seem to stem the tide of disaster in the failures. Most of the recent success in the world economy is happening in Eastern and Southern Asia, not as a result of some global plan to end poverty, but for homegrown reasons.

Moreover, the success stories follow a variety of formulas, perhaps an indication of an exploration that reflected each country's unique history and characteristics (see Hausmann and Rodrik, 2003). South Korea's government intervened in guiding its corporations, while Hong Kong was the poster-child for *laissez-faire* capitalism. China is a unique blend of Communist party dictatorship, state enterprises, and partial free market liberalization. India is a longstanding democracy, South Korea and Taiwan more recent democratic converts, while Singapore is not a democracy. All of these cases did realize most of their success from markets – and thus subjected their reforms to a market test – but some were far from a *laissez-faire* model. While most people believe that free markets and democracy are a big part of the success story of the West, other countries sometimes take a circuitous route to get there, or they may conceivably have their own unique recipe.

Of course, the success story of the West itself was a completely homegrown discovery, rather than following ideal formulas dictated by outsiders. Political scientist Charles Lindblom in a classic article described rich country politics as the "science of muddling through:" He noted in rich democracies that "actual policy practice is a piecemeal process of limited comparisons, a sequence of trials and errors followed by revised trials, [and] reliance on past experience."[6] In their history, rich country democracies did not have to put up with a team of outside experts trying to impose a "Washington Consensus" on them.

[6]Quoted in Scott (1998), p. 327.

Anecdote: Right reform, wrong conditions

Let me illustrate the principles that the above three facts suggest with an anecdote. Mexico for complex historical reasons has failed to evolve good financial laws. Take the example of privatization of Mexican state banks beginning in 1991. Privatization is one of the staples of free market reform urged by the World Bank and IMF. But things did not go according to plan. The problem began with the privatization program itself, in which buyers of the banks could use loans from the banks they were buying to purchase the banks. One buyer covered 75 percent of the purchase price with this trick. Normally, savers would not want to deposit in banks with such shaky financing, but savers had deposit insurance from the Mexican government. The newly privatized banks thus expanded credit rapidly, with little regard for risk.[7] Lax banking regulations allowed them to roll-over loans that borrowers did not repay without even having to declare the loans in default. Bank credit grew by over 20 percent per year in real terms from 1991 to 1994, while past due loans grew by over 40 percent per year.[8] If the banks did try to collect from borrowers, they ran into Mexico's tortuous (civil law) bankruptcy laws, in which it took between three and seven years for banks to recover collateral from borrowers. The reckless credit expansion contributed to the collapse of the peso beginning in December 1994, in which the peso lost half of its value, and Mexico had a severe recession.

In the aftermath of the peso crisis, the government designed a bailout of the banking system's bad loans. Unfortunately, the government (with World Bank and IMF acquiescence) dragged its feet on the bailout. With an anticipated bailout, the banks' owners had incentives to lend to themselves and then default. During 1995–98, the banks gave 20 percent of large loans to individuals on their own boards of directors. The looting of the banks raised the cost of the bailout to the government, which in the end amounted to 15 percent of Mexican annual GDP.

Since 1998, regulation of banks has been much tougher and the government has allowed foreign banks to enter to put competitive pressure on Mexican banks. The bad loan problem has finally been solved, but mainly because banks lend less to the private sector. Because of the still-shaky bankruptcy laws, banks are now extremely cautious about private borrowers – the share of private loans in bank assets declined from 49 percent in 1997 to 30 percent in 2003 (most of the rest goes to government lending). Mexico has still not solved the problem of getting financial markets to

[7]The Chilean banking crisis of 1982 happened even though there was no deposit insurance, but depositors and banks may have expected a government bailout anyway.

[8]Figures from Ross Levine, private communication.

work because of the difficulty in getting the bottom-up rules and incentives right (Haber, 2004). This story may give some insight into why the payoff to Latin America's "free market" reforms was disappointing. In terms of the previous facts, it illustrates how structural adjustment can misfire, it highlights all of the complex ingredients for "miracles," and it shows the dangers of outsiders like the IMF and World Bank imposing a universal blueprint instead of homegrown reformers searching for what works in local conditions.

Conclusions

A number of common-sense prescriptions follow from this rather sweeping and uneven review of recent experience. The first one is for economic policy advisers and international development economists: be humble!

If this sounds like useless moral exhortation, let me quote Karl Popper again on how humble policy advice (piecemeal engineering) proceeds differently from hubristic advice (utopian social engineering): The piecemeal engineer knows, like Socrates, how little he knows. He knows that we can learn only from our mistakes. Accordingly, he will make his way, step by step, carefully comparing the results expected with the results achieved, and always on the look-out for the unavoidable unwanted consequences of any reform; and he will avoid undertaking reforms of a complexity and scope which makes it impossible for him to disentangle causes and effects, and to know what he is really doing. Holistic or Utopian social engineering, as opposed to piecemeal social engineering aims at remodeling the "whole of society" in accordance with a definite plan or blueprint.

When the Yale political scientist and anthropologist James C. Scott summarizes why utopian schemes fail, he goes right to lack of humility: "If I were asked to condense the reasons behind these failures into a single sentence, I would say that the progenitors of such plans regarded themselves as far smarter and farseeing than they really were and, at the same time, regarded their subjects as far more stupid and incompetent than they really were."

Scott's advice for reformers is then to take an experimental approach to social change, and presume that we cannot know the consequences of our interventions in advance. Given this postulate of ignorance, prefer wherever possible to take a small step, stand back, observe, and then plan the next small move.

If this sounds too much like recommending partial equilibrium analysis, so be it! Economic reformers have been seduced by general equilibrium analysis, which is great as a theory but a disaster as a guide to policy reform, given the severe lack of information on the properties of the general equilibrium. Better to take a small step based on partial equilibrium analysis, see what happens in general equilibrium, then adjust accordingly.

Economic intuition will give some insights into the sequence of reforms – as the Mexico example showed, you should probably fix financial laws and regulation before privatizing banks.

Lack of humility also creates unrealistic expectations, which does damage of its own. Reformers promise miracles, and then there is a backlash against market reforms when the miracle does not arrive. Economic development advice should set reasonable expectations instead of promising every country they can grow like the East Asian miracles. The IMF and World Bank routinely over-predicted growth rates in response to reforms.

The industry of studying success stories has failed to generate the ability to replicate them. Indeed, the only common thread to the success stories of the past few decades – the East Asian tigers, China, India, Mauritius, Chile,[9] Botswana, etc. – is that the experimenters in each of these countries (which again were often far from *laissez faire* market economies) subjected their experiments to a market test, often through international markets. Would private foreign investors invest? Would the rest of the world buy what you are producing? The answer was yes in the success stories, which gave them feedback to move in the direction of prosperity, although their paths toward market successes varied drastically from the simplistic visions of shock therapy.

Economics and history yield good intuition into what piecemeal reforms are likely to pay off. The mantra of markets, democracy, and institutions became a mantra because this combination has a long and distinguished historical record and theoretical pedigree. But how to move towards more effective operation of markets, democracy, and institutions is a task for the pragmatic local reformer to experiment with, always sensitive to local conditions, getting lots of feedback on what's working and what's not, and accountable for adjustments when something is not working. Many countries can make gradual progress towards a better tomorrow in this way. Just don't expect to grow like South Korea when you do so!

References

Acemoglu, D., S. Johnson, J. Robinson (2004) "Institutions as the fundamental cause of long-run growth," *Handbook of Economic Growth*, forthcoming http://elsa.berkeley.edu/~chad/handbook9sj.pdf

Acemoglu, D. (2002) "Reversal of fortune: geography and institutions in the making of the modern world income distribution," *Quarterly Journal of Economics*, 117(4), pp. 1231–94, November.

[9]Chile is a good example of the long and torturous road to free market democracy, with reforms beginning under a brutal dictatorship and punctuated by two acute recessions, then some "reform of the reforms," followed by democracy and relatively stable growth. See Ffrench-Davis (2002, 2005).

Acemoglu, D. (2001) "The colonial origins of comparative development: an empirical investigation," *American Economic Review*, 91, pp. 1369–401, December.

Birdsall, N., D. Rodrik, and A. Subramanian (2005) "How to help poor countries," *Foreign Affairs*, pp.136–52, July/August.

Brock, W.A. (1999), "Scaling in Economics: a reader's guide," *Industrial and Corporate Change*, 8(3), pp. 409–46.

Buchanan, M. (2001) *Ubiquity: Why Catastrophes Happen*, Three Rivers Press, New York.

Burke, E. (1790) "Reflections on the Revolution in France", reproduced in I. Kramnick, *The Portable Edmund Burke*, Viking Portable Library, Penguin Putnam, New York, 1999, p. 443.

Cooter, R.D. (1996) *The Rule of State Law and the Rule-of-Law State*, Annual World Bank Conference on Development Economics, 1996.

Di Guilmi, C., E. Gaffeo, and M. Gallegati (2003) "Power law scaling in the world income distribution," *Economics Bulletin*, 15(6), pp. 1–7.

Dixit, A.K. (2004) *Lawlessness and Economics: Alternative Modes of Governance*, Princeton University Press, Princeton NJ.

Easterly, W. (2006) *The White Man's Burden: Why the West's Efforts to Aid the Rest Have Done So Much Ill and So Little Good*, The Penguin Press, New York, forthcoming.

Easterly, W. (2005) "What did structural adjustment adjust? The association of policies and growth with repeated IMF and World Bank adjustment loans," *Journal of Development Economics*, 76, pp. 1–22, February.

Easterly, W. (2001) *The Elusive Quest for Growth: Economists' Adventures and Misadventures in the Tropics*, MIT Press, Cambridge MA.

Easterly, W. and R. Levine (2003) "Tropics, germs, and crops: the role of endowments in economic development," *Journal of Monetary Economics*, 50(1), pp. 3–39, January.

Engerman, S.L. and K.L. Sokoloff (2002) "Factor endowments, inequality, and paths of development among New World economies," *NBER Working Paper* no. 9259.

Fafchamps, M. (2004) *Market Institutions in Sub-Saharan Africa*, MIT Press, Boston, MA.

Ffrench-Davis, R. (2005) *Reforming Latin America's Economies after Market Fundamentalism*, Palgrave Macmillan, Basingstoke.

Ffrench-Davis, R. (2002) *Economic Reforms in Chile: From Dictatorship to Democracy*, University of Michigan Press, Ann Arbor, MI.

Glaeser, E.L., R. La Porta, F. López-de-Silanes, and A. Shleifer (2004), "Do institutions cause growth?," *NBER Working Paper* no. 10568, June. http://papers.nber.org/papers/w10568.pdf

Haber, S. (2004) *Mexico's Experiments with Bank Privatization and Liberalization, 1991–2003*, mimeo, Stanford University, draft of October 18.

Hausmann, R.L. Pritchett, and D. Rodrik (2005) "Growth accelerations", Harvard University, revised, August.

Hausmann, R., D. Rodrik, and A. Velasco (2004) "Growth diagnostics", Harvard University, October.

Hausmann, R. and D. Rodrik (2003) "Economic development as self-discovery", *Journal of Development Economics*, 72(2), pp. 603–33, (revised April 2003).

Hayek, F.A. (1988) *The Fatal Conceit: The Errors of Socialism*, W.W. Bartley III (ed.), University of Chicago Press, Chicago, p. 76.

Hayek, F.A. (1973) *Law, Legislation, and Liberty*, vol. 1, "Rules and Order", University of Chicago Press, Chicago.
Levine, R. (2005) "Law, endowments, and property rights", *Journal of Economic Perspectives*, forthcoming.
Maddison, A. (2003) *The World Economy: Historical Statistics*, OECD.
McMillan, J. (2002) *Reinventing the Bazaar: A Natural History of Markets*, Norton.
Popper, K. (1971) *The Open Society and its Enemies*, Princeton, Princeton University Press, 1971. Quoted in P. Murrell, "Conservative Political Philosophy and the strategy of economic transition," *East European Politics and Societies*, vol. 6(1), Winter 1992.
Pritchett, L. (2005) *Reform is Like a Box of Chocolates: An Interpretive Essay on Understanding the Pleasant and Unpleasant Surprises of Policy Reform, World Bank mimeo.*
Pritchett, L. (1997) "Divergence, big time", *Journal of Economic Perspectives*, 11(3), pp. 3–17.
Przeworski, A. and J.R. Vreeland (2000) "The effect of IMF programs on economic growth," *Journal of Development Economics*, 62, pp. 385-421.
Quadrini, V. and J.-V. Ríos-Rull (1997) "Understanding the U.S. distribution of wealth", Federal Reserve Bank of Minneapolis, *Quarterly Review-Federal Reserve Bank*, Spring, 21(2), ABI/INFORM Global, p. 22.
Rauch, J. (2001) "Business and social networks in international trade," *Journal of Economic Literature*, 39, pp. 1177–03, December.
Rodrik, D., A. Subramanian, and F. Trebbi (2004) "Institutions rule", *Journal of Economic Growth*, No. 2.
Scott, J.C. (1998) *Seeing Like a State: Why Certain Schemes to Improve the Human Condition Have Failed*, Yale University Press, New Haven and London.
Seabright, P. (2004) *The Company of Strangers: A Natural History of Economic Life*, Princeton University Press, Princeton.
World Bank (2002) *Building Institutions for Markets: World Development Report 2002*, ("Institutions for Prosperity"), Oxford University Press, New York.

4
The Dual Divergence: Growth Successes and Collapses in the Developing World Since 1980

José Antonio Ocampo and María Angela Parra[1]

Introduction

Cross-country econometrics has been the preferred tool of empirical growth analysis over the past 20 years. This literature has tended to focus on long time periods, ignoring the instability and volatility of growth patterns in developing countries. Because shocks play a central role in explaining variations in growth patterns in the developing world (Easterly *et al.*, 1993), the meaning of the statistical coefficient estimated for long periods of time is unclear. In this sense, the use of panel data econometrics for shorter periods may be more appropriate, although, for many reasons, not ideal (Pritchett, 2000). Another route is to examine factors that determine growth spurts (accelerations) and collapses. Country-specific historical analysis is a third route (see, for example, Rodrik, 2003, among others), but the comparability of such analyses is a significant limitation in this regard.

This chapter takes the second route, focusing on growth surges and collapses in developing countries and their relation to common external factors that affect the economic performance of these countries. It also looks at the role of patterns of specialization in explaining relative growth performance in recent decades. The first section presents a survey of the still limited empirical literature on growth spurts and collapses. This is followed by a look at the incidence of accelerations and collapses of growth

[1]We are very grateful to Ricardo Ffrench-Davis, Stephany Griffith-Jones, Daniel Heymann, Jorge Katz, Jomo Kwame Sundaram, Rafael López Monti, José Luis Machinea, Stefania Piffanelli, Jaime Ros, Verónica Silva and Lance Taylor for their comments and suggestions, as well as to participants in the Seminar held at ECLAC on September 1–2, 2005.

in developing countries since 1950. We find a "global development cycle" that circumscribes the growth possibilities of developing economies. The third section focuses on the role in this context of specialization patterns and production development strategies. The final section presents some conclusions. Some of the facts that are mentioned are well known, yet, curiously enough, have been generally disregarded in the growth literature.

Survey of literature on growth spurts and collapses

In one of the best known studies on economic growth instability in the developing world Easterly *et al.* (1993) show that a large part of the variance of growth rates of developing countries, even in periods as long as a decade, can be directly explained by shocks – in the terms of trade, in debt crises and sharp changes in net external transfers, and in the form of wars. Furthermore, shocks have an indirect influence on growth by inducing policy changes. In turn, Easterly (2001) underscores the greater vulnerability of poor countries to natural disasters, compared to middle- and high-income countries. The greater sensitivity of low-income countries – particularly Sub-Saharan African countries – to these problems, as well as to civil wars, explains the greater dispersion of growth rates among them.

Looking at discontinuities in the growth experience is important for several reasons. First, the hypothetical determinants of economic growth may have non-linear effects, which imply that the same policy may have different effects in different countries and time periods. Non-linear interactions as well as (positive or negative) feedbacks are involved, for example, in the interaction between human capital and economic development (Ranis *et al.*, 2000).[2] As a result of non-linearities and the inconclusiveness of existing econometric results,[3] it may be impossible to draw policy implications from cross-country econometrics (Brock and Durlauf, 2001; Easterly, 2004; Rodríguez, 2005; Rodrik, 2005).

The second reason is that in economies experiencing substantial shocks, it may be impossible to isolate long-term trends from observable short-term trajectories. The major explanation for this is the path dependence generated by dynamic economies of scale: the close association between technological learning and production experience (i.e. "learning by doing" in a

---

[2]See the analysis of the variable effects of education in different countries and time periods in Azariadis and Drazen (1990).

[3]Indeed, the voluminous literature on cross-country econometrics has identified nearly 150 variables that have statistically significant effects on growth (Durlauf *et al.*, 2004). Because these variables do not necessarily exclude each other, with that technique alone it is impossible to know what priority should be given to each one of them (Brock and Durlauf, 2001).

broad sense), as well as similar processes related to the development of marketing networks and the growth of firms' reputation (goodwill). This means that both negative shocks (an external crisis, a natural disaster, or a war) and positive shocks (the discovery of new natural resources) may have long-term implications.[4] A related issue is that the formation of expectations in economies facing recurrent shocks necessarily involves a learning process (Heymann, 2000).

The origins of shocks are obviously important in this regard. Given the emphasis of the existing growth literature on the *domestic* factors that determine the growth performance of developing countries, the role of *external* shocks affecting performance generally has been downplayed or even ignored in cross-country econometrics. In contrast, external factors have been the focus of the structuralist tradition, with its emphasis on the asymmetries that characterize the functioning of the world economy (Ocampo and Martin, 2003). As we will see, the role of external factors is critical, for major breaks in the growth process in the developing world tend to cluster around specific time periods, indicating that developing economies tend to follow a common cycle, with major breaks clearly associated with the world economy.

The third reason why discontinuities are important is institutional in character. Although all forms of institution-building follow an evolutionary process, this feature is particularly important in *State* institution-building, again due to the "learning" processes involved. An interruption in the process of State building caused by a major economic crisis may thus have long-term implications, as a cursory look at the problems of Latin America following the "lost decade" indicates. The mix of an economic crisis with civil conflict may be particularly problematic, as the experience of several Sub-Saharan African countries over the past quarter century shows. In turn, major political discontinuities, such as revolutions (capitalist as well as socialist) can unleash an institutional restructuring that takes time to mature and may have unexpected twists. The experience of Central and Eastern Europe is the most relevant recent story in this regard. A major implication of this analysis is that, even if a major structural reform eventually has positive long-term effects, it also has transitional costs that may swamp its favorable impacts for a long time. In terms of the debates of the 1980s, this implies that "big bangs" are much less attractive than was believed during the period of structural reforms. Nonetheless, the discussion below will concentrate on economic issues, largely leaving aside these institutional dimensions.

[4]PSee, for instance, Easterly (2001, ch. 10), or the analysis of "Dutch disease" by Krugman (1990, ch. 7), and Van Wijnbergen (1984).

Finally, in terms of the evolution of economic structures, long-term growth should be understood as the result of sequential sector-specific growth spurts, of their intensity and of the domestic linkages that they generate. The noticeable discontinuities that characterize the evolution of production structures and specialization patterns imply that these factors may be crucial to understanding growth dynamics. Cross-country econometrics has failed to give adequate attention to this issue, emphasized in the structuralist tradition (see, for example, Amsden, 2001; Lall, 2001; Palma, 2004). The Kaldorian links running from growth to productivity, associated with the presence of underutilized resources during the growth process, have also been disregarded, as well as the links between productivity convergence, domestic production linkages and external balances (Cimoli and Correa, 2005; Ocampo, 2005a; Rada and Taylor, 2004).

Several attempts have been made in recent years to understand the role of discontinuities in the growth process. Hausmann *et al.* (2004) explore the determinants of episodes of economic growth acceleration since the 1950s. According to their results, accelerations are associated with increases in investment and trade, as well as with real exchange rate depreciation. Accelerations also appear to be linked to changes in political regimes. Positive terms of trade shocks have positive short-term effects, but they are not a significant predictor of sustained accelerations. On the contrary, standard economic reform measures play no role in explaining growth accelerations, although they can help to explain whether or not growth is sustained. The major conclusion of that paper, however, is that most of the variables used in mainstream growth analyses do not seem to play an important role as determinants of growth spurts and, in this sense, growth spurts are highly unpredictable.

Ros (2005), in contrast, considers the factors determining growth collapses. He finds three factors that affect the incidence of such episodes. The first is size: small economies are more likely to face collapses. The second is the pattern of specialization: dependence on raw material exports – particularly mineral exports – is associated with the incidence of reductions in per capita income. The third is income distribution: more unequal societies are likely to face growth collapses. According to Ros, political-economy issues are involved in the latter two links, whereas vulnerability to shocks clearly shows in the first two.

Reddy and Minoiu (2005) examine a similar phenomenon: namely, real-income stagnation, which they define as negligible or negative per capita real-income growth for a significant uninterrupted sequence of years. They find that countries that suffered spells of real income stagnation were more likely to be poor, dependent on primary commodity exports, conflict ridden, and located in Latin America or Sub-Saharan Africa. A majority of landlocked developing countries also tend to be more likely to face long-term stagnation. Stagnation is also very likely to persist over time: countries afflicted with stagnation in the 1960s had a 75 percent likelihood of being afflicted by stagnation in the 1990s as well.

Jones and Olken (2005) claim that changes in physical capital accumulation are not important in explaining growth accelerations and that, at best, they explain only a quarter of the magnitude of growth collapses. Both events instead reflect changes in productivity. Structural breaks are also associated with accelerations or decelerations in the allocation of labor to manufacturing, particularly to advanced manufacturing. Upturns are associated, in turn, with the evolution of trade shares, whereas inflation plays some role in downturns. The authors find that changes in productivity are the major determinant of both growth accelerations and collapses, but they fail to explain what determines major productivity shifts.

"Explaining" differences in growth rates as the result of differences in productivity growth, as do Jones and Olken (2005) and a voluminous literature, is however questionable, on at least two grounds. First, it ignores the short-term and perhaps even the medium-term Keynesian effects of changes in capacity utilization on productivity, which will bias analysis against the effects of capital accumulation.[5] Second, it ignores long-term Kaldorian growth-productivity dynamics, according to which strong positive and negative productivity trends are associated with the more or less intensive utilization of *existing* factors of production: variable *under*-employment of physical capital and of the labor force, including human capital; and variable underutilization of natural resources; and existing infrastructure. These Kaldorian links, recently brought back to the debate by Ocampo (2005a), Rada (2005) and Rada and Taylor (2004) imply that productivity improvements are largely the *result* of economic growth rather than an exogenous determinant of growth (as in the neoclassical development literature). More generally, to the extent that these Kaldorian links are valid, growth and productivity must be explained simultaneously.

The global development cycle

The widening income gap between different regions and countries has been a feature of the world economy for the past two centuries (see Figure 4.1, and Maddison, 1995 and 2001). The only exception to this trend is the

[5]Jones and Olken (2005) try to take this effect into account but do so using rather rough measures of labor force participation and electricity consumption. Their results indicate that there is little change in labor force or capital utilization around either up-breaks or down-breaks. Contrary to this result, Ffrench-Davis (2005) shows that total factor productivity (TFP) estimates tend to be biased in a context of significant changes in capacity utilization. He finds that, once this factor is taken into account, capital stock reappears as the main determinant of growth in most Latin American countries.

Figure 4.1 Per capita GDP growth and dispersion, OECD and developing countries, 1870–2001

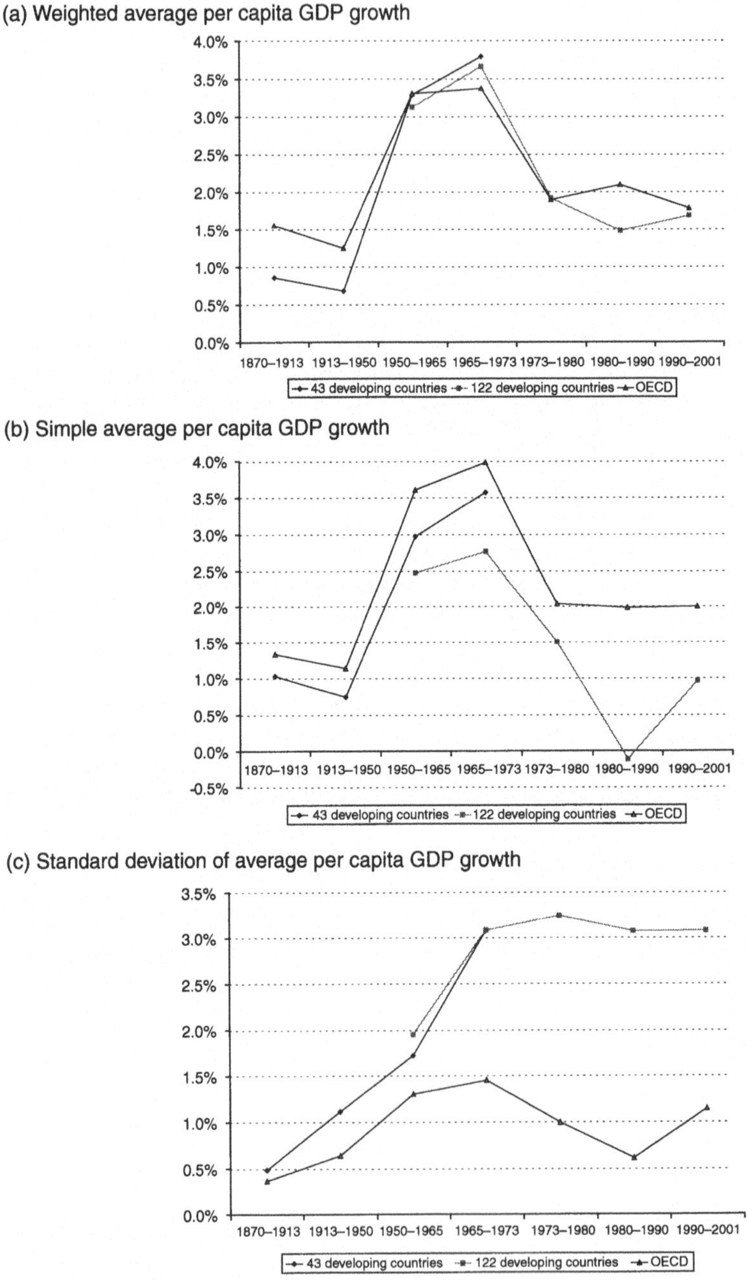

Source: Author's calculations based on Maddison (2001).

period 1965–1973, in which the international per capita GDP gap decreased slightly (as we will point out below, the mid-2000s may be the beginning of another phase of this type, but it is too soon to say whether this reflects a longer-term trend). The story of the developing countries is thus one of "divergence, big time" *vis-à-vis* the industrial world (Pritchett, 1997), with the late phase of the "golden age" the only exception so far in history. This is also the conclusion of the analysis of the effects of inter-country inequality in world income distribution (Bourguignon and Morrison, 2002); growing divergence among countries has also been a major contributor to the growing inequality of world income distribution over the past quarter century, if we isolate the effects of the rapid growth of China and, to a lesser extent, India (Berry and Serieux, 2004).

History has also shown considerable divergence *among* developing countries, particularly since the mid-1960s (Figure 4.1.c). Part of this divergence has been the result of several success stories ("miracles") at different times in various parts of the developing world (China and India being the most recent ones). There are, however, very few instances of "peripheral" countries that have joined the industrial "center" (Japan being the notable exception in this regard, perhaps with some of the "first-tier" Asian NICs). This implies that "miracles" have been more commonly followed by either stagnation at middle- or even low-income levels (a phenomenon that can be called "truncated convergence") or by outright collapses.

Figure 4.2 Percentage of developing countries with per capita GDP growth (five-year moving average) by intervals

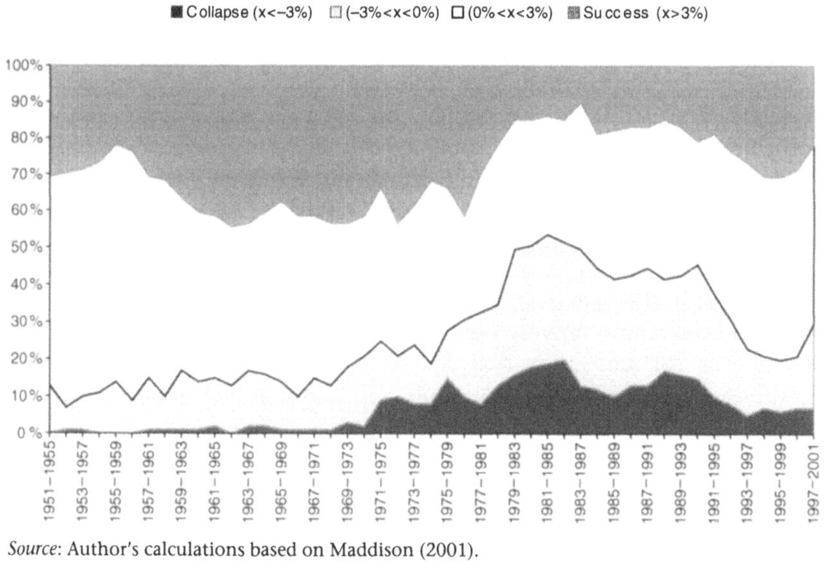

Source: Author's calculations based on Maddison (2001).

This brief overview of historical trends helps to underscore the basic "stylized fact" about the post-war development experience which serves as the starting point of this chapter: unlike the "golden age" (1950–73) when there was fairly *widespread* growth in the developing world and, in its last phase (1965–73), some convergence of the real incomes of developing countries *vis-à-vis* the industrial world, the period since 1980 can be characterized as a "dual divergence," involving both lower growth rates of developing *vis-à-vis* industrial countries, but also strikingly different growth experiences *among* developing countries (Figure 4.1). The intermediate period, covering the years between the two oil shocks of the 1970s, was a mixed story: still high average growth in the developing countries, but very high divergence among them.

The story can best be told in terms of the frequency of episodes of sustained economic growth and collapses over time. In the 1960s and 1970s, about 40 percent of developing countries could be considered success stories (annual average per-capita GDP growth greater than 3 percent at least over a five-year period), but this proportion fell to less than 20 percent through most of the past quarter century (Figure 4.2). In contrast, less than 15 percent of the countries had negative growth during the 1960s and 1970s, but that proportion increased to over 40 percent in the 1980s and early 1990s. Collapses (defined in this graph as growth rates of –3 percent per capita or less over at least a 5-year period) were rather nonexistent during the "golden age" but then shot up and became frequent during the "lost decade" of the 1980s (in several parts of the developing world and not only in Latin America) and in the early 1990s (when collapses were common in the former USSR, Central and Eastern Europe, and Sub-Saharan Africa).

A similar story arises in Pritchett (2000), who catalogues countries according to the growth pattern followed before or after a statistically determined structural break, which, on average, fell around 1977–78. According to this classification, out of the 88 countries included in his analysis, 7 followed a steep hill;[6] 13 followed a hill pattern, with steady growth around 1.5 percent, generally insufficient for convergence with the industrial center; and 7 accelerated[7] after the break. The majority of developing countries fall under the less appealing categories of growth followed by stagnation (12 plateaus), growth followed by contraction (32 mountains) and stagnation, or very slow growth in both periods (17 plains). This means that, for more than half of developing countries, growth slowed down after the structural break, while very few experienced the opposite trend.

[6]Fast growth, above 3% per capita, before and after the break.
[7]GDP growth below 1.5% before the break, followed by growth above 1.5%.

Figure 4.3 Frequency of sustained growth and contractions in the developing world

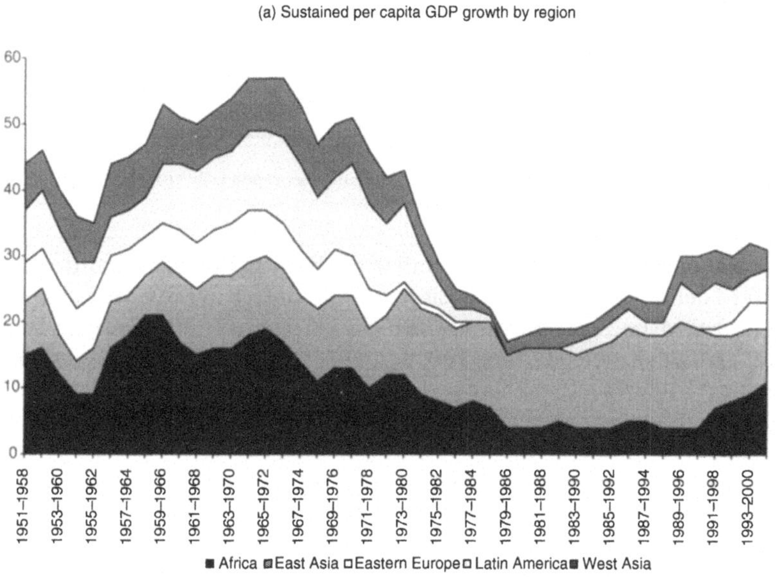

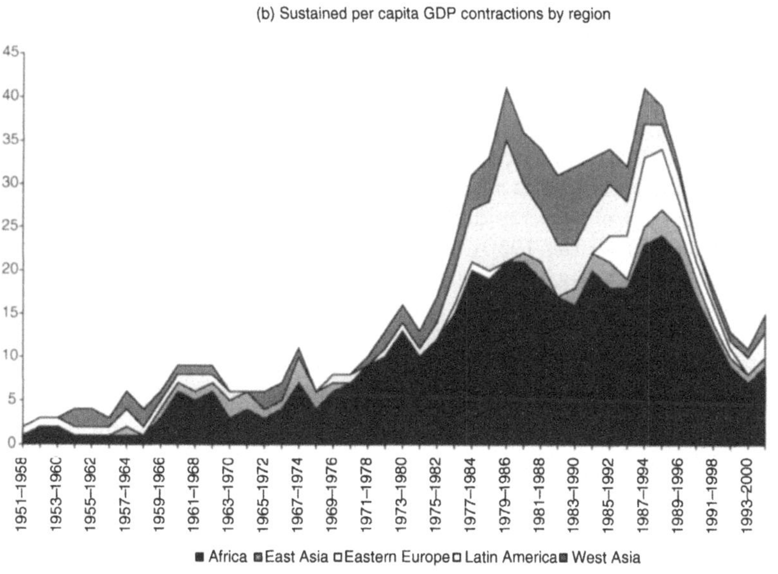

Source: Author's calculations based on Maddison (2001).

Note: First, 5-year moving averages of per capita GDP growth rates were calculated. Then we counted the number of countries that experience a rate below 0% and of those which experience a rate above 2%. Finally, we only consider the cases in which 4 of those moving averages fulfill consecutively those conditions.

Table 4.1 Developing countries successes and collapses[a]

		1950–1960	*1960–1970*	*1970–1980*	*1980–1990*	*1990–2000*
Cumulative growth	X > 25	42.6	49.5	45.5	15.8	30.7
of which:	X > 50	13	17	18	6	5
Cumulative growth	X < 0	6	7	27	54	31
of which:	X < -10	1	3	16	28	19

Source: Author's calculations based on Maddison (2001).
[a]Percentage of total number of countries whith cumulative per capita GDP growth rate (101 countries, 1990 Geary-Kamin dollars, PPP).

Using a criterion of "success" similar to that used by Hausmann *et al.* (2004) to define "sustained expansions" (four consecutive five-year periods with growth over 2 percent per capita[8]), we get again a similar picture: successful growth clustered in the 1960s and 1970s (Figure 4.3.a). Those experiences were widespread in the developing world during the "golden age," tended to disappear in the 1980s, except in East Asia, and became somewhat more common in the 1990s, but at levels far below those of the "golden age." A similar criterion to define "sustained contractions" (four consecutive five-year periods with negative GDP growth per capita) indicates that they were rather infrequent before the first oil shock, then tended to appear more frequently in Africa between the two oil shocks, to become widespread during the "lost decade" of the 1980s and the first half of the 1990s (Figure 4.3.b).

The cumulative effect of successes and collapses is summarized in Table 4.1. Between two-fifths and one-half of developing countries experienced a fair rate of growth (25 percent per capita over a decade) from the 1950s to the 1970s; this fell to less than one-fifth during the "lost decade" and increased again in the 1990s, although at levels far below those of the "golden age". Experiences of very rapid growth (over 50 percent in a decade) were quite common from the 1950s to the 1970s, yet very infrequent since. In turn, experiences of negative or highly negative growth were very infrequent in the 1950s and 1960s, started to become more common in the 1970s, shot up in the 1980s and were still very frequent in the 1990s. Seen as a whole, therefore, the era of structural reforms in the developing world still has a long way to go to match the performance of the period of high State intervention in development. And the transition from one era to the next has already been registered in history as a long and costly one.

A clear way to summarize the evidence is that *growth successes and collapses tend to cluster in specific time periods*. It is unlikely that the domestic

[8]Four consecutive five-year periods are equivalent to an eight-year period. For example, if the first period is 1964–1968, for it to be considered a sustained expansion or contraction, the periods 1965–1969, 1966–1970 and 1967–1971 also have to be periods of 2% average growth (expansion) or negative growth (contraction).

Figure 4.4 The global development cycle, 1951–2004

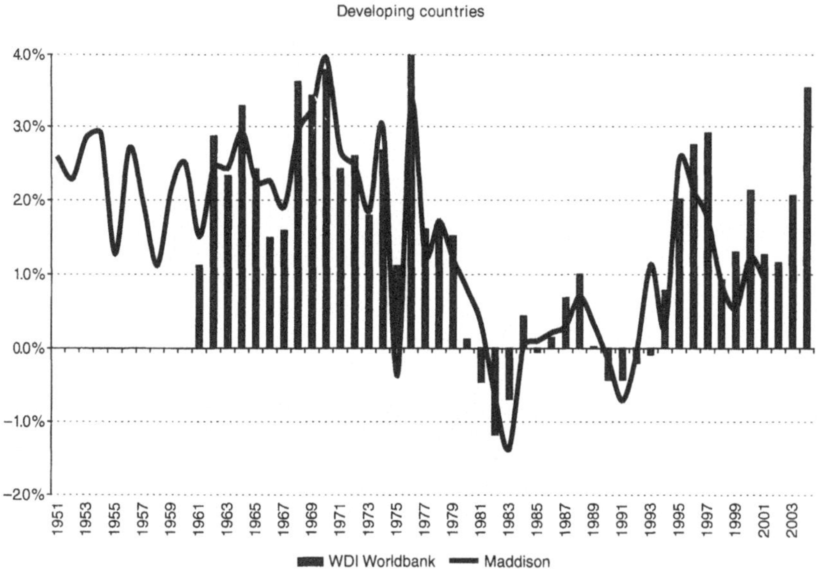

Source: Author's calculations of per capita GDP growth based on Maddison (2001) and World Bank World Development Indicators Online.

factors explored in the growth literature can explain such clustering. Thus, we have to rely on common external factors, as well as on domestic policies that transmit their effects in developing countries (particularly procyclical macroeconomic policies that tend to reinforce, rather than smooth out, the domestic effects of external shocks; see Ocampo, 2005b). The outstanding difference between "the dual divergence" and the "golden age" has been the significant increase in the frequency of growth collapses and the much lower frequency of growth successes over the past quarter century (1980–2005).

The clustering of both successes and collapses implies that a *global development cycle* has dominated the medium-term trajectory followed by developing countries. This cycle should be understood as the average growth performance of developing countries resulting from a set of external factors that affects all or large clusters of them, and thus constrains each country's growth possibilities. While, historically, these factors have been associated with dynamic processes originating in the industrial world, they have also increasingly encompassed the *global* effects of events originating in developing countries with systemic importance. These determinants of the cycle may have diverging effects on different countries and regions. In this sense, the average growth trajectory is not inconsistent with variable performance within the developing world and, particularly, with strong regional dimensions.

Figure 4.5 External debt sustainability and interest rates, 1970–2004

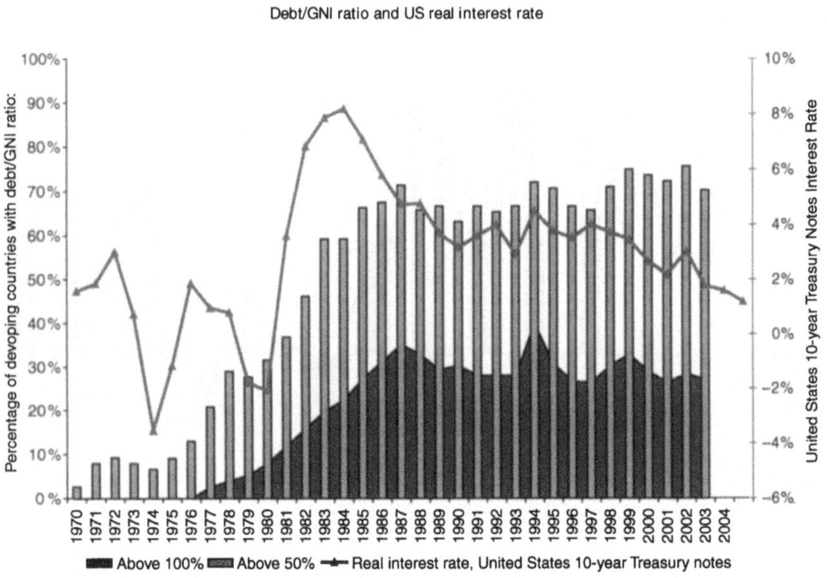

Source: Author's calculations based on World Bank Global Development Finance Online.

Figure 4.6 Primary commodities and developing countries terms of trade, 1900–2005

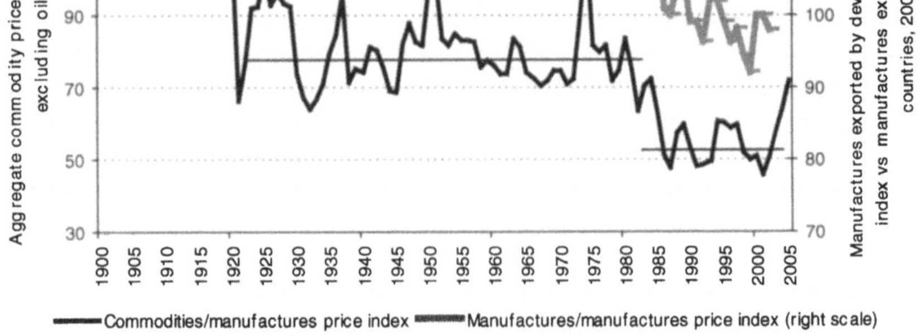

Source: Grilli and Yang (1988); Ocampo and Parra (2003); and United Nations (2003).

Given the leading role played by the industrial world in determining the global development cycle, it is not surprising that the cycle coincides, to some extent, with the average growth performance of industrial countries. Thus, the end of the "golden age" in industrial countries also marked the end of the "golden age" of development. Nonetheless, other determinants of the cycle are more specific and relate to global trade trends (including those associated with commodity markets) and with boom–bust cycles in international financing to developing countries.

The *global development cycle* is depicted in Figure 4.4, in terms of the evolution of the unweighted average per capita GDP growth of developing countries. The oil shocks of 1973 and 1979 disturbed the normal functioning of developed countries' economies, generating inflation and recession, and had important effects in developing countries as well (directly and through the recycling of petrodollars). Nonetheless, the dynamics of oil markets had different effects on different countries and thus cannot explain the general downturn observed by 1980. To explain that, we turn to two major and largely unexpected shocks that severely affected several parts of the developing world.

The first was the *permanent effect of the interest rate shock* of 1979 (Figure 4.5). The second was the *structural downward shift of the terms of trade* (Figure 4.6). The interest rate shock had no historical precedents. As inflation promptly receded, real interest rates in the US (using the 10-year Treasury note rate as a benchmark) increased from –1.8 percent in 1979 to 3.6 percent in 1981, reaching a peak of 8.2 percent in 1984. The rate faced by developing countries was even higher: the average risk premium paid by developing countries added to the LIBOR rate rose from 2.5 percent in 1979 to 22 percent in 1981 in real terms. Having profited from the recycling of petrodollars, developing countries suffered a substantial shock that implied, for many of them, significant balance of payments distress. The non-oil commodity terms of trade shock did have precedents, but only in the distant past (in the 1920s). Real non-oil commodity prices experienced a structural downward shift of over 30 percent, breaking the long stretch since the 1920s when they had been essentially trend-less (Ocampo and Parra, 2003). The price index of manufactures exported by developing countries, relative to manufactures exported by developed countries, experienced a simultaneous downturn. The unprecedented character of the interest rate shock and the distant memory of a comparable terms-of-trade shock explain the unexpectedly large magnitude of *ex-post* risks that developing world had to confront.

The debt dynamics of developing countries turned explosive after the interest rate shock and had both short-term and long-term effects. The proportion of developing countries with moderate debt ratios (over 50 percent of GDP) had been rising from the mid-1970s but was still low prior to the shock, whereas the proportion with critical debt ratios (over 100 percent of

GDP) was very low (Figure 4.5). Both increased sharply *after* the interest rate shock and remained at high levels for the next quarter century, for three basic reasons. The first is that real interest rates remained high: over 4.5 percent for almost 20 years for that same US interest rate; in fact, they only returned to low real levels in the early 2000s. The second was the lack of international institutions to manage debt overhangs; this is in sharp contrast to the 1930s, when one such "institution" was available: broad based moratoria. Eventually a few solutions emerged, but had only weak effects: the Brady Plan of the late 1980s and the Heavily Indebted Poor Countries (HIPC) Initiative of the mid-1990s (still not fully implemented). The third was that, together with the hike in interest rates, net financial flows became negative. Thus, net resource transfers remained highly negative until the early 1990s for a vast number of developing countries. The Asian crisis, and its contagion effects, interrupted the recovery of the 1990s, although the crisis had weaker and more temporary effects than the debt crisis of the 1980s.

Interestingly, the two factors that generated the "lost decade" may at long last be waning. Low real interest rates and the HIPC Initiative may finally break the long-term debt overhangs, while Chinese-led growth has strengthened commodity markets. These are some reasons why the global development cycle may be experiencing an upward shift (see Figure 4.4). It is still unclear, however, if these recent trends and their effects on the global development cycle will be sustainable, as the disturbance in global financial markets associated with the correction of current global imbalances may lead to higher interest rates or risk premia, and commodity prices may have already reached a plateau (United Nations, 2006). To the extent that ODA to the poorest countries of the world increases, based on the commitments made in recent years, ODA may also become a positive determinant of the global development cycle.

The central role played by the global development cycle does *not* render regional and country-specific factors insignificant. Indeed, these factors play an important role, particularly in explaining why a country or region departs from the average trend in either phase of the cycle – i.e., why it does not experience rapid growth during periods of growth success in the developing world as a whole, or why it can mitigate or entirely avoid a growth collapse. Nonetheless, this is an entirely different question than that raised in cross-country econometrics. This means that the relevant country- and region-specific factors depend on those affecting the global development cycle and its domestic transmission mechanisms – and may thus be time-bound. It also implies that short-term dynamics, including the way macroeconomic policy is done, can play a more prominent role than the one usually attributed in the growth literature. It means, finally, that long-term determinants of growth – such as institutions, or the level of human capital – largely play a role to the extent that they help explain the capacity of individual countries to benefit from upward phases and their vulnerability to external shocks during the downward phase of the global development cycle.

This can be illustrated by the variable performance of different developing countries during the "lost decade," when, under similar adverse circumstances, some countries ended up in major crises, while others did not. Variance in performance among developing countries has been analyzed from two different angles. The first is through characteristics of the macroeconomic adjustment mechanism, and the second is through the institutional effects of the massive shocks coming from financial and commodity markets. The literature that has analyzed different adjustment mechanism has underscored the virtues of a broader set of macroeconomic instruments, including mixing orthodox with less orthodox instruments (see, for example, Taylor, 1988). The degree of trade liberalization, as measured by the levels of tariff and non-tariff protection, did *not* play a role in the relative performance of different countries during the 1980s (see, for example, UNCTAD, 1992, Part II, Ch. I), but the degree of macroeconomic instability, defined in orthodox terms, did have significant effects. This is, furthermore, the correct interpretation of the effects of several measures of "openness" used in cross-country econometrics, as emphasized by Rodríguez and Rodrik (2001). The possibility and existence of national strategies to profit from the growing markets in the industrial world for manufactures produced in developing countries did have importance as well (see the next section). But, as indicated in the voluminous literature on East Asian industrialization, the strategy followed by these countries has been quite different from trade liberalization, in the traditional sense (see, for example, Amsden, 2001, and Wade, 1990).

The adverse effect of inflation on growth has been used to show the incidence of macroeconomic instability on the relative performance of different countries. Seen in this light, however, inflation is partly an *effect* of external shocks. This is reflected in the frequency of episodes of high inflation in the developing world during the "lost decade." That frequency resulted mainly from the broad-based foreign exchange gaps that developing countries faced, which had direct and indirect impacts on domestic inflation (via devaluation).

As Rodrik (1999) has argued, institutional factors, particularly institutions for managing conflict, may help explain why, of countries facing the same adverse circumstances, only some ended up with this type of macroeconomic disequilibria. This argument gives strong indirect backing to the old Latin American structuralist idea that distributive conflicts underlie inflation. Other structural factors may have been at work, too. A typical debate in the Latin American literature of the 1980s focused on the "domestic transfer problem" (transferring resources to the government to service the foreign debt). This transfer was made more difficult in those countries in which the government did not have direct access to foreign exchange (i.e., did not directly or indirectly control the foreign exchange generated by exports), and thus had to guarantee access to foreign exchange through indirect means (see, for example, ECLAC, 1996). Inflationary crises were more common in countries where internal transfer was more difficult.

These arguments indicate that external factors have a direct, as well as an indirect, effect on performance in developing countries. The indirect links are associated with the capacity of individual countries to manage vulnerability, but vulnerability would not have played an important role unless the countries faced an external shock. Thus, the features of the relevant domestic factors are not independent of those of the external variables that determine the global development cycle. Furthermore, the interaction between external and domestic factors may be contingent on the circumstances surrounding a specific period, and their joint effect may have long-term implications associated with path dependence.

The large and unexpected shocks that the developing world faced in the early 1980s provide the best explanation of the poor average performance of developing countries during the "lost decade," while the relatively direct impact of the shocks, as well as the way economies adjusted to them,

Figure 4.7 Trade specialization by region, 1980, 2002

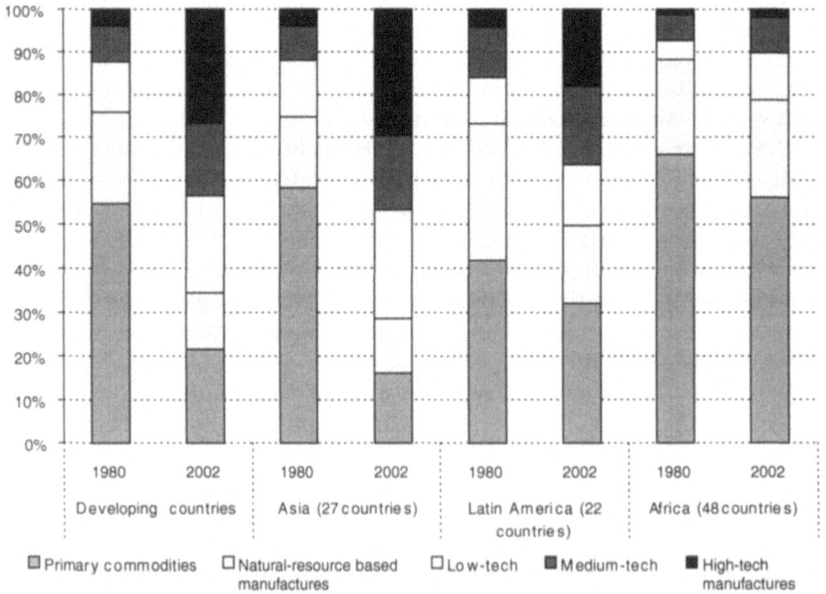

Source: Author's calculations based on UNCTAD Handbook of International Statistics Online. Classification following Lall (2001).

provide a first explanation of diverging performance among countries. A second explanation focuses on how domestic institutions or other domestic factors may have affected the domestic response to massive shocks. We will concentrate in the next section on a third factor, highlighted in much of the structuralist literature, yet generally ignored in mainstream growth analysis: the role of specialization patterns.

Patterns of specialization

As we have pointed out, the experience of developing countries indicates that growth takes place not in steady flows, but in spurts and collapses of different magnitude and frequency. The transformation of production structures and the role of specialization patterns are crucial in this context. In a broad sense, long-term growth can be understood as a sequence of sector-specific growth spurts, their intensity and the domestic linkages they generate (Ocampo, 2005a). These spurts are the result of innovations and the transformation of production structures that they induce.

In developed countries, innovations are associated with technological waves – or, perhaps using Schumpeter's (1961) terminology, different forms of innovations or "new combinations." In developing countries, innovations are more closely linked to the attraction of sectors, activities and technologies previously developed in the industrial world. Historically, this has involved processes of import substitution, export promotion or a mix of both strategies. In this context, although macroeconomic policy can certainly block or promote it, steady growth can be essentially seen as the result of a successful sequence of innovations in production structures (i.e., of micro and, particularly, *meso*economic processes). These sectoral dynamics are ignored or assumed to play a passive role in growth analyses that concentrate on institutional or macroeconomic features and policies. In contrast, it plays a central role in the "structuralist" tradition of economic thinking, broadly defined, where growth is viewed as the result of success in managing the dynamic transformation of production structures.

Seen in this light, the major issue over the past quarter century has been the rapid transformation of the structure of developing country exports: primary goods and natural-resource intensive manufactures fell relative to low-, mid- and high-technology manufactures (see Figure 4.7). All developing country regions diversified into the more dynamic components of world trade, but East and South Asia diversified much faster (including into low-technology manufactures), followed by Latin America. The success stories of the East Asian countries have been related to their achievements in entering external markets, profiting from dynamic economies of scale and transforming their production structures accordingly.

Three factors are important in understanding the links between the evolution of international trade over the past quarter century and the record of economic growth in the developing world. The first is the rate of growth of global markets for developing countries' exports. Dynamic markets for such exports can be generated by high income-elasticities of final demand for them in the industrial world, by economies of diversification (i.e., high and rising demand for diversity of designs), or by the transfer of activities to the developing world due to cost factors (particularly wage costs). The second factor is the strong dynamic economies of scale that characterize sectors with large technological content. In this regard, it can be expected that specialization in sectors with greater technological content will lead to faster growth. The first two factors are linked in practice, as higher technology products are the most dynamic in world trade (Lall, 2001; UNIDO, 2002). The third is the spatial agglomeration that may result from static or dynamic economies of scale. This has long been a key issue in regional economics and has taken center stage in the recent literature on economic geography (see, for example, Fujita *et al.*, 1999).

In the face of the diverse dynamics that characterize world markets, developing countries can adopt either of two broadly defined export strategies: increasing market shares in sectors where a specific country has an established position and diversifying into higher technology products. The first strategy is widely available; the second may only be available to a limited number of developing countries. This is particularly true for high technology exports, where opportunities may be subject to agglomeration effects. Opportunities for producing primary goods and resource-intensive manufactures are more broadly available, but the dynamism of international markets is limited and can therefore lead to "fallacy of composition" effects. Consequently, the simultaneous entry of several countries into these markets will lead to an oversupply of exports that will be reflected in falling terms of trade for developing countries as a whole and/or to high-cost producers being displaced from the market. Low-tech manufactures fall in between these two cases.

Individual countries can succeed with any of these strategies, especially if they implement appropriate productive strategies (see, for example, the success of Chile with the first, or that of the Republic of Korea with the second). However, *as a group*, developing countries can only succeed, in any market, if final demand is elastic and/or if developed countries lose market shares – provided of course that the process is not hampered by protectionism in the developed countries.

The existing literature has explored these issues in different ways. Lall (2001) argues that export structures, being path-dependent, have important implications for growth and development, with highest technology products having the greatest benefits in terms of learning and spillover effects, as well as being more dynamic in world trade. Palma (2004) expresses a similar view based on the different capacity that low- vs. high-technology products have in inducing medium- and long-term productivity growth in the economy as a whole, as well as their relative dynamism in world trade. Hausmann *et al.* (2005) have argued, in turn, that the quality of exports, as indicated in the "income level" of a country's exports (i.e., an estimate of the weighted average income of countries exporting specific products, which may be seen to reflect their technological content), is an independent determinant of economic growth.

These relations have been used to explain East Asia's much superior growth performance. According to Lall (2001) and Palma (2004), among others, that performance is closely associated with the continuous effort, both by the State and the corporate sector, to upgrade export production capacities. UNCTAD (2003) provides a detailed analysis of the significant divergence in the growth of developing countries along these lines. The East Asian economies have experienced persistent industrialization drives. In contrast, in Sub-Saharan Africa, the share of manufacturing in GDP fell in the 1980s and stabilized in the 1990s at relatively low levels. South America has experienced premature deindustrialization, while Mexico and Central America avoided this trend by specializing in high-import intensive manufacturing exports, but with limited benefits in terms of growth (see also, in this regard, ECLAC, 2004; Ocampo and Martin, 2004; Palma, 2005).

Some of the transformation processes involved have links to the external shocks experienced by developing countries – i.e., to the dynamics of the global development cycle. Thus, UNCTAD (2003) argues that the impact of integration into the world economy largely depends on the circumstances under which it takes place and on the policies pursued during the integration phase. Integration of Latin America and Africa (as well as Central and Eastern Europe) marked a sharp shift in development strategy, occurring in a "big-bang" manner and following the debt crisis (i.e., a period of weakness). This contrasts with the integration process in East Asia, which occurred from a position of strength and was characterized by a continuous and purposeful strategy of gradual opening up. Expressing it in the Schumpeterian terminology used by Ocampo (2005a), in East Asia, the "creative" elements prevailed ("creative destruction"), while in other regions of the world, the "destructive" components of the restructuring process were stronger ("destructive creation"), reflecting the destruction of many import-substitution activities and the weak domestic linkages generated by new export sectors.

The development impact of the strategy of a given country would depend not only on success in entering markets, but also on the capacity to capture a share of the value added in the production chain. This is, in a sense, obvious and even tautological, for GDP is nothing else but "value added", but it can have broader implications, as those activities with limited value added (e.g., maquila) are also likely to be footloose. In the terms used by Palma (2004), unless the industries are firmly "anchored" in the domestic economy, their growth-enhancing capacity evaporates. Ocampo (2005a) refers to these specialization patterns as "shallow."

According to UNIDO (2002), middle- and high-tech products represent more than 60 percent of world total manufacturing exports, mainly due to the dynamic growth of high-tech exports. This comes intertwined with the growth of the integrated production systems of multinational firms, which have located different parts of the production chains in different locations and countries (UNCTAD, 2002). Moreover, although the direct and indirect import content of the manufactured exports of developing countries are generally high, and have been rising in recent years, the capacity to capture certain activities (such as assembly tasks) may not lead to rapid growth (UNCTAD, 2002). This is also linked to the relationship the country establishes with FDI: if the strategy to attract FDI is focused, not on creating assets (by providing human resources and infrastructure), but on offering special incentives to multinational investments, the process can ultimately be counterproductive (Mortimore and Peres, 2001).

According to Mayer *et al.* (2002), becoming part of an international production network broadens the range of sectors on which developing countries can base their quest for industrialization. Given relative factor endowments, developing countries may begin by acquiring competence for the more labor-intensive components of complex products and gradually move to more skill- and technology-intensive activities. Nonetheless, due to the geographically dispersed production sites, the package of technology and skills available at any one site is narrower, and, more generally, the spillovers from subcontracting or hosting affiliates of multinational enterprises are reduced. As a result, cross-border backward and forward linkages are strengthened at the expense of domestic ones.

Mayer (2003) reviews the literature on the "fallacy of composition" with an emphasis on labor-intensive manufactures. The analysis indicates a potential problem in this market, as competition among different developing countries for export shares may reduce the benefits from manufacturing exports. The likelihood that a country that exports labor-intensive manufactures would be subject to adverse price trends and protectionism in the North has risen with the increasing integration of several highly populated low-income countries into world markets. According to this author, experience in this regard differs across different groups of countries. The group of countries with the lowest proportion of skill- and technology-intensive manufactures and the greatest proportion of labor-intensive products in their manufactured exports has faced declining terms of trade for its manufacturing exports. Others appear to have succeeded in improving their terms of trade *vis-à-vis* other developing countries by shifting their exports into higher skill- and technology-intensive manufactures. UNCTAD (2002) also shows that there are signs that the prices of the manufactured exports of developing countries have been weakening in the past 20 years *vis-à-vis* those of industrial countries, especially for the less skill-intensive manufactured exports (see Figure 4.6).

"Fallacy of composition" effects are even more important in primary goods, most of which face low income-elasticities of demand in world markets. Indeed, the downward structural shift of non-oil commodity prices in the 1980s may be viewed as the result of the massive export supply generated by developing countries trying to adjust to the debt crises (see Figure 4.6). A similar phenomenon may have affected manufactures exported by developing countries to the industrial world. According to this analysis, the deterioration of the terms of trade can be better explained by differences among countries (developed versus developing countries, different levels of technological capacity, different organization of labor markets, presence or absence of surplus labor, different position in international debt and trade markets, etc), rather than by the characteristics of the goods they export. In other words, the manufactures exported by a large number of developing countries – i.e., labor-intensive manufactures – share some of the disadvantages originally highlighted by the Prebisch–Singer hypothesis in relation to commodity markets (see Ocampo and Parra, 2006, who also survey the relevant literature).

The terms-of-trade debate has essentially been about the need for developing countries to industrialize. As Sarkar (2001) stated, the policy implication of the classical hypothesis on the evolution of commodity prices[9] was that an agricultural country did not need to industrialize to enjoy the gains from technical progress taking place in manufactures; free play of international market forces would distribute the gains from the industrial countries to the agricultural countries through favorable terms of trade. Prebisch (1950) argued that the asymmetries between the center and the periphery of the world economy destroyed the basic premise of the international division of labor, making the transmission of technical change in the world economy highly uneven. Thus, for developing countries, industrialization was not an end in itself, but the principal means at the disposal of the countries for obtaining a share of the benefits of technical progress and for progressively raising the standard of living of their population.

This has generated another debate in which the point of contention is whether there are "commodity-like" characteristics in manufacturing processes in developing countries that place these countries in double jeopardy in their attempts to escape from unequal exchange in world trade. This debate has generated what Athukorala (2000) calls the "new terms of trade

[9]We refer here to the belief, dating back to Adam Smith, that the terms of trade of primary products would show long-term improvement *vis-à-vis* manufactures, based on the law of diminishing returns in primary production and the law of increasing returns in manufactures.

Figure 4.8 Specialization vs. growth: simple correlation patterns, 1980–2002

(a) Primary commodities and natural resource based manufactures

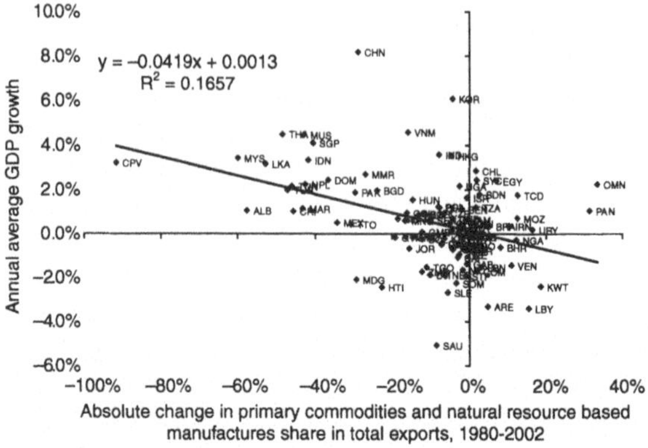

(b) Low-tech manufactures

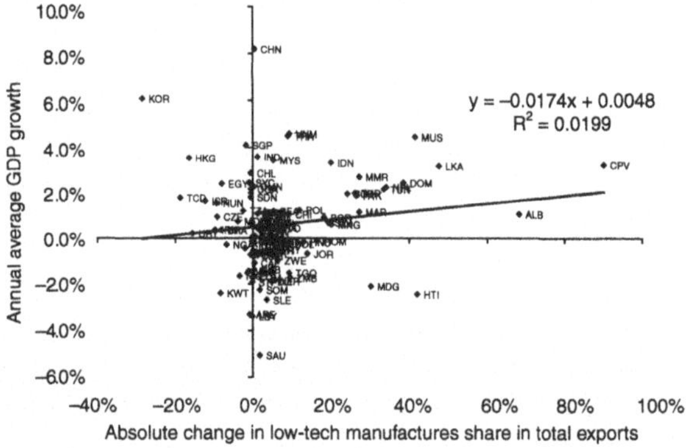

(c) Medium-and-high-tech manufactures

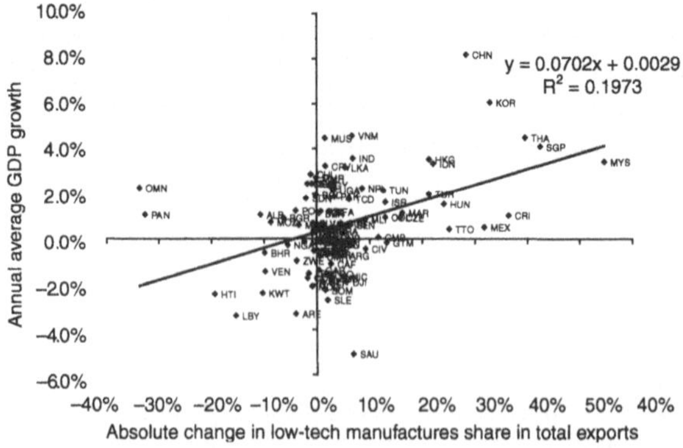

Source: Author's calculations based on UNCTAD Handbook of International Statistics Online and UN data.

Table 4.2 Share of exports by technological content and economic growth in countries that specialized in primary commodities and natural resource-based manufactures

	Code	Continent	Region	Primary products: Share in country exports 2002(%)	Primary products: Annual average increase 1980–2002(%)	Natural resource-based manufactures: Share in country exports 2002(%)	Natural resource-based manufactures: Annual average increase 1980–2002(%)	GDP growth 1980–2002(%)	Average GDP growth(%)
Increasing market shares									
Chile	152	2	9	51.6	6.8	39.1	5.4	2.86	
Seychelles	690	1	1	20.2	1.8	73.2	29.8	2.44	
Oman	512	3	13	86.0	9.6			2.26	
Uganda	800	1	1	83.9	0.3			2.16	
Sudan	736	1	3	31.7	0.7	65.3	11.7	1.81	
Chad	148	1	2	92.2	5.5			1.78	
United Republic of Tanzania	834	1	1	66.5	1.0	26.6	1.5	1.21	
Burkina Faso	854	1	5	79.4	2.4			1.20	
Benin	204	1	5	82.2	8.3			1.13	
Panama	591	2	8	66.7	7.1			1.07	
Colombia	170	2	9	52.1	3.4			0.96	
Mali	466	1	5	81.3	5.5			0.88	
Mozambique	508	1	1	86.8	6.5			0.74	
Jamaica	388	2	7			83.1	0.3	0.64	
Senegal	686	1	5			58.9	3.4	0.64	
Guinea	324	1	5			90.6	0.5	0.49	
Mauritania	478	1	5	50.3	3.8	46.4	3.6	0.42	
Iran, Islamic Republic of	364	3	11	89.7	9.3			0.37	
Brazil	76	2	9	28.6	6.1	30.1	4.7	0.36	
Syrian Arab Republic	760	3	13	83.9	5.3			0.30	
Ecuador	218	2	9	76.0	2.8			0.15	
Guinea-Bissau	624	1	5	95.7	7.9			0.05	
Malawi	454	1	1	77.8	1.8			−0.13	
Congo	178	1	2	79.4	1.9			−0.14	
Paraguay	600	2	9	68.7	4.8			−0.50	
Peru	604	2	9	48.6	2.1	33.8	3.5	−0.54	
Angola	24	1	2	89.3	5.4			−0.56	
Bahrain	48	3	13			73.3	3.8	−0.62	
Argentina	32	2	9	50.3	4.4	27.3	5.9	−0.72	
Cameroon	120	1	2	75.5	1.0	21.3	3.0	−0.77	
Zimbabwe	716	1	1	41.8	0.0	27.1	6.3	−0.96	
Gabon	266	1	2	82.1	0.7			−1.38	
Venezuela	862	2	9	83.1	3.9			−1.43	
Nicaragua	558	2	8	62.1	1.1	22.5	3.4	−1.65	
Comoros	174	1	1	92.2	1.6			−1.72	
Somalia	706	1	1	58.4	2.9	35.1	4.1%	−2.25	
United Arab Emirates	784	3	13	62.9	3.5			−3.30	0.20
Decreasing market shares									
Egypt	818	1	3	28.5	−0.6	41.6	5.9	2.41	
Cuba	192	2	7			85.0	−4.8	0.70	
Ghana	288	1	5	54.4	−0.4	37.2	1.2	0.47	
Gambia	270	1	5	76.4	−4.1			0.08	
Algeria	12	1	3	83.3	−0.6			−0.04	
Guatemala	320	2	8	45.6	−1.0	26.9	5.1	−0.16	
Kenya	404	1	1	36.7	−1.1	47.3	0.1	−0.21	
Rwanda	646	1	1	61.6	−4.9	35.7	−1.5	−0.22	
Bolivia	68	2	9	54.9	1.4	30.7	−1.1	−0.24	
Nigeria	566	1	5	99.8	−0.4			−0.28	
Côte d'Ivoire	384	1	5	59.4	3.4	22.3	−0.8	−0.45	
Burund	108	1	1	79.8	−4.2			−0.61	
Central African Republic	140	1	2			86.8	−1.3	−1.09	
Togo	768	1	5	46.6	−2.7	38.4	−0.6	−1.52	
Zambia	894	1	1	63.1	−2.7	21.8	−0.9	−1.73	
Niger	562	1	5	32.3	−0.1	59.5	−6.4	−1.87	
Djibouti	262	1	1	34.4	−1.4	39.4	0.7	−1.87	
Sao Tome and Principe	678	1	2	96.2	−5.6			−1.92	
Kuwait	414	3	13	62.3	1.0	32.7	−1.2	−2.38	
Sierra Leone	694	1	5	91.1	−5.7			−2.68	
Libyan Arab Jamahiriya	434	1	3	81.5	−1.4			−3.38	
South Arabia	682	3	13	87.0	−3.0			−5.06	−1.00

Source: Author's calculations based on UNCTAD Handbook of International Statistics Online and UN data.

Table 4.3 Share of exports by technological content and economic growth in countries diversifying exports to non-resource based manufactures

	Code	*Continent*	*Region*	*Primary products*		*Natural resource-based manufactures*		*Low-tech manufactures*		*Medium-tech manufactures*		*High-tech manufactures*			
				Share in country exports 2002(%)	*Annual average increase 1980–2002(%)*	*Share in country exports 2002(%)*	*Annual average increase 1980–2002(%)*	*Share in country exports 2002(%)*	*Annual average increase 1980–2002(%)*	*Share in country exports 2002(%)*	*Annual average increase 1980–2002(%)*	*Share in country exports 2002(%)*	*Annual average increase 1980–2002(%)*	*GDP growth 1980–2002(%)*	*Average GDP growth(%)*
Diversifying to low, medium or high-tech manufactures															
China	156	3	10					39.0	14.1			27.4	25.1	8.20	
Republic of Korea	410	3	10							30.9	10.7	38.4	17.0	6.09	
Thailand	764	3	12					20.4	14.1			31.4	31.5	4.50	
Singapore	702	3	12									58.6	15.9	4.11	
HongKongSAR, China	344	3	10					37.2	9.4	20.6	10.5	35.2	17.3	3.54	
Malaysia	458	3	12									52.7	18.0	3.44	
Turkey	792	3	13					49.6	15.5	20.7	18.5			2.00	
Israel	376	3	13			45.3	10.3					26.6	14.5	1.64	
Hungary	348	4	14							33.3	22.2	31.5	17.2	1.55	
Poland	616	4	14					30.6	6.6	30.4	3.8			1.24	
Costa Rica	188	2	8	26.6	2.6							26.7	22.4	1.04	
Czech Republic	200	4	14			20.4	4.0	26.0	2.9	27.7	4.3	21.9	10.5	0.94	
Mexico	484	2	8							26.6	12.1	33.1	15.3	0.52	
TrinidadandTabago	780	2	7	20.6	–3.3	46.6	–1.1			25.2	14.3			0.44	
Philippines	608	3	12									70.6	29.5	0.22	
Romania	642	4	14					48.0	2.9	21.5	0.4			–0.12	2.5
Diversifying to low-tech manufactures															
Viet Nam	704	3	12	50.4	18.3			31.9	20.7					4.59	
Mauritius	480	1	1			24.6	1.5	62.9	11.9					4.47	
India	356	3	11			32.1	11.6	36.2	9.4					3.58	
Indonesia	360	3	12	31.9	0.1	24.6	5.9	20.6	21.5					3.34	
Cape Verde	132	1	5					93.1	25.7					3.23	
Sri Lanka	144	3	11	22.8	2.2			59.1	15.3					3.18	
Myanmar	104	3	12	53.0	10.2			27.9	28.0					2.71	
Dominican Republic	214	2	7					61.4	4.1					2.45	
Nepal	524	3	11					74.0	11.2					2.25	
Tunisia	788	1	3					53.2	10.0					2.16	
Bangladesh	50	3	11					88.8	10.2					1.97	
Pakistan	586	3	11					76.0	8.3					1.89	
Morocco	504	1	3	22.6	1.2	20.1	3.6	38.5	11.5					1.15	
Albania	8	4	16					80.8	8.7					1.07	
El Salvador	222	2	8			28.3	10.8	34.2	5.0					0.69	
Mongolia	496	3	10	26.6	– 4.7	37.9	12.0	34.5	4.1					0.61	
Uruguay	858	2	9	41.5	3.4	22.3	5.2	29.2	0.6					0.21	
Honduras	340	2	8	31.2	– 0.1	43.6	5.5	20.2	8.1					–0.16	
Jordan	400	3	13	24.7	5.2			29.3	10.2					–0.68	
Madagascar	450	1	1	55.2	– 3.1			32.8	10.6					–2.08	
Haiti	332	2	7					85.3	4.1					–2.42	1.6

Source: Author's calculations based on UNCTAD Handbook of International Statistics Online and UN data.

Figure 4.9 Specialization vs. growth: 1980–2002

(a) Gains or losses in market share in 1980–2002

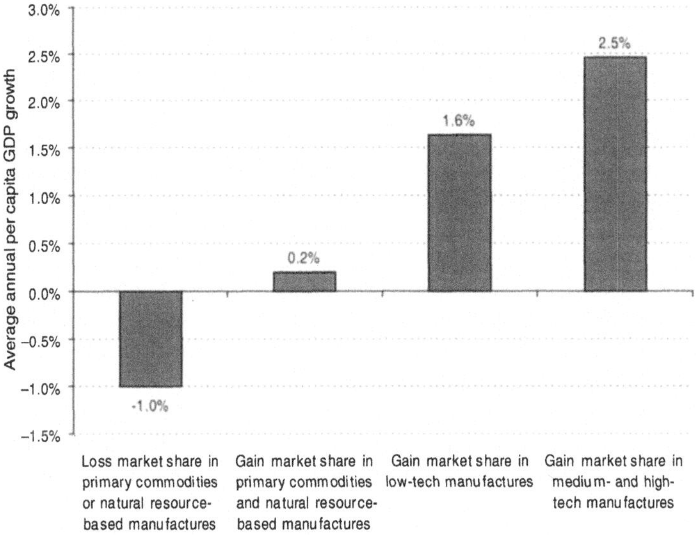

(b) Sector share in 2002

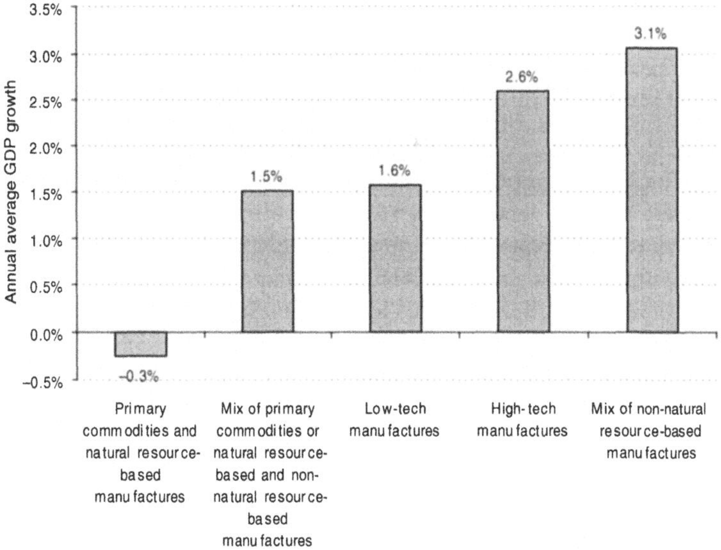

Source: Tables 4.2 and 4.3.

pessimism," in the sense that it could be self-defeating for developing countries to try to industrialize. But several individual case studies for Asia show that this is not necessarily true. Some countries have in fact achieved significant terms of trade gains. Could other developing countries also avoid this "curse"? There are, indeed, grounds for optimism, but only in so far as developing countries take a more pro-active attitude towards promoting technological improvements, industrialization, and export diversification.

The simple correlation between specialization patterns and growth presented in Figure 4.8 provides a first look at the relevance of the previous arguments. Economic growth in the developing world is negatively correlated with continued reliance on the exports of primary goods and natural resource-intensive manufactures, but positively correlated with diversifying into mid- and high-tech manufactures, with no clear pattern when we look at low-tech manufactures. There are, however, significant differences in performance around the average pattern.

A closer look at this issue shows the interaction between two different variables: success in increasing market shares and specialization patterns. Tables 4.2 and 4.3 provide a detailed look at the evidence on the interaction between these two factors. The first shows countries that have continued to rely on natural-resource-based manufactures or primary commodities, while the second looks at countries able to increase market shares in non-resource-based manufacturing categories. In both cases, we restrict the analysis to sectors that represent at least 20 percent of the exports of a country in 2002.

The evidence presented by these two tables is striking and can be summarized in four major conclusions.[10] First, most countries that have failed to increase shares in world markets are exporters of primary goods or natural resource-intensive manufactures, and all of them experienced either low growth or per-capita GDP contraction. Second, success in increasing market shares in these sectors has been generally associated with weak growth. Indeed, Chile, Seychelles, Oman, Uganda, and Egypt are the only cases in the sample of 96 countries analyzed that extracted GDP per capita growth above 2 percent during 1980–2002 from a strategy based on natural resources (Table 4.2). Other countries that had rapid rates of growth mixed this strategy with low-tech manufactures (Vietnam, Mauritius, India, Indonesia, Sri Lanka, and Myanmar) or high-tech manufactures (Costa Rica, which had, in any case, a much lower rate of growth). Third, there are cases of countries (Cape Verde, Dominican Republic, Nepal, and Tunisia)

[10]The analysis is based on the structure of exports of goods. Therefore, it does not include diversification into services, which may be behind some of the rapid success stories.

that have extracted rapid growth from a specialization pattern based on low-tech manufactures or, as previously mentioned, by mixing it with natural-resource-intensive goods, but most developing countries that have grown fast have been increasing market shares in mid- or high-technology exports (Table 4.3). Finally, there is, in any case, a significant difference in the capacity of Asian countries to extract growth out of these sectors *vis-à-vis* Latin American (Costa Rica and Mexico), Central European (Hungary and Poland) and West Asian (Turkey) countries. This may be related to the "destructive" features of productive restructuring underway outside Asia, but also to the stronger linkages associated with new technology exports in Asia, which are in some cases national, but more generally regional in character.

Figure 4.9 summarizes in a simple way the evidence provided in Tables 4.2 and 4.3. Panel a shows the very large difference in average growth rates between countries undergoing a transformation of specialization patterns into higher technology exports vs. those specializing in natural resource-intensive sectors, even when they increased market shares in those sectors. Those gaining market share in low-tech manufactures fall in between. Panel b shows that countries that still based their exports mainly on primary commodities and natural-resource-based manufactures in 2002 did not grow in the previous two decades. Countries that grew the most had specialized in two (out of three) non-natural resource based manufacturing categories or only in high-tech manufactures. Mixes involving natural resource exports with non-natural resource intensive manufactures, as well as specialization in low-tech manufactures, fall in between. This indicates that specialization patterns, and their evolution over time, do matter. Indeed, few factors among those explored in standard growth regressions can explain differences as large as those captured in Tables 4.2 and 4.3 and Figure 4.9, which are in the order of 3 percentage points per year.

Although the conclusions are not necessarily very encouraging for all developing countries, they indicate that any country wanting to speed up growth should learn from the NIEs' State and corporate efforts to consistently upgrade export production capacities. Although diversifying into mid- and high-technology exports is not feasible for many developing countries, and there may be agglomeration forces at work that benefit the already dynamic East Asian regional cluster, there could be opportunities for some of them that should not be disregarded.

Most developing countries would have to compete in primary goods, natural resource, or low-tech manufacturing exports, where they may face "fallacy of composition" effects. The medium-term option is clearly to promote the continued opening of markets for these products by industrial countries. In the long term, countries should not hesitate to enter the export learning process, always having in mind the objective of upgrading export capabilities and avoiding stagnation around primary commodities and perhaps even labor-intensive manufactures.

Conclusions

This chapter analyzes major factors explaining the transition from the "golden age" of fairly widespread growth in the developing world in 1950–73 to the "dual divergence" since 1980, involving both lower growth rates of developing *vis-à-vis* developed countries and strikingly different growth experiences among developing countries. It builds from a growing body of literature emphasizing discontinuities in the growth experience of developing countries – growth spurts and collapses – that render traditional cross-country econometrics involving long time periods a rather useless analytical tool. The chapter builds also on issues traditionally emphasized by the structuralist literature, yet frequently ignored by mainstream development economists.

A clear way to summarize the evidence is that *growth successes and collapses tend to cluster in specific time periods*. It is unlikely that the domestic factors explored in the mainstream growth literature can explain such clustering; so, we have to rely on common external factors. The significant increase in the frequency of collapses and the much lower frequency of successes in the past quarter century (1980–2005) is the significant difference between the period of the "dual divergence" and the "golden age." The clustering of successes and collapses implies that a *global development cycle* has dominated development trends. The global development cycle is partly determined by that of the industrial world countries. Thus, the end of the "golden age" in industrial countries also marked the end of the "golden age" of development. However, other determinants of this cycle are more specific, and have to do with the functioning of financial markets *vis-à-vis* developing countries (and, more particularly, emerging markets) and with the major structural downturn experienced by the terms of trade in the 1980s.

Of course, country-specific factors still play a role, explaining why a country does not experience rapid growth during periods of growth success in the developing world as a whole, or why it can better manage vulnerabilities during downswings of the global development cycle. And domestic policies, particularly pro-cyclical macroeconomic policies, are crucial for transmitting the effects of external shocks. Nonetheless, the relevant domestic factors are not independent of the external factors that determine the global development cycle. Furthermore, this interaction between external and domestic factors may be contingent on the circumstances surrounding a specific period.

Discontinuities in the growth experience are important, due to the path dependence generated by dynamic economies of scale, which reflect the links between technological learning and production experience. An additional issue, not explored in this chapter, is associated with the effects of shocks and major institutional changes on State institution-building, due to the complex "learning" process involved.

Discontinuities are also important for development in the sense that long-term growth should be understood as the result of a sequence of sector-specific growth spurts, their intensity and the domestic linkages they generate. This implies that *specialization patterns are crucial to understand growth dynamics*. Overall, the evidence presented in this chapter underscores the very large difference between the average growth of countries undergoing a transformation of specialization patterns into higher technology exports and that of countries experiencing success in primary goods sectors.

This conclusion is not necessarily very encouraging for developing countries as a whole, for the opportunity to diversify into medium- and high-technology exports may not be available to many of them, given the agglomeration forces at work. In any case, more developing countries should learn from the NIEs' substantive State and corporate sector efforts consistently to upgrade export production capacities.

Most developing countries would have to compete in primary goods, natural resource or low-tech manufacturing exports, where they are likely to face "fallacy of composition" effects. The medium-term option is clearly to promote the continued opening of markets for these products by industrial countries. In the long term, countries should be aware of the risk of fallacy of composition, yet simultaneously promote a process of export diversification that creates dynamic comparative advantages and "climbs the ladder" towards more technologically advanced products.

References

Amsden, A. (2001) *The Rise of the Rest: Non-Western Economies' Ascent in World Markets*, Oxford University Press, Oxford.

Athukorala, P.-Ch. (2000) "Manufactured exports and terms of trade of developing countries: evidence from Sri Lanka," *The Journal of Development Studies*, 36(5), June, pp. 89–104.

Azariadis, C. and A. Drazen (1990) "Threshold externalities in economic development," *The Quarterly Journal of Economics*, 105(2), May, pp. 501–26.

Berry, A. and J. Serieux (2004), "All about the giants: probing the influences of world growth on income inequality at the end of the 20th century," *CESifo Economic Studies*, 50(1), Munich, ifo Institute for Economic Research.

Bourguignon, F. and Ch. Morrison (2002) "Inequality among world citizens: 1820–1992," *American Economic Review*, 92(4), September, pp. 727–44.

Brock, W. and S. Durlauf (2001) "What have we learned from a decade of empirical research on growth? Growth empirics and reality," *The World Bank Economic Review*, 15(2), pp. 229–72.

Cimoli, M. and N. Correa (2005) "Trade openness and technology gaps in Latin America: a 'low-growth trap,'" in J.A. Ocampo (ed.), *Beyond Reforms, Structural Dynamics and Macroeconomic Vulnerability*, ECLAC, Stanford University Press and World Bank, pp. 45–70.

Durlauf, S., P. Johnson and J. Temple (2004) "Growth econometrics," *Vassar Economics Working Paper*, 61, October.
Easterly, W. (2004) "National policies and economic growth: a reappraisal," draft chapter for forthcoming *Handbook of Economic Growth*, edited by P. Aghion and S. Durlauf.
Easterly, W. (2001) *The Elusive Quest for Growth: Economists' Adventures and Misadventures in the Tropics*, The MIT Press, Cambridge, MA.
Easterly, W., M. Kremer, L. Pritchett, and L. Summers (1993) "Good policy or good luck? Country growth performance and temporary shocks," *Journal of Monetary Economics*, 32(3), December, pp. 459–84.
ECLAC (1996) *The Economic Experience of the Last Fifteen Years: Latin America and the Caribbean, 1980–1995*, Santiago.
ECLAC (Economic Commission for Latin America and the Caribbean) (2004) *Productive Development in Open Economies*, Santiago.
Ffrench-Davis, R. (2005) *Reforming Latin America's Economies after Market Fundamentalism*, Palgrave Macmillan, Basingstoke.
Fujita, M., P. Krugman and A.J. Venables (1999) *The Spatial Economy: Cities, Regions and International Trade*, The MIT Press, Cambridge, MA.
Grilli, E.R. and M.Ch. Yang (1988) "Primary commodity prices, manufactured goods prices, and the terms of trade of developing countries: what long run shows," *The World Bank Economic Review*, 2(1), pp. 1–47.
Hausmann, R., J. Hwang and D. Rodrik (2005) "It is not how much but what you export that matters," Working Paper, Harvard University, John F. Kennedy School of Government, December.
Hausmann, R., L. Pritchett and D. Rodrik (2004) "Growth accelerations," *National Bureau of Economic Research*, Working Paper no. 10566, June.
Heymann, D. (2000) "Major macroeconomic upsets, expectations and policy responses," *CEPAL Review*, 70, April, pp. 13–29.
Jones B. and B. Olken (2005) "The anatomy of start-stop growth," *National Bureau of Economic Research*, Working Paper no. 11528, August.
Krugman, P. (1990) *Rethinking International Trade*, The MIT Press, Cambridge.
Lall, S. (2001) *Competitiveness, Technology and Skills*, Edward Elgar, Cheltenham.
Maddison, A. (1995) *Monitoring the World Economy 1820–1992*, Development Centre Studies, Organization for Economic Co-operation and Development (OECD), Paris.
Maddison, A. (2001) *The World Economy – A Millennial Perspective*, Development Centre Studies, OECD, Paris.
Mayer, J. (2003) "The fallacy of composition: A review of the literature," *UNCTAD Discussion Papers*, 166, February.
Mayer, J., A. Butkevicius and A. Kadri (2002) *UNCTAD Discussion Papers*, 159, May.
Mortimore, M. and W. Peres (2001) "Corporate competitiveness in Latin America and the Caribbean," *CEPAL Review*, 74, August, pp. 37–59.
Ocampo, J.A. and M.A. Parra (2006) "The commodity terms of trade and their strategic implications for development," in K.S. Jomo, *Economic Globalization, Hegemony and the Changing World Economy During the Long Twentieth Century*, Oxford University Press, New Delhi and Oxford, pp. 164–94.
Ocampo, J.A. (2005a) "The quest for dynamic efficiency: structural dynamics and economic growth in developing countries," in J.A. Ocampo (ed.), *Beyond Reforms, Structural Dynamics and Macroeconomic Vulnerability*, ECLAC, Stanford University Press and World Bank, pp. 3–44.

Ocampo, J.A. (2005b) "A broad view of macroeconomic stability," *DESA Working Paper*, No. 1, October.

Ocampo, J.A. and J. Martin (2004) *América Latina y el Caribe en la Era Global*, CEPAL and Alfaomega, Bogotá.

Ocampo, J.A. and J. Martin (2003) *Globalization and Development*, ECLAC and Stanford University Press, Palo Alto.

Ocampo, J.A. and M.A. Parra (2003) "The terms of trade for commodities in the twentieth century," *CEPAL Review*, 79, April, pp. 7–35.

Palma, G. (2005) "Four sources of 'de-industrialization' and a new concept of the 'Dutch Disease,'" in J.A. Ocampo (ed.), *Beyond Reforms, Structural Dynamics and Macroeconomic Vulnerability*, ECLAC/Stanford University Press and World Bank, pp. 71–116.

Palma, G. (2004) "Flying-geese and lame ducks: regional powers and the different capabilities of Latin America and East Asia to 'demand-adapt' and supply-upgrade' their export productive capacity," unpublished manuscript, August.

Pritchett, L. (2000), "Understanding patterns of economic growth: searching for hills among plateaus, mountains and plains," *World Bank Economic Review*, 14(2), May, pp. 221–50.

Pritchett, L. (1997) "Divergence, big time," *Journal of Economic Perspectives*, 11(3), Summer, pp. 3–17.

Prebisch, R. (1950) *The Economic Development of Latin America and its Principal Problems*, United Nations, New York.

Rada, C. (2005) "A growth model for a two-sector open economy with endogenous employment in the subsistence sector," *Schwartz Center for Economic Policy Analysis*, New School University, New York.

Rada, C. and L. Taylor (2004) "Empty sources of growth accounting, and empirical replacements à la Kaldor with some beef," *Center for Economic Policy Analysis*, New School University, November.

Ranis, G., F. Stewart and A. Ramírez (2000) "Economic growth and human development," *World Development*, 28 (2), February, pp. 197–221.

Reddy, S.G. and C. Minoiu (2005) "Real income stagnation of countries, 1960–2001," unpublished manuscript, March.

Rodríguez, F. (2005) "Cleaning up the kitchen sink: on the consequences of the linearity assumption for cross-country growth empirics," unpublished manuscript, August.

Rodríguez, F. and D. Rodrik (2001) "Trade policy and economic growth: a skeptic's guide to the cross-national evidence," in B.S. Bernanke and K. Rogoff (eds), *NBER Macroeconomics Annual 2000*, MIT Press, Cambridge.

Rodrik, D. (2005) "Why we learn nothing from regressing economic growth on policies," unpublished manuscript, March.

Rodrik, D. (2003) *In Search of Prosperity: Analytic Narratives on Economic Growth*, Princeton University Press.

Rodrik, D. (1999) "Where did all the growth go? External shocks, social conflict and growth collapses," *Journal of Economic Growth*, 4, December, pp. 385–412.

Ros, J. (2005) "Divergence and growth collapses: theory and empirical evidence," in J.A. Ocampo (ed.), *Beyond Reforms, Structural Dynamics and Macroeconomic Vulnerability*, ECLAC, Stanford University Press and World Bank, Palo Alto, pp. 211–32.

Sarkar, P. (2001) "The North-South terms of trade debate: a reexamination," *Progress in Development Studies*, 1(4), pp. 309–27.

Schumpeter, J. (1961) *The Theory of Economic Development*, Oxford University Press, New York.

Taylor, L. (1988) *Varieties of Stabilization Experience: Towards Sensible Macroeconomics in the Third World*, Clarendon Press, New York.

United Nations (2003) *International Trade Statistics Yearbook, volume II: Trade by commodity*, New York.

United Nations (2006) *World Economic Situation and Prospects*, New York.

UNCTAD (2003) *Trade and Development Report 2003, Capital Accumulation, Growth and Structural Change*, New York and Geneva.

UNCTAD (2002) *Trade and Development Report 2002, Developing Countries in World Trade*, New York and Geneva.

UNCTAD (1992) *Trade and Development Report 1992*, New York and Geneva.

UNIDO (2002) *Industrial Development Report 2002/2003: Competing through Innovation and Learning*.

Van Wijnbergen, S. (1984) "The Dutch disease: a disease after all?," *Economic Journal*, 94(373), March, pp. 41–55.

Wade, R. (1990) *Governing the Market: Economic Theory and the Role of Government in East Asian Industrialization*, Princeton University Press, Princeton.

Part II

Interrelations Between Growth and Equity

5

Is Greater Equity Necessary for Higher Long-Term Growth in Latin America?

François Bourguignon and Michael Walton[1]

Introduction

This chapter explores the relationship between equity and the growth process. It argues that equity, in the sense of equality of opportunity, is, in some fundamental respects, complementary to long-run growth. Sustained growth is likely to be much more problematic in highly inequitable societies. This is of central concern for Latin America because of the continued large inequities prevalent throughout the continent.

The extensive literature on the relationship between inequality and growth goes back in time – notably, in the second half of the twentieth century to Kuznets and Lewis for the effects of growth on inequality and to Kaldor for the effects of inequality on growth. There was then a major expansion of both theoretical and empirical work in the 1990s. The empirical part of this literature has primarily concerned with interactions between inequality of *outcomes* – and especially incomes – and growth. Our reading is that it is rich in theoretical insight, but with weak empirical results.

Lewis (1954) and Kuznets (1955) postulated that income inequality would rise and fall in the process of development from poverty to wealth, income differentials initially rising as high-productivity and high-wage

[1]This chapter draws on two recent publications undertaken under the auspices of the World Bank, with which we were involved, one focused on inequality in Latin America (De Ferranti *et al.*, 2004) and especially the *World Development Report* for 2006 on Equity and Development (World Bank, 2005). We are grateful to colleagues on the team that prepared the 2006 Report, especially Abhijit Banerjee, Francisco Ferreira, Peter Lanjouw, Tamar Manuelyan-Atinc, Marta Menéndez, Berk Özler, Giovanna Prennushi, Vijayendra Rao, James Robinson and Michael Woolcock. We are also grateful to David de Ferranti, Yasuhiko Matsuda, Guillermo Perry and Kenneth Sokoloff for contributions to earlier work on Latin American inequality (in De Ferranti *et al.*, 2004).

production took off in the context of a labor surplus, and then eventually falling as the bulk of labor became absorbed into the modern sector. Kuznets – drawing on the very limited historical data available at that time – found an empirical confirmation of that inverted U-shape relationship between inequality and development. The "Kuznets Curve" came to be the best-known stylized "fact" of income distributional change in relation to development. However, with the collection of better data across countries and over time, it became evident that this was not a fact at all: there is essentially no evidence for the Kuznets Curve as a general empirical phenomenon (see, for example, Bruno *et al.*, 1998, and Kanbur, 2000). In effect, there are many reasons to believe that, in view of the complexity of the mechanisms that determine the evolution of the distribution of income, no general pattern is likely to emerge.[2]

Most of the theoretical literature of the past 15 years points to a negative relationship between inequality and growth. It is common to organize this literature into two types of channel (see Aghion *et al.*, 1999; Bénabou, 1996; and Bertola, 2000 for reviews.) A first strand focuses on a positive relationship between wealth and investment: with lumpy investment and credit market failures, people below a certain level of wealth will invest less (early work in this direction is associated with Galor and Zeira, 1993). This can lead to significant dynamic effects on occupational choice (as in Banerjee and Newman, 1993). If the distribution of wealth were more equal, overall investment and labor productivity would be higher. A second strand focuses on political economy channels. Where wealth distributions are more unequal, political processes can lead to worse economic outcomes. This may occur for various reasons: a) weak incentives for elite power to redistribute wealth so as to increase economic efficiency (Bénabou, 2000); b) greater likelihood of the populace imposing inefficient income redistributive measures, for example under a median voter model (for early models see Alesina and Rodrik, 1994); or c) because there is an increased likelihood of distributional fights.

Note that in both strands of the theoretical work the variable that is focused on – *wealth* and *power* – is more closely related to influences on future possibilities, than to the distribution of *opportunities* (see Ferreira and Walton, 2006). By contrast, most of the empirical estimation has involved examining the links between measures of initial *income* inequality and subsequent growth. Initial results were seemingly consistent with the theory, but these have been increasingly questioned on econometric grounds. We share the view of Banerjee and Duflo (2003) that, at this point, there is little that can be said of value on the overall relationship between income

[2]See Bourguignon *et al.* (2004).

inequality and growth, owing to pervasive problems of omitted variables and measurement error.[3]

These, inconclusive, empirical results are often explicitly or implicitly taken to support the view that distribution should not be of significant concern in the design of growth-oriented strategy. Growth is a matter for policymakers concerned with finance, trade, infrastructure and other determinants of competitiveness and innovation. Equity should be dealt with separately, most notably through social policies, with, of course, careful attention to tradeoffs between equity and efficiency that are almost second nature to economists.

We present a very different position here. We argue that equity has a central role in providing the basis for long-run growth. It is both bad economics and bad policy to separate questions of equity from questions of growth. In developing this argument, we make two departures from past literature. *First*, in line with the recent theoretical literature, we focus on a concept of equity that is essentially *ex ante*, that is, concerned with *equal access of all individuals to opportunities* to pursue a life of their choosing, including the pursuit of economic activities. The intuition is straightforward: if significant parts of the population have restricted opportunities for investment and innovation, while those at the top have extensive opportunities to pursue their private interests, then there will be both efficiency losses and adverse dynamic effects.

Second, we emphasize that interactions of equity with efficiency and growth have to be understood in terms of *specific* inequalities of opportunities, in economic, social and political spaces, and of their interactions with market and non-market institutions. Once this prism is adopted, there is evidence for a negative relationship between inequity and economic processes affecting efficiency or growth in two areas: in the inefficient results from the interaction between market imperfections and inequalities of assets, status or influence; and in the effects of extreme political inequalities on the design of economic institutions, with a tendency to form institutions that promote predation, rent-seeking, or protection of economic (and other) privileges, rather than broad-based incentives for investment and innovation.

This analysis forms the basis for the view that equity forms an essential part of the framework for long-run growth, of direct relevance to Latin

[3]Forbes (2000) and Li and Zou (1998) sought to control for these problems using panel regression techniques with country fixed effects and adaptive effects of inequality on growth. In both case, it was found that the relationship between inequality and growth was in fact positive. Yet, it is likely that the lags between distributional changes and changes in growth rates are too long for standard econometric techniques on 5-year data to be of real significance.

America. However, neither the conceptual approach, nor the types of evidence available, imply any *general* empirical relationship between some overall proxy for equity and growth episodes. Some ways of providing for greater equity can be growth-sapping, and there are different institutional ways of assuring the greater equity that underpins long-run growth.

The chapter is organized into two parts. The first part elaborates on the definition and measure of inequity and on the theoretical mechanisms mentioned above that may provide a link between equity and growth. It also discusses the available evidence of these mechanisms and concludes with some country experiences that illustrate the link between equity and development. The second part turns to policy. It outlines the implications for development strategy in three areas: policies designed to expand opportunities for the bottom part of the distribution; approaches to policy and institutions designed to reduce the influence and privileges at the top of the distribution; and the management of transitions.

Equity and channels of influence on growth

Equity: concept and evidence

Inequality refers to a distribution of a characteristic in a population, with income being the most commonly used characteristic in economic analysis. It is thus essentially a descriptive concept of an outcome variable. Equity, by contrast, is an intrinsically normative concept, related to some notion of fairness. Drawing on thinking in the tradition of John Rawls, Ronald Dworkin, Amartya Sen, and John Roemer, we adopt a concept of equity that is primarily concerned with equality of opportunity.[4] Every individual should have equal opportunities to pursue a life of their choosing, irrespective of circumstances outside their control, such as the wealth of their parents, the social group into which they are born, their gender, and country of birth. With equal opportunities, outcomes will differ, owing to differences in talent, preferences and effort, as well as pure luck.

We recognize that many societies do care about outcomes, and in particular suggest a complementary criterion of minimizing absolute deprivation, irrespective of causes, in the spirit of a Rawlsian maximin principle. This is important for policy design, but is not the focus of this chapter, for which the primary interest is equity in terms of equality of opportunities.

How large is inequity? Direct measurement of a "set" of opportunities is difficult because opportunities are not directly observed, and because of the inherent multi-dimensionality of this set. But there is widespread indirect evidence of enormous inequities in the world (World Bank, 2005). Here we

[4]The concept adopted is closest to that developed by Sen and Roemer; see, for example, Sen (1992) and Roemer (1998).

Figure 5.1 Divergence in human capital according to family circumstances starts in early childhood

Cognitive developement for children aged three to five in Ecuador differs markedly across different family backgrounds

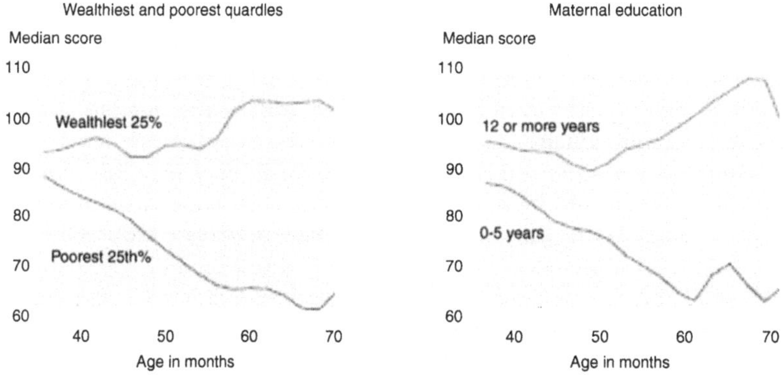

Source: Paxson and Schady (2005).

Note: Median values of the test of vocabulary recognition (TVIP) score (a measure of vocabulary recognition in Spanish, standardized against an international norm) are plotted against the child's age in months. The medians by exact month of age were smoothed by estimating regressions of the median score on age (in months), using a bandwidth of 3.

provide selected illustrations. Inequities start in early childhood. A measure of infant mortality, that is a good proxy for the general health status of young children, varies substantially both across countries, and within countries, in relation to measures of parental characteristics, such as wealth or maternal education. The average mortality rate in Bolivia is almost three times that of Colombia or Brazil, but so is the difference between infant mortality of children born of uneducated in relation to secondary educated Bolivian mothers. Country of birth and parental characteristics are clearly out of a child's control. Furthermore, the health status of young children is strongly associated with physical and cognitive abilities exhibited later in life.

Paxson and Schady (2005) find a major divergence across Ecuadorian children between 3 and 6 years old in a measure of cognitive development (based on a vocabulary recognition test), associated with a measure of the wealth of the household and the education of the mother (see Figure 5.1). As is well-established in longitudinal studies of the US, such differences in early childhood are typically magnified, rather than offset, by differences in the quality of formal education, in rich and poor countries alike.

It is also well known that investments in education are strongly influenced by the income, wealth, and educational level of parents. In Brazil, the share of the variance in the years of education of the population at working age that is explained by parent's characteristics ranges between 37 and 50 percent, depending on gender or year of birth. That share is still higher when considering earning rates that incorporate inter alia the quality of education. It ranges between 48 and 63 percent. In other words, around 50 percent of human capital formation may be explained by family background, whether the link is through early childhood development, parental preferences, or liquidity constraints faced by the parents.

Parental background continues to matter later in life. Still in the case of Brazil, it was found that the probability for labor-force participants 30 years and more to be employed in the formal labor market depended on the education of their parents, even after controlling for the age, gender, and own education of individuals.[5]

Liquidity constraints and lack of access to credit may also limit opportunities to invest in productive ventures. Here, too, there is plenty of evidence on such limits. The Investment Climate surveys conducted by the World Bank in more than 50 countries and approximately 60,000 firms, show that only 7.6 percent of micro enterprises had bank loans (against more than 60 percent for large firms) (see World Bank, 2004).

Examples of inequality of opportunities exist in other areas – barriers to entry in some sectors of activity or some professions, lack of voice in public decision making, lack of access to specific infrastructure – to give just a few categories.

Are inequities such as these of concern? Societies may be concerned with equity for both intrinsic and instrumental reasons. There is in fact considerable evidence of an intrinsic concern with equity, from the teachings of religions and other sources of moral leadership, from moral philosophy, from attitudes expressed by individuals and from behavioral experiments (for example those involving real money in game settings). We recognize the importance of such intrinsic, moral concerns, and believe they should form part of debates over practical policy design. But this is again not the main concern here. Our focus in this chapter is essentially instrumental. It is concerned with the relationship between equity and growth-related economic processes.

Interactions between equity and economic processes

The thesis is that many inequities interact with economic processes in ways that reduce growth, and that this works through specific inequalities of opportunities and their manifestation in economic and non-economic institutions. It is useful to loosely organize the interactions into two sets: *opportunity-restricting* and *privilege-preserving*. *Opportunity-restricting* is used to refer to the processes that curtail the economic opportunities for groups, especially those in the bottom and middle of the distribution.[6] This applies

---

[5]Both sets of evidence are drawn from regressions reported in Bourguignon *et al.* (2005), based on data from 1996.

[6]"Distribution" is used loosely to refer to distributions of wealth, power, status and influence that shape rankings of opportunities across the population.

both to human capital formation (perhaps especially for the poor) and to investment in productive activities (by farmers, the self-employed and entrepreneurs – often in the middle of the distribution).

Privilege-preserving refers to processes that favor economic and political elites in ways that channel the efforts both of themselves and aspirants to higher status into predatory, rent-creating or rent-preserving behaviors, as opposed to wealth-creation. These mechanisms typically restrict the opportunities of others. Obvious examples include measures that restrict entry into activities by competitors, or allow entry only against payment. Opportunity-restricting and privilege-preserving mechanisms are thus intimately related, typically reflecting different sides of the same political coin. But the distinction is often of practical use, and we make use of it in the policy section.

Supporting this intuitive account of processes are three analytical elements: first, the reproduction of inequalities leading to the persistence of inequality of opportunity; second, specific ways in which market imperfections interact with some particular types of inequality; and third, interactions between political inequalities and the formation of economic and non-economic institutions, that influence both the two preceding processes.

Inequality "traps"

We draw on literature in a variety of disciplines to support the view that inequalities of opportunities, and, therefore, of results, tend to reproduce themselves, both within a lifetime and across generations. We refer to these processes as inequality "traps." These work through interactions between the inheritance and processes of formation of inequalities of economic resources and human capital. Lack of access to credit or education is a source of inequality trap. People with limited access to these facilities end up with a level of resources that does not permit their children to do better on that account. Such a reproduction of the inequality of opportunity ends up being deeply embedded in political and socio-cultural processes (see Rao and Walton, 2004, for a survey and examples of the interactions between inequalities of power, economic and socio-cultural structures.) Absent this persistence we would be less concerned about interactions with efficiency and growth.

The persistence of inequalities is a phenomenon that is commonly observed, whether in terms of wealth differences, social status, political and economic influence, and of course income. This is true across castes in India, between racial or ethnic groups, in the US, South Africa, and in all Latin American societies with significant Afro- and indigenous groups or high levels of income inequality. There is evidence of considerable inter-generational persistence of incomes, in countries as diverse as Brazil and the US. Even in the land of opportunity of the US, recent work by Mazumder (2005) finds an intergenerational elasticity of incomes between fathers and sons of 0.6. Such a figure implies it would take some five generations for a family with half the average income to substantially close the gap. There is also evidence that mobility is lower at the bottom of the distribution, and especially so for Afro-Americans (Hertz, 2005).

Market imperfections and inequalities

The second analytical element is based on interactions between inequalities and market imperfections – drawing on a tradition of analysis associated with the work of Akerlof, Spence, and Stiglitz. Market failures, notably of information or agency, are profound in many markets that shape opportunity, notably for credit, insurance, land, and human capital. These interact with the distribution of wealth, status, and influence to reduce efficiency: lenders use wealth or connections to guide lending or provide collateral for credit; those with wealth have better options for managing risk and so on. This both increases the cost of investment, innovation, or risk-taking among groups without these initial endowments, and lowers the cost for the privileged. Inefficiencies can occur because good investment opportunities of poor and middle groups don't get financed and less good investment opportunities of the rich do.

Evidence for interactions between market failures and inequalities come from a variety of microeconomic evidence. One important category of evidence concerns the widespread disparities in lending rates across wealth categories, even after adjusting for risk and repayment probabilities. Investment in education is systematically biased to wealthier households. Poor people have limited access to insurance instruments and manage risks by inefficiently diversifying their activity. These and other categories of evidence lead to lower and middle parts of distributions having curtailed opportunities, leading to underinvestment and foregone innovation. By contrast, households in the top of the distribution have relatively cheap

Figure 5.2 Returns to capital decline with firm size for small firms in Mexico

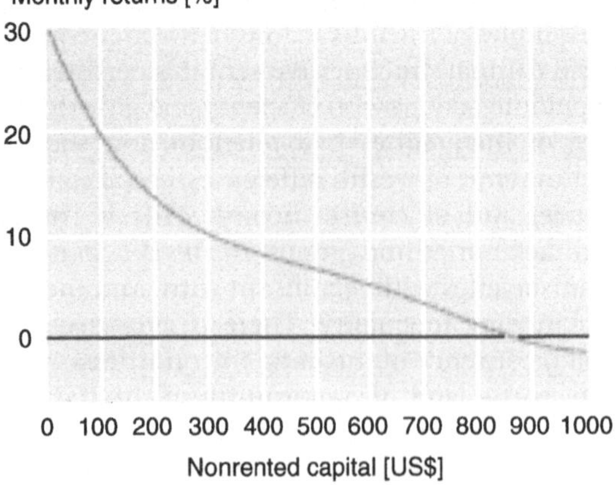

Source: McKenzie and Woodrulf (2003).

access to resources, can self-insure and may overinvest, as when relatively unintelligent rich kids get access to high quality education, or well-connected firms are able to borrow resources at low rates and invest them in relatively unproductive projects.

An illustration of the inefficiency of these market imperfections in the presence of initial inequalities of wealth is provided for a Latin-American country by McKenzie and Woodruff (2003). These authors were able to calculate returns to investment across the size distribution of Mexican firms, starting with micro-enterprises. They find very large returns (above 10 percent per *month*) for small firms, that decline significantly with firm size (Figure 5.2).[7] Such enormous discrepancies are suggestive of large inefficiencies: they should be bid away if equal access to credit markets allowed small firms to expand their capital and larger firms to downsize theirs.

Political inequalities and institutions

The third analytical element flows from traditions of thought that recognize that economic opportunities are shaped by formal and informal institutions, and that institutions are both endogenous and display persistence. This draws on work in economics associated with Douglass North, as well as extensive traditions in other social sciences. We emphasize the relationship between institutional design and inequalities of power, recognizing

Figure 5.3 Countries with better governance grow faster

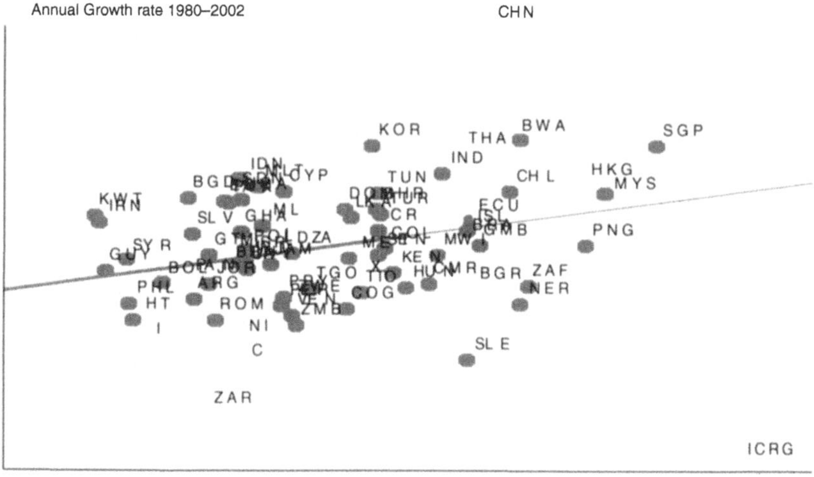

Source: Knack (2005).

[7]This result holds when controlling for the risk of business (cross-sectional variance of monthly returns) and for the quality of the entrepreneurs (using prior wages).

that institutions are shaped by distributional struggles. Unequal power structures are more likely to create extractive, predatory, or rent-preserving institutions that are good for elites, but are bad for provisioning of property rights and investment finance.

Note how these three elements interact. Institutions shape both inequality traps and the ways in which societies respond to market failures. For example, provision of free and compulsory public schooling is a response to a market failure, but whether it is adopted is a function of political choice.

Evidence on the role of political inequality and quality of institutions in growth and economic efficiency has been intensively researched over the past years. A point of departure is the correlation between measures of the quality of institutions in a country – for example protection of property rights or constraints on the executive – and its level of income. While debate on econometrics continues, a significant strand of recent literature argues for a causal relationship between historically formed institutions and contemporary *levels* of income.[8] In support of this, Knack (2005) finds 1980–2002 *growth rates* to be positively – although less strongly – associated with the initial value of an index of institutional quality after controlling for the initial level of income (Figure 5.3).

The difference between evidence on income levels and growth rates is important. Results on levels are very much of an historical nature. This is the perspective adopted in the influential recent paper by Acemoglu *et al.* (2002), a perspective that is highlighted by the instrumental variables they use to correct for the endogeneity of institutions and support the authors' view that the relationship is causal. In particular, the use of settlers' mortality during the colonial period as an instrument for today's institutions, suggests a rather long period of gestation. By contrast, using growth rates for recent decades and the quality of institutions at the beginning of that period does not run into this kind of difficulty. At the same time, the correlation is much weaker. It is also not clear that the time sequencing of the dependent and independent variables is sufficient to correct for endogeneity. It is possible for instance that an unobserved variable is responsible for both the quality of institutions at time t and the growth rate observed between t and t + 1.

Another type of evidence comes from in-depth case studies – the particularly influential work by Stanley Engerman and Kenneth Sokoloff (and co-authors), that uses the natural experiment of European colonization of the Americas to analyze different paths of institutional and economic development. Two results are highlighted here. First, this work explores the interaction between resource endowments, political inequalities and

[8]For examples see Acemoglu *et al.* (2001, 2002); Kaufmann and Kraay (2002); and Rodrik *et al.* (2002). Their interpretations of causal influences of historically formed institutions has been contested, in, for example, Glaeser *et al.* (2004).

institutions. For the early period of colonization, the authors argue that the combination of production potential for resource-based extraction – notably in silver, gold, and sugar – plus access to pools of subordinate, unskilled labor, led to the formation of extractive, oligarchic, and inequitable political and social institutions in Latin America. By contrast, in Northern America, English colonists tried to impose oligarchic structures and extractive economic institutions but failed to do so: there was neither the natural resource base nor ready supplies of subordinate labor (Engerman and Sokoloff, 2002; De Ferranti *et al.*, 2004).

Second – and perhaps more directly relevant to contemporary concerns – this work discusses how political inequalities were associated with a range of *choices* over institutional design in the nineteenth and early twentieth centuries, which tended to perpetuate inequity or to attenuate it. These included suffrage institutions, property rights in intellectual capital, public schooling, taxation and the shape of the financial system.[9]

Tradeoffs

The framework sketched above supports a potential causative influence of greater equity on both efficiency and growth. We see this as an important corrective to the dominant response of economists to questions of equity in terms of a tradeoff with efficiency. But we are not suggesting that tradeoffs do not exist. They certainly do. Achieving greater equity (for example through public education or more extensive road networks) will often require taxation or reallocation of public spending. Taxation (almost) always involves distortions to decision-making. The same is true for reducing public spending in public infrastructures that may be essential for productivity gains. These have to be assessed in the analysis of policy options.

A specific version of a tradeoff, that is of great practical importance for policymaking, concerns the management of transitions from more to less inequitable institutions and policies. To the extent that an inequitable initial position intrinsically protects the privileges of some, there will be losses to those privileged by the existing system, at least in the short-run. Such changes will be resisted, and the ensuing distributional struggle can lead to greater uncertainty and lower investment and innovation, with open conflict only the most extreme manifestation of such struggles.[10]

[9]See, for example, Engerman and Sokoloff (2005); Haber (2004); and Haber *et al.* (2003); Sokoloff and Zolt (2005).

[10]A full framework would deal explicitly with the role of distributional struggle and conflict. This is an area in which there are likely to be important interactions with growth, especially with respect to the management of crises (see for example Rodrik, 1999) and the possibility of perpetuation of a high-conflict equilibrium with polarized groups fighting over the distribution of existing assets or spoils (see García-Montalvo and Reynal-Querol, 2006).

In addition, even where existing structures are inefficient, for example via favored lending to inefficient business elites, or highly unequal landholdings, equity-enhancing reforms may lead to losses of organizational capital and economic networks, that lead to transitional, but potentially large, economic losses.

There is a considerable empirical micro-economic literature on the disincentive effect of taxes (on labor supply, savings, or investment behavior), which would seem to provide evidence of the existence of the preceding tradeoffs. However, this literature is not without critique. At the aggregate level, it is not clear that a higher level of taxation leads to less efficiency and slower growth. As emphasized by Lindert (2004), several European countries have shown remarkable long-run economic successes along with high levels of tax efforts. The empirical literature on the productive impact of various types of public spending is not without ambiguity either. In both cases, the ambiguity arises essentially from the econometric difficulty of identifying precisely the net effects of taxation or changes in the composition of public spending. However, this is not a reason for dismissing a priori the existence of short-run tradeoffs between equity-enhancing reforms and economic growth.

Do communist experiences provide evidence of a powerful tradeoff between equity-enhancing policies and economic growth? This experience is only of limited relevance to the above arguments, which refer to market rather than command economies. Most communist regimes did indeed do a very good job on equity in the domain of social provisioning. But at the same time they drastically restricted economic opportunities for the bulk of the population, preventing them from expressing their economic potential and condemning them to economic stagnation. In a Latin American context, it would be equally inappropriate to consider populist policies that have often been pursued in the name of greater equity, but have typically been bad for growth, as demonstrating an unavoidable tradeoff. The problem is that these policies were often oriented towards mere income redistribution, which we have seen may have a negative impact on growth, rather than enhancing the opportunities of the poor, and were macroeconomically unsound.

Country experiences of the link between equity and sustained growth

The evidence discussed in the previous section is supportive of specific channels of influence from equity to economic processes affecting growth. However, this evidence is only partial. The arguments in this chapter would be much stronger if they could rely on a positive aggregate relationship between some proxy for equity and medium to long-term growth rates across countries. It is unlikely that such a relationship could be identified, however. On the one hand, equity is a concept that has many dimensions which can hardly be "proxied" by a single indicator. On the other hand, as in other cross-country analyzes, country heterogeneity is extremely difficult to take satisfactorily into account. In effect, it is most likely that some components of the equity concept are of different relevance depending on the country that is analyzed. For this reason, there probably is very much to learn from case studies, but this is a research line that is still largely to be developed. In any case, it is not the purpose of this chapter to promise a new, generalized elixir for growth accelerations that would be embedded in the goal of equity. For none of these general elixirs work, with the cross-country work providing little support for the influence of specific policies on getting growth going, as recently discussed by Hausmann *et al.* (2005).

The absence of a generalized aggregate relationship need not imply pessimism, however. It rather takes us to a diagnostic perspective that emphasizes both specific pathways of causation, and the possibility of varied institutional resolutions to core principles affecting equity and associated economic process.[11] Scandinavia, Korea, and Taiwan (province of China) are obvious and well-documented cases of success in provisioning for equity and sustained growth. In particular, it is striking that in all these countries, sustained growth relied on heavy initial investments in the education of the whole population and a rather egalitarian distribution of land. In other words, sustained growth in these countries relied on an early drive towards equity. Of course, these may be found to be rather extreme examples of the link between equity and growth. But, the same lesson may be drawn from the history of economic growth in many of today's developed countries – starting with the historical experience of the US.

These examples may not constitute specific institutional models for Latin America, but the general lesson of successful growth on a foundation of equity may be relevant. However, all successful growth stories do not necessarily fit well the equity causation paradigm, countries like China, and Chile, in Latin America, being apparent exceptions to that relationship. Before discussing briefly these cases and showing that they are not necessary exceptions to the basic ideas in this chapter, we will briefly focus on two other categories of country experiences that look, at first glance, to be at variance with the analysis presented here: episodes of growth with *inequity*; and the (lack of) association between democracy and growth.

Inequitable growth episodes

Some Latin American countries have experienced periods of sustained growth apparently under significantly inequitable conditions. This included extended periods of growth in Brazil and Mexico in the middle of the

---

[11]It may be worth noting that the view that there can be different institutional forms for the resolution of common (equity) principles is broadly consistent with Rodrik (2003) on the interpretation of growth.

twentieth century. While specific factors were associated with these episodes, there is an overarching account. In each of these cases, economic elites had significant investment opportunities that were supported by the *partial and selective* provisioning of property rights. For Mexico, Haber *et al.* (2003) have developed the argument that "credible commitments" between political and economic elites involved the provision of the selective guarantee of property rights to specific elite groups, despite the lack of general protection of property rights. This was reflected in a highly concentrated banking system, with a significant degree of connected lending. Such inequitable provisioning was consistent with periods of growth, but brought dynamic costs through the restriction of entry and competition, and raised the stakes for distributional struggles over rents. Brazil had an authoritarian closure of the political system for extensive periods. Mexico had a semi-authoritarian form of corporate inclusion that effectively managed conflicts for several decades. But in none of these cases did the inequitable growth model prove to be sustainable over the long term.

Democracy and growth

We have emphasized that greater political equality should underpin the design of institutions that support broad-based investment and innovation. Isn't democratization a fundamental means of achieving greater political equality? Historical work by Engerman and Sokoloff and Lindert, referred to above, does indeed link the timing of the extension of the suffrage to expanded provision of education and other social programs. But, given the high multi-dimensionality of equity, democracy, while desirable, is neither necessary nor sufficient for greater equity. In some cases there may have been sufficient political or economic need to deliver to poorer groups to induce greater equity under authoritarian auspices. This may lie at the heart of the success of authoritarian East Asian cases: actual communist revolutions in China, the political base of the government in a poorer ethnic group as in Malaysia, or perceived positive development impact of education as in South Korea in the 1960s. On the other hand, formal democracy alone is no guarantee of either sufficient pressures for change in favor of poorer or middle groups, or of constraints on the power and privileges of political and economic elites, as Latin America's history amply illustrates.

The case of China

China looms large in any attempt to interpret development, and especially one that seeks to understand the role of equity in development processes. Hasn't it moved from a highly equitable form of communism to extensive use of domestic and international markets? And didn't this lead to *both* rising income inequality (Figure 5.4) *and* the most extraordinary pace and scale of reduction in poverty and expansion in social welfare in history?

Figure 5.4 The rise in income inequality in China, 1981–2002

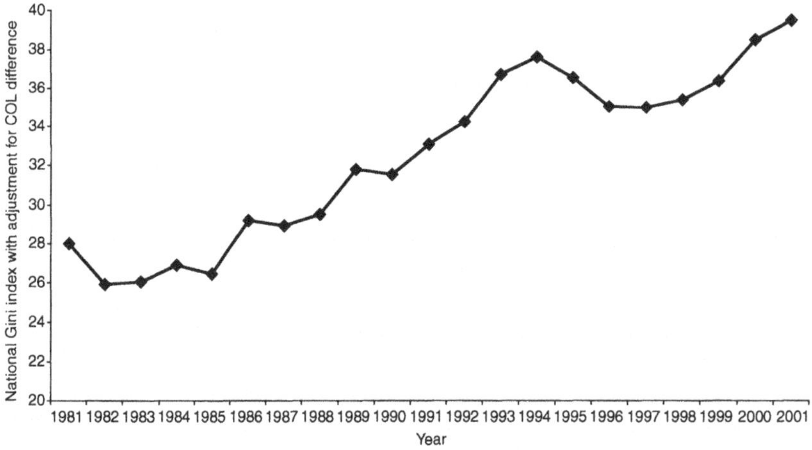

Source: Ravallion and Chen (2004)

Finally, did this not occur within the context of restricted democratic practices? This looks, at first glance, like a refutation of the central argument of this chapter: that equity, in the political and economic arenas, is necessary for prosperous development over the long term.

We believe that an account along these lines is an important misreading of change in China. Take some of the major shifts in Chinese policy that the literature interprets as having driven growth and income poverty: the institutional shift to the household responsibility system allowing peasants to produce for themselves (1979–early 1980s); massive indirect effects of opening to international trade (whole period); opening to inward FDI (especially in the 1990s); and huge internal migration flows. All these were essentially "equitable" in the sense of spreading of opportunity, from a situation of extensive restrictions on opportunities. In terms of equality of opportunities, China was indeed equitable before the reforms, but this was an *equality of restricted opportunities*. Reforms undertaken in 1978 and after contributed to expand the set of individual opportunities to market economy based opportunities, and *they initially did so more or less equally* among individuals, thus preserving initial equity. Ever since the end of the 1970s, this has been an important source of growth. At the same time, it is remarkable that it may be the initial equity in restricted opportunities that allowed for a swift opening of the economy to trade and FDI. Indeed, such a reform might not have been possible in the presence of an economic elite controlling entire sectors of the economy as in many other countries.

At a somewhat later stage, there were indeed aspects of Chinese development that increased inequity. The prevalence of investment linked to connections, and extensive corruption, is clearly inequitable, in the sense of both unfair process and inequalities of opportunity to all potential investors. While these have not had a major adverse effect on aggregate growth to date, introducing more transparent and fairer process will be important to sustained growth in the long term.

There were also periods in which policy-related shifts were associated with biases either against inner provinces or rural areas. These were factors behind the rise in inequality in outcomes and stagnating income poverty between the late-1980s and early-1990s. This unequal regional development coupled with restrictions on migration was inequitable in terms of rising inequality of opportunity. For these cases there may have been some tradeoff – or alternatively a more balanced policy stance might have achieved greater equity without significant growth losses.

Few observers argue that such policy-induced biases were essential to Chinese growth, in contrast to the overall institutional change and economic opening. Moreover, even using the narrower prism of income inequality, it is noteworthy that the periods when inequality fell (notably the early 1980s and the mid-1990s) actually had the highest growth rates, not the lowest. Also, provinces that experienced greater increases in inequality had lower growth (Ravallion and Chen, 2004).

With respect to patterns, there are also rising concerns within China over the adverse consequences for development of areas where there has been rising inequality, including in some areas of social provisioning (in health for example) and concentrations of wealth through connections. But there is no evidence that these brought benefits in income growth. On the contrary, for some years the Chinese government has seen this as an area where policy could be improved – see for instance the reference to "constructing a harmonious society" in the 11th 5-year plan.

Of course, democracy as part of an equitable society remains patently absent in China, even though decentralization might seem to be a first step towards this objective. Whether the transition towards a more effective democracy can take place without growth being temporarily slowed down is uncertain. The same is true of whether a democratized China could sustain the highest growth rates consistent with its economic evolution – which at some stage will necessarily involve a slowing down of the pace observed today.

A note on Chile

Chile remains the most important successful transition to sustained growth in Latin America (growth has been positive over the past 20 years except in 1999). Did equity contribute? Income inequality, a marker of inequity, has remained persistently high – especially following regressive resolutions of macroeconomic shocks in 1975 and 1982[12] – and is comparable to other high-inequality Latin American countries today. However, on a number of dimensions, post-democratization Chile seems more equitable than most other Latin American societies: there is greater equality before the law and more generalized protection of property rights (according to indices that seek to capture these factors); the return to democracy was associated with the re-formation of relatively programmatic political parties, in contrast to the vertical, clientelistic pattern so typical of Latin America; and, social provisioning is relatively equitable, according to incidence and sectoral studies. Judging from school enrollment rates, education is more equitably distributed within the population. Fifteen years ago, Chile ranked highest – with Uruguay – in Latin America in terms of net secondary school enrollment, despite lagging behind countries like Brazil or Mexico in terms of income per capita. This logically implies that education is more equally distributed within the population today than in other countries.[13] With respect to social spending, a push for more extensive and more equal provisioning was central to the democratic governments' political program. Work by Bravo *et al.* (2002) finds that the substantial and progressive levels of social spending led to a reduction in an augmented measure of distribution, which included incomes and the value of transfers, during the 1990s.[14] Also noteworthy are innovative activities, such as the *Puente* program, designed to break poverty traps.

Are the preceding factors sufficient to explain the superior growth performance of Chile in Latin-America over the past 20 years? This cannot be excluded. At the same time there also are issues of concern with respect to equity in Chile, fully comparable to other countries in the region, notably in areas ranging from health provisioning to the role of conglomerates. A more thorough comparison of the degree of equity in Latin American countries along the various dimensions of that concept is necessary before a more robust test can be made of the hypothesis that more equity in Chile is an important factor behind the sustained higher growth rates observed in that country.

[12]See Ffrench-Davis (2002), Ch. 9, for a discussion on the evolution of the Chilean income distribution, including links to macroeconomic conditions and policies.

[13]Another important difference between Chile and many Latin-American countries is the greater ethnic homogeneity of society, which logically contributes to more equity. However, this difference has been there for a very long time and may not be the most relevant to explain Chile's recent higher sustained growth rate

[14]This assumed that the value of social spending to recipients was equivalent to the cost to the government.

Implications for development strategy

The above diagnosis or hypotheses concerning the role of equity in development has substantial implications for the design of a growth-oriented strategy for Latin America. It implies, in particular, moving away from the dichotomy between growth and equity-oriented policy that has been a feature of discourse and practice in the region (as elsewhere). This dichotomy has scant theoretical support, but persists in the mind of many practical economists and development practitioners: ministers of finance and trade for growth; ministers of social development for equity.

We outline here some implications for public action. As noted earlier, it is useful to divide areas of action into two categories: those that expand opportunities for poor and middle groups – tackling the opportunity-restricting policies and institutions of the past; and those that seek to take on economy-wide conditions produced by the history of protection of privileges of elites (and other corporatist groups).

In moving to considerations of public action we need to consider the bogy of determinism. We have emphasized the importance of history, of inequality traps, and of institutional persistence. Does that imply there is little or no scope for action, that historically formed power structures and market imperfections are given, and that much of Latin America, that had a bad historical draw, is condemned to persistent inequity and low growth? Answering positively to that question would be a misreading of an approach informed by history and institutions. First, institutions are always products of contested interests and perspectives – recognizing institutional inertia is fully consistent with a role for political and social agency. Second, the underlying political and global context for Latin America is arguably less constraining than in the past, especially in the political domain – with universal suffrage and the spread of democracy at local levels, there are popular demands for *both* more equity and more growth. In most Latin American countries it is increasingly the case that individual interests can be aggregated and political coalitions can be formed that can support alternative designs for greater equity. Accordingly, after describing the two categories of action, we look at the question of managing transitions in relation to these categories.

Expanding opportunity for poor and middle groups

The first category involves using public action to remove restrictions on opportunities for poor and middle groups. As noted above, restrictions on opportunity often flow from interactions between market failures and inequalities of wealth, status or power. In economic terms, this implies measures that either deepen and extend markets (especially credit and insurance markets) or involve public action to offset the adverse effects of missing and imperfect markets. This involves an agenda of broadening

Figure 5.5 The impact of early childhood interventions on child development in an experiment in Jamaica

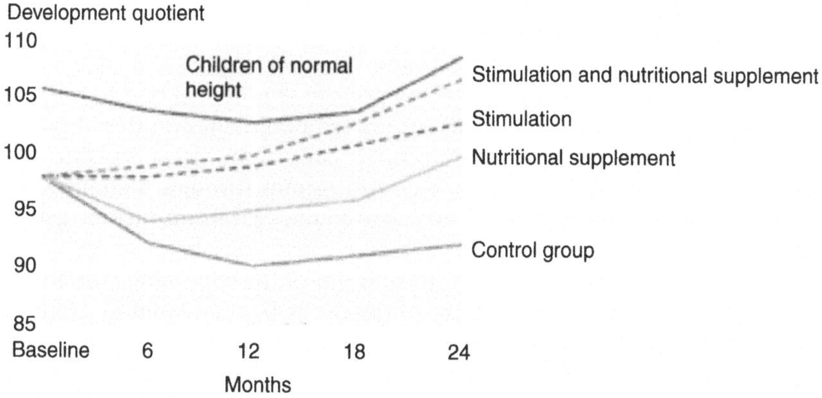

Source: Grantham-McGregor *et al.* (1991).

Note: The Development Quotient is an index composed of ratings in four behavioral and cognitive development indicators: locomotor (large-muscle activities, running and jumping), hand-eye coordination, hearing and speech performance (shape recognitiion, block construction, and block patterns).

access to the financial system, especially by small and medium entrepreneurs, developing comprehensive risk-management structures – including for health- and employment-related shocks – and educational systems that assure access to quality basic education for all, meritocratic entry to tertiary education, and effective training systems. For both politically supportable policies and effective implementation, such "technocratic" areas of design will need to be underpinned by tackling problems of lack of local voice, including inherited structures of social exclusion that curtail opportunities for particular groups (notably indigenous and Afro-Latino groups).

We illustrate with three specific policy areas where there are evaluated results. First, we noted earlier that the restriction of opportunities starts in early childhood, citing evidence from Ecuador. This is an area where there are known packages of interventions that can offset adverse family conditions through a mixture of nutrition and behavioral interactions and stimulation. Figure 5.5 provides the results of one randomized experiment in Jamaica. Infants with a significant developmental deficit associated with under- nutrition (and other correlated factors) were provided with different mixes of nutritional supplement and stimulation. After 24 months in the program those who received both interventions had almost caught up with children of normal height on an index of behavioral and cognitive development, those with no interventions actually suffered an increase in the deficit.

Second, the use of cash transfers to poor families, conditional on school and/clinic attendance, is proving an effective tool for both reducing current income poverty and improving access of children of poor families to school. This was pioneered in the region in the 1990s in Brazil (with *Bolsa Escola*) and Mexico (with PROGRESA, now *Oportunidades*).[15]

A third example of equity-enhancing policies is provided by rural roads that serve to reduce transport costs of isolated poor communities. A good example is the expansion of access to rural roads in the Sierra, in Peru. An evaluation that sought to obtain a control group through matching of communities without increased road access found significant income gains (Escobal and Ponce, 2002).

The preceding examples are only illustrations of the wide variety of interventions that can expand the opportunities of the poor and middle groups. Some of them mostly relate to human capital accumulation in segments of the population that did not have access to schools or health care. The effects of these interventions on growth will thus be delayed until the generations that have benefited from them are in the labor force. Other interventions that correct for existing market imperfections – improved access to infrastructure, to credit, to insurance – have been shown to have a more direct income impact on beneficiaries.

Tackling privilege-preserving mechanisms

The second category concerns institutions and policies that are the product of privilege-preserving processes. Because they have more power than others, elites are able to bias policy decisions in their own interest. And because their own interest does not necessarily coincide with that of the community, they are thus responsible for socially sub-optimal situations, which most often lead to slow growth. In effect, most of the action by the elites consists of creating market imperfections – for instance through barriers to entry in some sectors of economic activity – from which they can draw rents, or influencing tax and public spending decisions in their favor. Such privileges often concern political and economic elites but also corporate groups who have achieved success in "opportunity-hoarding," for example public sector unions or the beneficiaries of loss-making formal social security systems.

Privileges enjoyed by the elites or specific corporate groups have a direct impact on the opportunities offered to the poor and middle-groups. Barriers to entry stifle entrepreneurship among the poor and the middle

---

[15]See Székely (ch. 6, in this volume); Skoufias and McClafferty (2001) and Skoufias *et al.* (1999) for syntheses. It is true that a large share of the transfer is going to infra-marginal families – whose children would have attended in any case (de Janvry and Sadoulet, 2003). But to the extent a value is placed on the transfer itself – for its effects on reducing the income poverty– this is of less concern.

class, resistance to tax increases prevents implementation of opportunity-expanding policies for those groups, closed-shop practice by unions or pressure on wages restrict employment opportunities for the non-union part of the society. Knowing that they contribute to slow down development will not lead the elites to spontaneously forego their privileges, however. If they control political power, governments will not undertake equity and growth-enhancing policies that reduce the privileges of the elite. This fundamental issue of the "transition" towards more equity is tackled in the final section of this part of the chapter. Before considering it, however, it is helpful to give some examples of reforms that would break some privilege-preserving mechanisms and facilitate opportunity-enhancing policies. Such reforms do exist. In effect, many of them have been dealt with extensively in the economic literature (although generally not in the context of equity) from Adam Smith's attacks on the trade and entry-restricting impulses of powerful industrialists to the recent book on *Saving Capitalism from the Capitalists* by Rajan and Zingales (2003). In a Latin-American context, we look here at three areas: finance and taxation, and more briefly the conduct of macroeconomic stabilization policy.

Capture of the financial sector

Many of Latin America's financial systems are narrow, and consequently, access is relatively restricted. As Figure 5.6 shows, credit to the private sector is lower in Mexico than India as a share of GDP. In Brazil it is about the same as much-poorer India and less than a third of Korea's. This is an indirect indicator of the lack of availability of credit for many new and

Figure 5.6 Credit to the private sector, various countries

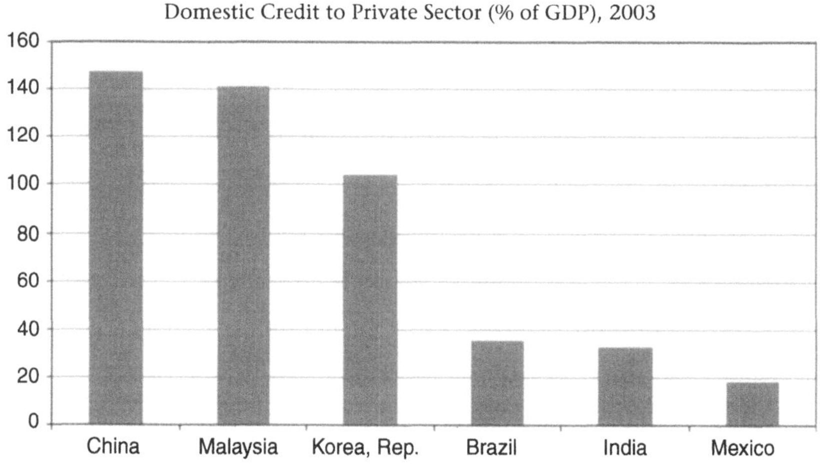

Source: World Development Indicators.

existing firms as well as for households. It is supported by other indicators. Only 25 percent of households in Mexico City (a relatively affluent part of the country) make use of banking services. Analysis of the historical evolution of Mexico's banking system (Haber, 2004) shows how a narrow financial system was a product of an effective deal struck amongst political and economic elites, that led to a concentrated and protected banking system and industrial and service sector, with connected lending important, leading to low asset quality.

The standard answer to protected, narrow financial systems would seem to be liberalization. But there is a paradox: rapid economic liberalization in a context of unequal influence can lead to the continued concentration among economic elites and further distortions (see Claessens and Perotti, 2005, for discussion of international evidence.) Such an increase in loan concentration was observed in Chile after the across-the-board liberalization of 1975. This was accompanied with a shortening of credit maturity and a surge in the rate of interest (Ffrench-Davis, 2002). This is also the story of Mexico's privatization of the early 1990s (Haber and Kantor, 2004). The privatization of banks was designed to favor influential domestic interests, to the extent that new owners could get away with modest levels of own-equity (with lax rules on borrowing to finance purchases). The incentive structure favored rapid credit growth, continued connected lending, and low asset quality. This was a central conditioning factor for the Tequila crisis. The subsequent late 1990s reforms, which led to an overwhelmingly foreign-owned banking system, led to better asset quality but a

Figure 5.7 Coverage of micro finance: various countries and regions (micro-finance clients as proportion of the population)

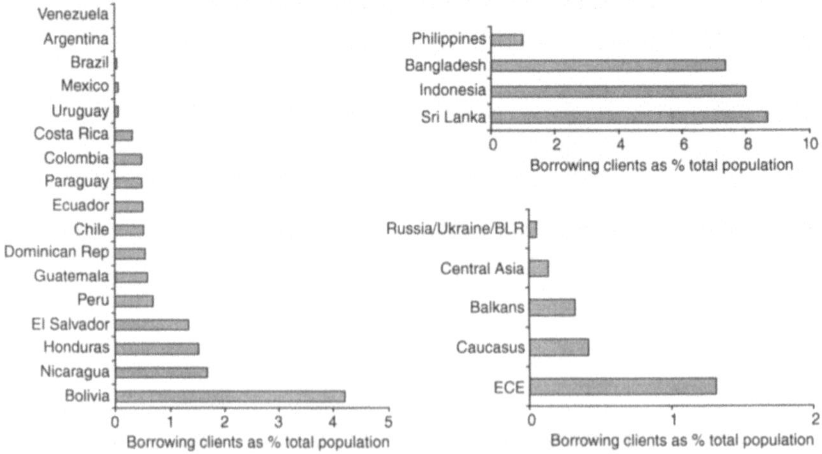

Source: Honohan (2004).

highly risk-averse, and still very narrow, system. In one interpretation, part of the reason is that the context of weak property rights – for dispute resolution and collection of bad loans – persists (Haber and Kantor, 2004).

There are many dimensions to financial sector reform; the purpose here is to emphasize the role of (unequal) political context, and to design reform processes in ways that both pursue technical approaches to broadening of access (mobile banking, reverse factoring, using Internet platforms) and develop the accountability structures to prevent re-capture by narrow groups (Claessens and Perotti, 2005). Micro-finance has probably a role here, at the same time that it is part of the more targeted opportunity-expanding measures discussed above. Currently coverage is very low in Latin America, with Bolivia, at 4 percent of the population the highest, whereas it is close to negligible in Brazil or Mexico (Figure 5.7).[16] In contrast, three poor Asian societies have attained coverage of the order of 8 percent. There is opportunity for expansion, it can bring benefits to the self-employed and micro-enterprise sector, but is a complement, and by no means a substitute for the broadening of access in the core financial system (Honohan, 2004).

Taxes

As stated earlier, most opportunity-expanding reforms require an increase in public spending, which in turn should be financed either by reallocating spending or by raising taxes. To be effective, both policies must necessarily reduce the privileges of the elite. In the first case, the elite lose free access to some services or infrastructure. In the second case, they suffer net income losses. The focus here will be on taxes, but most of the argument also applies to public spending benefiting the elite.

The central story on taxes in Latin America is that elites get away with paying little, sustaining an equilibrium of relatively low provision of social and economic services, often of low quality, and consequently low support in the general population for higher tax efforts. The overall tax effort is low as a share of GDP for most countries – with some exceptions (Brazil has high taxes, in part due to high social security contributions, but also very unequal spending.) And the most striking difference in tax structures is the much lower take on individual income taxes than in rich countries: on average Latin American countries get less than 1 percent of GDP, while developed countries receive over 7 percent (Table 5.1). Also of importance are the very low receipts on property taxes – less than half the share of rich countries. This contrast has long historical roots, linked to the size of local government: in the nineteenth and early twentieth centuries, local governments in the US and Canada accounted for a major

[16]Note that no distinction is made between public (subsidized) and private micro-finance operations in those figures.

Table 5.1 Tax structure in the 1990s, Latin America and developed countries (% of GDP, consolidated central government)

	Latin America and the Caribbean		*Developed countries*
Tax category	*1990–94*	*1995–99*	*1991–2000*
Income taxes	*3.6*	*3.4*	*9.7*
Individual	0.5	0.9	7.1
Corporate	1.9	1.7	2.3
Social security	*2.5*	*2.9*	*7.8*
Taxes on goods and services	*5.6*	*7.4*	*9.5*
VAT and sales	3.2	4.8	6.5
Excises	2.1	2.3	3.0
Trade taxes	*2.2*	*1.8*	*0.3*
Imports	1.9	1.8	0.3
Exports	0.1	0.0	0.0
Property taxes	*0.4*	*0.3*	*0.8*
All taxes	*14.2*	*16.1*	*28.7*

Source: Stotsky and WoldeMariam (2002); and International Monetary Fund (IMF) Government Financial Statistics (GFS) database.

share of total government revenues, with property taxes a primary source (Sokoloff and Zolt, 2005). In Latin America, local governments raised lower revenues, and primarily from taxes other than on property.

Some of the constraints on taxation are greater than in the past – especially with greater mobility of capital and skilled labor. But individual income tax rates (let alone taxes paid) are in many countries less than the US, which would seem to be a reasonable benchmark for skilled labor. The more fundamental issue is re-shaping the tax-spending contract within society that is central to the overall accountability relationship between government and citizenry. The VAT, which is also considerably lower in Latin America than in rich countries, is reasonably at the core of this, but extending income and property taxes, and raising the take from elites, is an important complement.[17]

Macroeconomic policy

The conduct of macroeconomic policy may not seem to be a domain in which entrenched privileges and associated inequities play a major role.

[17]Of course, the issue is not only that of the tax code but of its implementation. A key issue is that of tax elusion and tax evasion in the country itself or in tax havens.

However, recent work indicates that there are significant connections. First, there is evidence that distributional conflicts, and weak conflict-management institutions, can increase the proclivity of countries to suffer crises, and then suffer more long-lasting growth effects of crises.[18] Second, when crises occur, there is evidence of regressive distributional resolutions. For example, case studies of financial crises in a number of Latin American countries, including Argentina, Chile, Ecuador, and Mexico, find that workouts tend to benefit those within the financial system, at the expense of those outside, and larger and better connected interests at the expense of smaller and less-influential agents (Halac and Schmukler, 2003). Under these conditions, the conduct of short-run macroeconomic policy offers scope for equity-enhancing reforms. In particular, the use of contra-cyclical instruments, stronger and more independent supervision and regulation of financial systems, and *ex ante* deposit insurance for small and medium depositors (De Ferranti *et al.*, 2004) could go a long way in avoiding crises that reinforce the privileges of the elite and reduce the opportunities of the poor.

Managing transitions

The central message of this chapter is the need to shift from inequitable initial conditions and institutions in ways that broaden economic opportunities. Some of these changes may benefit all groups in society. Such Pareto-improving reforms should be implemented spontaneously by governments, unless all groups in society are not well informed about the direct and indirect effects of these reforms. Analysis and dissemination would then be all that is needed for a transition to a more equitable and faster growing society. But many of the changes we discussed will typically not be Pareto-improving, at least in the short to medium term. The political economy of transitions is thus central. There is a difference between the two categories of intervention – especially under contemporary democratic conditions, and we look at each in turn.

Many of the opportunity-expanding interventions involve additional services to the poor, or improving the quality of universal services. Over the long term they should improve the productivity of poorer groups, and this is potentially complementary to the interests of economic elites. Measures such as these have the potential to command broad support. They typically do not involve direct attacks on privileges, but often do require spending. This implies raising taxes or reduce other spending, imposing a squeeze on

[18]Acemoglu *et al.* (2002) argue that there is a causal relationship between the historically shaped part of institutional weakness and macroeconomic instability; Rodrik (1999) finds that countries with greater latent distributional conflicts and weak conflict-management institutions do a worse job in managing exogenous shocks, with adverse effects on subsequent growth.

privileged groups now, but with the prospect of future gains for all. There is at least the possibility of shifts being Pareto-improving over the long term.

While this eases the overall structure of the political economy challenge, the politics of institutional change can still be complex. The introduction of PROGRESA/*Oportunidades* illustrates. This program was designed in the wake of widespread political reaction against the earlier PRONASOL program, a form of social fund that was an instrument of President Salinas' strategy to build political support via traditional patronage mechanisms. The reaction created the political space for a more "technocratic" program, space that was most skillfully used. Transfers in return for more education and health of poor children is more politically acceptable to both the broad populace and the elite than straight subsidies, since they have the potential to increase the productivity of the population and accelerate growth, possibly leading to some dynamic Pareto-improvement. Moreover, the carefully documented positive results from the randomized evaluation contributed to the credibility of the program and its bridging to the new administration. The Fox administration embraced and expanded the program under the new name of *Oportunidades*.

What of the second category of intervention, where reducing privileges is central to a shift to sustained growth? Change here is less likely to be Pareto-improving even in the long run, and even if growth does take off. Indeed, an essential part of a more dynamic Latin America society is likely to be greater downward mobility from the top than at present, as well as more upward mobility from the bottom and middle. What factors may influence politically feasible changes?

First, in some areas, some compensation of losers is relevant, though the relevance may be restricted by the need to reduce *permanent* privileges. One example, already commonly used, is the use of severance pay to compensate for layoffs in privatizing companies. Where the issue is protection from risks, a promising approach is to shift to *ex ante* insurance. Leaving risk management to the *ex post* working of unequal influence is highly inequitable and often economically costly. This is vividly illustrated by the typically unequal patterns of loss allocations via bailouts in Latin American financial crises (Halac and Schmukler, 2003). Shifting to defined rules of the game, notably over deposit insurance, can help ameliorate this.

Second, forming coalitions for privilege-reducing change has to be central to the structure of a political economy resolution. These may involve alliances between the bottom and middle, or with parts of the elite, since in most countries the elite is unlikely to be monolithic. In theory, the existence of some minimum democratic mechanisms should permit such outcomes to emerge. But forming such alliances for change may be one of the challenges within Latin America's political system. The dominant heritage is of vertical political structures, working through both the state and political parties. This takes the form of clientelism and patronage, or the inheritance of corporatist structures of inclusion of the twentieth century. With such practices, democracy is incomplete and forming alliances for change is more difficult. The transition to programmatic parties, that was central to successful transitions from clientelism in Europe and American cities, remains incomplete and weak. Chile is relatively unusual in having essentially programmatic parties, in a tradition going back to before the Pinochet regime.

As members of the elite partly control the way the political system works, they may impede or at least delay such a transition from clientelism to more democratic political practices based on programmatic parties. Whether they would actually oppose such a change depends on what costs them more: keeping a patronage system that permanently will draw on their resources or shifting to more democratic mechanisms that will terminate some of their privileges. This situation differs from the Pareto-improvement case considered earlier. It essentially involves the elite maximizing its long-run welfare, by choosing the least costly of various possible institutions. Here, too, information is essential. The main actors in that game may not always have perfect knowledge of the actual cost for them of various reforms that would expand opportunities in the rest of the population.

A third set of factors for change are exogenous or controlled by external actors. For instance, technological change imported from abroad may in some cases modify the costs and benefits of equity-enhancing reforms. Also, external competition through international trade or capital flows can be a potent force for lowering internal barriers to entry and increasing access to finance (for developed countries see Rajan and Zingales, 2003). The increasing easiness with which societies can compare with each other due to rapid progress in information technology should also contribute to facilitating equity-enhancing reforms by expanding the information set of all local political actors.

Conclusion

In this chapter we have argued that one of the major issues faced by Latin America is not about how to achieve growth with equity. It is rather about *understanding the relationship* between equity – understood in terms of equal opportunities in the economic, social, and political realms – and the growth process. This relationship works through specific inequalities, shaped by market and political institutions. There are important positive links between equity and efficiency, and between equity and incentives for investment and innovation. Latin America is characterized by a wide array of institutional structures that are both opportunity-restricting for the poor and middle groups and privilege-preserving for elites and corporatist groups (including some unions), at national and local levels. Failure to address these inequities undercuts long-run growth, and this is a central part of the long-run Latin American malaise.

The transition to democracy, the broadening of information flows, the vitality of the press and deepening of civil society, all these phenomena provide a more hospitable political basis for tackling inequities in ways that are supportive of sustained growth. But there are many ways of striving for equity: some, such as communist economic strategies and populist macro policies have proved to be disastrous for growth, the former by eliminating market opportunities and the latter by ignoring basic macroeconomic constraints. It is of great importance that policy design and public debate be shaped by an understanding both of the fundamental positive links between equity and growth and the risks of misguided strategies. Getting rid of the typical dichotomization of analysis of growth and equity – at least in economic discourse – is a necessary step.

Finally, we would note that this analysis has important implications for empirical work in the future. The approach presented here has argued for a relationship between equity and sustained growth exclusively through interactions between *specific* inequalities (including political inequalities), market functioning and economic and non-economic institutions. Future work needs to build on analysis of microeconomic, political and social processes, both to deepen our diagnostic base and to inform policy design.

References

Acemoglu, D., S. Johnson, and J.A. Robinson (2002) "Reversal of fortune: geography and institutions in the making of the modern world income distribution," *Quarterly Journal of Economics*, 117(4), pp. 1231–94.

Acemoglu, D., S. Johnson, and J.A. Robinson (2001) "The colonial origins of comparative development: an empirical investigation," *American Economic Review*, 91(5), pp. 1369–401.

Aghion, Ph., E. Caroli, and C. García-Peñalosa (1999) "Inequality and economic growth: the perspective of the New Growth Theories," *Journal of Economic Literature*, 37, pp. 1615–60.

Alesina, A. and D. Rodrik (1994) "Distributive politics and economic growth," *Quarterly Journal of Economics*, 109, pp. 465–89.

Banerjee, A. and E. Duflo (2003) "Inequality and growth: what can the data say?," *Journal of Economic Growth*, 8(3), pp. 267–99.

Banerjee, A. and A.F. Newman (1993) "Occupational choice and the process of development," *Journal of Political Economy*, 101(2), pp. 274–98.

Bénabou, R. (2000) "Unequal societies: income distribution and the social contract," *American Economic Review*, 90(1), pp. 96–129.

Bénabou, R. (1996) "Inequality and growth," in B. Bernanke and J. Rotemberg (eds), *National Bureau of Economic Research Macroeconomics Annual 1996*, MIT Press, Cambridge, MA.

Bertola, G. (2000) "Macroeconomics of distribution and growth," in A. Atkinson and F. Bourguignon (eds), *Handbook of Income Distribution*, North-Holland, Amsterdam.

Bourguignon, F., F. Ferreira, and M. Menéndez (2005) "Inequality of opportunity in Brazil?," World Bank, Washington, DC.

Bourguignon, F., F. Ferreira, and N. Lustig (2004) *The Microeconomics of Income Distribution Dynamics in East Asia and Latin America*, Oxford University Press for the World Bank, New York.

Bravo, D., D. Contreras, and I. Millán (2002) "The distributional impact of social expenditure: Chile 1990–1998", in *Chile's High Growth Economy: Poverty and Income Distribution 1987–1998*, World Bank Country Study, World Bank, Washington, DC, pp. 73–114.

Bruno, M., M. Ravallion, and L. Squire (1998) "Equity and growth in developing countries: old and new perspectives on the policy issues," in V. Tanzi and Ke-young Chu, (eds), *Income Distribution and High-quality Growth*, MIT Press, Cambridge, MA.

Claessens, S. and E. Perotti (2005) "The links between finance and inequality: channels and evidence," background paper for the *World Development Report 2006*, World Bank, Washington, DC.

De Ferranti, D., G.E. Perry, F.H.G. Ferreira, and M. Walton (2004) *Inequality in Latin America: Breaking with History?*, World Bank, Washington, DC.

De Janvry, A. and E. Sadoulet (2003) "Targeting and calibrating educational grants: focus on poverty or on non-enrolment risk?", University of California, Berkeley.

Engerman, S.L. and K.L. Sokoloff (2005) "The evolution of suffrage institutions in the New World," *Journal of Economic History*, 65(4), pp. 891–921.

Engerman, S.L. and K.L. Sokoloff (2002) "Factor endowments, inequality, and paths of development among New World economies," *Economía*, 3(1), pp. 41–88.

Escobal, J. and C. Ponce (2002) "The benefits of rural roads: enhancing income opportunities for the poor," paper presented at the fifth meeting of the LACEA/IDB/World Bank Network on Inequality and Poverty, Madrid.

Ferreira, F.H.G. and M. Walton (2006, forthcoming) "Inequality of opportunity and economic development," in G. Kochendorfer-Lucius and B. Pleskovic (eds), *Equity and Development*.

Ffrench-Davis, R. (2002) *Economic Reforms in Chile: From Dictatorship to Democracy*, University of Michigan Press, Ann Arbor.

Forbes, K.J. (2000) "A reassessment of the relationship between inequality and growth," *American Economic Review*, 90(4), pp. 869–87.

Galor, O. and J. Zeira (1993) "Income distribution and macroeconomics," *Review of Economic Studies*, 60, pp. 35–52.

García-Montalvo, J. and M. Reynal-Querol (2006, forthcoming) "Why ethnic fractionalization? Polarization, conflict and growth," *American Economic Review*.

Glaeser, E., R. La Porta, F. López-de-Silanes, and A. Schleifer (2004) "Do institutions cause growth?," Harvard University, Cambridge, MA.

Haber, S. (2004) "Political institutions and economic development: evidence from the banking systems of the United States and Mexico," paper presented at the Economics, Political Institutions, and Financial Markets II: Institutional Theory and Evidence from Europe, the United States, and Latin America Conference, February 5, Palo Alto, CA.

Haber, S. and S. Kantor (2004) "Getting privatization wrong: the Mexican banking system, 1991–2003," paper presented at the World Bank Conference on Bank Privatization in Low and Middle-Income Countries, November 23, Washington, DC.

Haber, S., N. Maurer, and A. Razo (2003) *The Politics of Property Rights: Political Instability, Credible Commitments, and Economic Growth in Mexico: 1876–1929*, Cambridge University Press, Cambridge, UK.

Halac, M. and S.L. Schmukler (2003) "Distribution effects of crises: the role of financial transfers," *World Bank Policy Research Working Paper Series* no. 3173, Washington, DC.

Hausmann, R., L. Pritchett, and D. Rodrik (2005) "Growth accelerations," Harvard University.

Hertz, T. (2005) "Rags, riches and race: the intergenerational economic mobility of black and white families in the U.S.," in S. Bowles, H. Gintis, and M. Osborne Groves (eds), *Unequal Chances. Family Background and Economic Success*, Princeton University Press, Princeton, NJ.

Honohan, P. (2004) *Financial Sector Policy and the Poor: Selected Findings and Issues*, World Bank, Washington, DC.

Kanbur, R. (2000) "Income distribution and development," in A. Atkinson and F. Bourguignon (eds), *Handbook of Income Distribution*, North-Holland, Amsterdam.

Kaufmann, D. and A. Kraay (2002) "Growth without governance," *Economía*, 3(1), pp. 169–215.

Knack, S. (2005) "Lessons from the 1990s – Governance and growth," World Bank Development Research Department.

Kuznets, S. (1955) "Economic growth and income inequality," *American Economic Review*, 45(1), March, pp. 1–28.

Lewis, A.W. (1954) "Economic development with unlimited supplies of labor," *Manchester School of Economic and Social Studies*, 22(2), pp. 139–91.

Li, H. and H.-fu Zou (1998) "Income inequality is not harmful for growth: theory and evidence," *Review of Economic Development*, 2(3), pp. 318–34.

Lindert, P.H. (2004) *Growing Public: Social Spending and Economic Growth since the Eighteenth Century*, Cambridge University Press, Cambridge, UK.

Mazumder, B. (2005) "The apple falls even closer to the tree than we thought: new and revised estimates of the intergenerational inheritance of earnings," in S. Bowles, H. Gintis, and M. Osborne Groves (eds), *Unequal Chances: Family Background and Economic Success*, Princeton University Press, Princeton, NJ.

McKenzie, D. and Ch. Woodruff (2003) "Do entry costs provide an empirical basis for poverty traps? Evidence from Mexican microenterprizes," Cambridge, Mass., Harvard University, Bureau for Research in Economic Analysis of Development (BREAD) Working Paper 20. Available on line at: http://www.cid.harvard.edu/bread/papers/working/020.pdf.

Paxson, Ch.H. and N. Schady (2005) "Cognitive development among young children in Ecuador: the roles of wealth, health and parenting," *World Bank Policy Research Working Paper Series*, no. 3605, Washington, DC.

Rajan, R.G. and L. Zingales (2003) *Saving Capitalism from the Capitalists: Unleashing the Power of Financial Markets to create Wealth and Spread Opportunity*, Crown Business, New York.

Rao, V. and M. Walton (eds) (2004) *Culture and Public Action*, Stanford University Press, Stanford, CA.

Ravallion, M. and Sh. Chen (2004) "China's (uneven) progress against poverty," *World Bank Policy Research Working Paper Series*, no. 3408, Washington, DC.

Rodrik, D. (2003) "Growth strategies," paper prepared for the *Handbook on Economic Growth*, Harvard University Press, Cambridge, MA.

Rodrik, D., A. Subramanian, and F. Trebbi (2002) "Institutions rule: the primacy of institutions over geography and integration in economic development," *National Bureau of Economic Research Working Paper Series*, no. 9305, Cambridge, MA.

Rodrik, D. (1999) "Where did all the growth go? External shocks, social conflict, and growth collapses," *Journal of Economic Growth*, 4(4), pp. 385–412.

Roemer, J.E. (1998) *Equality of Opportunity*, Harvard University Press, Cambridge, MA.

Sen, A. (1992) *Inequality Reexamined*, Harvard University Press, Cambridge, MA.

Skoufias, E. and B. McClafferty (2001) *Is PROGRESA Working? Summary of the Results of an Evaluation by IFPRI*, International Food Policy Research Institute, Washington, DC.

Skoufias, E., B. Davis, and J.J. Behrman (1999) *Final Report: An Evaluation of the Selection of Beneficiary Households in the Education, Health, and Nutrition Program (PROGRESA) of Mexico*, International Food Policy Research Institute, Washington, DC.

Sokoloff, K.L. and E.M. Zolt (2005) "Inequality and the evolution of institutions of taxation: Evidence from the economic history of the Americas," University of California, Los Angeles.

Stotsky, J.G. and A. WoldeMariam (2002) "Central American tax reform: trends and possibilities," *Fiscal Affairs Department Working Paper* no. 02/227, International Monetary Fund, Washington DC.

World Bank (2005) *World Development Report 2006: Equity and Development*, Oxford University Press, New York.

World Bank (2004) *World Development Report 2005: A Better Investment Climate for Everyone*, Oxford University Press, New York.

6
Pro-Growth Social Policies for Latin America

Miguel Székely[1]

Introduction

Most governments in the developing world explicitly consider absolute poverty reduction as their main – or at least as one of their main – priorities in the agenda. In fact, all those endorsing the eight Millennium Development Goals (MDGs) have committed publicly to cut poverty by half between 1990 and 2015.[2]

The endorsement of the MDGs, and in particular, of the goal which is directly related to poverty, is in itself an advance in terms of acknowledging that poverty reduction should be at the center stage of policy decisions. Agreeing to specific targets and to the generation and use of concrete indicators to monitor progress, has additionally contributed to a revived debate on how to achieve the objective.

The level of poverty at any point in time depends, on the one hand, on the amount of resources available in an economy, and on the other, on the ways in which such resources are shared among the population. Therefore, most of the discussion about how to achieve the first of the MDGs has revolved around the use of policy tools that affect the level of economic growth and/or the distribution of resources over time – and, therefore, inequality.

Although few would argue that the policy choice is *either* to focus exclusively on growth-promoting policies, *or* alternatively, to focus only on redistributing the existing resources for reducing inequality, these two extremes tend to be in the background of the debate. For instance, there is a strand of literature that sustains that "growth will mostly do the job,"

[1]This chapter was initiated while the author served as Deputy Minister for Planning and Evaluation at the Ministry of Social Development of Mexico. We thank participants in the Conference organized by ECLAC for useful comments and suggestions.
[2]See, for instance, Machinea *et al.* (2005) for a more detailed description of the MDGs.

since there is evidence that when there is growth, the incomes of the poor generally rise, and there is poverty reduction.[3] Under this perspective, specific policies directed to the economically disadvantaged are not necessarily a priority. The priority is to guarantee growth in mean incomes.

The matter is much less clear in the case of the relationship between poverty and changes in the distribution of resources. At first sight it would seem straightforward that given a certain income level, a redistribution of resources to low income groups – with the consequent reduction in inequality – would reduce poverty, while regressive redistributions would make poverty rise.[4] The complication comes when it is realized that usually there are feedbacks between changes in the distribution and economic growth itself.

The literature has not been able to settle entirely on the question of which way the feed back goes, and there are mainly two opposing views:[5] one sustaining that more inequality is good for growth, and, therefore, good for poverty reduction at least to some extent, and another arguing that inequality is bad for growth and, therefore, bad for poverty reduction. The main argument behind the first of these positions is inspired by the Kaldorian view that since the rich generally have higher savings rates to finance investment, redistributions of resources towards these groups tend to trigger economic growth, which in turn reduces poverty by increasing all incomes through a trickle down effect. Under this argument, regressive redistributions may affect the poor negatively in the short run, but they will eventually be beneficial when growth spurs. Following this line of argument, income redistributions towards the poor will not only deviate resources towards those with lower propensity to save and invest, but will also introduce a series of distortions including adverse labor supply decisions, deadweight losses, and other inefficiencies in the economy that will reduce "the size of the cake" for all, and will, therefore, lead to greater poverty.

The second position is that higher inequality or regressive redistributions are bad for poverty, not only because they may reduce the lot of the poor directly, but also because inequality is bad for growth. As shown by Bourguignon and Walton (ch. 5, this volume), there are several theoretical arguments that explain why this may be the case, including imperfect markets, the political economy of redistribution, and the risks of social

[3]The paper by Dollar and Kraay (2002) is a good example of this. The authors argue that on average, the incomes of the poor rise at least proportionally with increases in GDP.

[4]Strictly speaking, this depends on the exact section of the distributions where the changes take place. For instance, there might be increases in inequality due to redistributions at the top end that do not affect the poor.

[5]See Aghion *et al.* (1999) for a review of the literature.

unrest. The central one for our discussion – put forward initially by Galor and Zeira (1993) and Banerjee and Newman (1993) – states that when inequality is the result of market imperfections affecting the poor, such as credit constraints, high return investment projects will not be undertaken by this group of society, and the potential of the economy will be restrained by inefficiency. If the market imperfection is relaxed or eliminated, the poor will increase their income through human and physical capital investment, and this in turn will increase overall output and will improve the distribution of resources at the same time. In other words, having a sector of the population with low economic capacity and productivity due to market imperfections (and not due to labor supply, investment, or other individual preferences), restrains economic activity through the impossibility of taking advantage of the opportunities offered by the environment.

As clearly explained by Bourguignon and Walton (ch. 5, this volume), the real world is somewhere in between the two extreme positions. There are continuous feedbacks between poverty, inequality and economic growth that depend on specific country conditions and that can vary over time. This makes it difficult to generalize on which of the effects is stronger, and, therefore, which way the net relationship goes. For instance, economic growth can directly or indirectly benefit the poor, and is certainly a pre-condition for sustained poverty reduction, but the extent to which the poor benefit varies widely across space and time.[6] It depends on changes in payments to factors of production, on the geographic location of economic activity, on the initial distribution of assets, and so on. Inequality also affects growth and poverty in different ways depending on the specific context, and leads to more or less poverty reduction in different circumstances. In the end, the relationship between these three variables can be viewed as a triangle, where poverty, inequality, and growth are in each of the axes, with multiple back and forth country- and time-specific effects.

The public policy question under this scheme is how to use policy tools to affect one or more of these dynamic relationships. In the case of poverty, one would want to identify interventions where apart from having no growth-equity tradeoff, or a low tradeoff, the intervention is pro-growth in the sense that by benefiting the poor, there is a positive net effect on overall output.[7] Following Bourguignon (2004), this can be achieved through reducing wealth inequality by eliminating or relaxing the market

[6]Foster and Székely (2000) present empirical evidence along these lines.
[7]For a discussion on the definition of *pro-poor* growth, see for instance, Kakwani *et al.* (2000).

imperfections that inhibit the accumulation of income-earning assets among the poor. By creating the conditions for enhanced human and physical capital accumulation among this group of society, overall investment and output increase, and the poor will be better equipped to take advantage of the opportunities that the economic context generates:[8] that is, greater human and physical capital accumulation among the poor increases their productivity, and with it, overall productivity rises and greater growth rates can be achieved.[9]

One of the most promising policy mechanisms explicitly designed along these lines, are the Targeted Conditional Cash Transfer Programs (TCCTPs). These kinds of programs have recently flourished in Latin America, and are now being considered by a wide set of countries in other regions. TCCTPs have been subject of growing interest precisely because they entail a long-term view on poverty reduction based on human capital accumulation for the new generations. They combine short-term relief with long-term investments aimed at breaking the poverty cycle among chronically poor families, and since they are financed through public budgets, they entail a redistribution of resources in favor of the poor through asset formation and greater productivity. In other words, they are *pro-growth social policies*.[10]

As with any new policy intervention, the implementation and operation of TCCTPs inevitably generates discussions about fundamental aspects of policy making. This chapter points out the issues that have been prone to the most intensive debates during their adoption and that are critical factors that determine the success or failure of these initiatives. The contribution is to highlight the paradigms that are challenged during the planning and implementation of these interventions, and that become either the obstacles or the keys for success.

The chapter is organized as follows. The next section describes TCCTPs and summarizes some of their effects on human capital accumulation and poverty. The following section identifies and discusses the paradigms that are usually challenged during their implementation and the final section presents some of the main challenges for TCCTPs for the future.

---

[8]This argument has also been developed in Székely (1998) and Attanasio and Székely (2001). The argument is supported by empirical evidence from Mexico.

[9]See Aghion and Armendáriz de Aghion (2004), and Hernández and Székely (2005) for the development of this argument.

[10]Evidently, TCCTPs cover one important part of the policy spectrum, but not all of it. They have been usually complemented with programs aimed at working age adults (i.e. training programs), and other interventions such as credit for small and medium enterprises.

TCCTPs: A new generation of pro-growth social policies

There is a long tradition of cash transfer programs around the world. According to Tabor (2002) the earliest of these types of interventions are the disability allowances introduced in the 1890s in industrialized nations. Cash transfers have evolved considerably ever since, and they are now quite widespread in developed and developing nations.

Cash transfers are part of safety-net systems that include social insurance and/or social assistance policies. Social insurance transfers tend to be linked to the formal sector of the economy, and they are characterized by playing an insurance role by preventing individuals and families from falling into poverty. They are typically financed by individual contributions, government funds, and employers. Commonly used mechanisms include unemployment insurance, disability benefits, pension funds for old age security, and medical and life insurance, among others. Social assistance transfers play more of a "corrective" role by supporting families and individuals either to alleviate poverty, or to exit poverty. They are typically not related to formal labor market participation, and they are financed from public budgets.[11]

TCCTPs are within the realm of social assistance transfers, but apart from providing immediate relief through cash, they introduce an innovation by imposing conditionality for beneficiary families, which is directly related to the accumulation of human capital. By imposing conditionality, they shift the scope from social assistance, to social investment. While standard social assistance is mainly linked to certain socioeconomic status, TCCTPs are also linked to this criteria, but they additionally require a change in behavior by the recipient – specifically, they condition cash to school attendance by children, greater use of health services by family members, better nutrition practices, etc. – in order to become and remain eligible for the benefit.

Conditionality is the key factor that distinguishes social assistance from these developmental policy instruments, because the accumulation of assets that it entails leads to long-term effects rather than only alleviating poverty until the cash transfer is consumed.[12] Families receiving standard pure cash transfers are likely to return to their original standard of living if the transfer is discontinued, or they might even end up worse off if the transfer generates dependency, lower labor supply, or other reactions that cannot be reversed immediately. In contrast, TCCTPs lead to the accumulation of a type of capital that is inherent to individuals, and so if they are

[11]Tabor (2002) provides a review of social insurance and social assistance programs around the world.

[12]This argument is well developed in Coady and Morley (2004).

discontinued, they nevertheless leave some kind of asset behind that can be used permanently (for example, one cannot take away an extra year of schooling when someone has already acquired it).

Another reason why TCCTPs are an attractive instrument to reduce wealth inequality, and in particular human capital inequality, is that human capital cannot be accumulated infinitely, in contrast to physical capital. Individuals can only accumulate a limited amount of this type of asset over their life time, so when successful conditionality is build in a transfer program and this is combined with a targeting criteria, the education gap between the rich and poor will close through speeding up the accumulation rate by the poor.

TCCTPs fit in naturally into the poverty–inequality–growth debate discussed in the introduction. As already explained, one of the theoretical explanations for inequality and poverty is the existence of market imperfections that impede the poor from investing in economically viable and profitable activities, such as human capital accumulation. The cash provided by TCCTPs is designed precisely to strengthen the demand for education, health, and nutrition services by the poor. Take for instance, the case of education; it is well known that even when public schools, teachers, school materials and other inputs for human capital accumulation are available at no cost, many of the poor can still not afford to send their children to school because under imperfect capital markets, they are unable to access resources to cover the private expenses and forgone incomes that schooling assistance entails. By providing them with cash to cover these expenses (investing from the demand-side) households are empowered to benefit from the service and to engage into accumulating income-earning assets for the future. The same applies for health services, and for access to quality food for nutrition.

Description of TCCTPs

Large, cash driven, and comprehensive programs have been recently introduced with different variations in Bolivia, Brazil, Chile, Colombia, Ecuador, Honduras, Jamaica, Mexico, and Nicaragua. The first of these programs were introduced in Mexico and Brazil in the mid-1990s, and the others have proliferated ever since.

Figure 6.1 describes a prototype of what would be the most comprehensive version of a Latin American TCCTP. The first step in the implementation of these programs is geographic targeting. By mapping incomes, poverty rates, schooling levels, health outcomes, nutritional levels, household infrastructure, access to public services, and other indicators, the regions with the greatest needs are identified. A second step consists on identifying through means testing the households in the selected areas that fall below certain predefined standard. In many cases, community participation is used to validate and refine the selection of the neediest households.

Figure 6.1 Prototype of a Latin American TCCTP

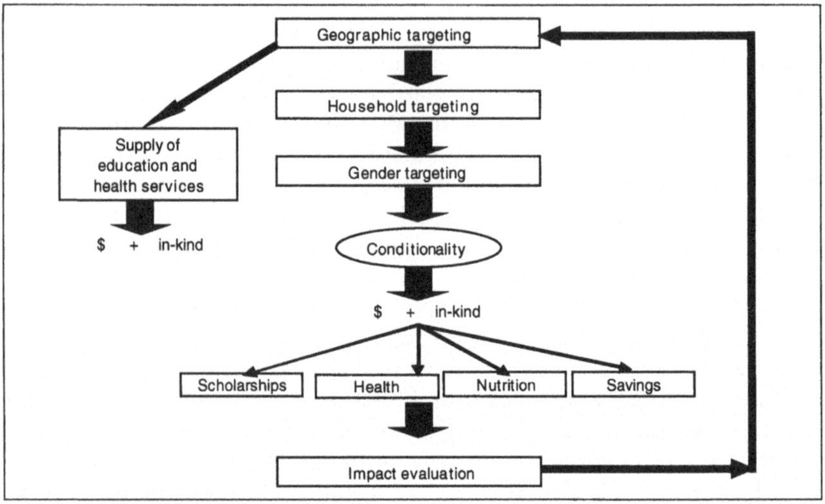

The third step in targeting introduces another innovation. It identifies the female head of the household, and entitles her to receive the cash transfers directly, and to verify the compliance of the conditionality. Conditionality is directly linked to the contents of the benefit package: transfers for education are linked to school attendance, transfers for health are conditional on using health services periodically, nutrition and food support requires monitoring of height and weight of children and attendance to training and workshops by the female head, while savings benefits are also aligned to school attendance. Apart from cash transfers, several programs provide in kind benefits such as food allowances. In some countries, support for families is also combined with mechanisms to strengthen the supply of education and health services including allowances for teachers, infrastructure provision, or incentives on performance.

Specifically, the educational component of TCCTPs include cash scholarships that in some cases vary by gender and by schooling level, and sometimes they additionally include in-kind support through the provision of school materials. The health component normally consists on providing a prevention health package with some curative basic services, and weight and height monitoring for young children. Food support usually combines cash allowances with in-kind transfers of enriched products aimed at young children. Typically, cash and in-kind benefits are designed in such a way that they cover the opportunity cost of each activity. For instance, school grants are calculated by acknowledging the opportunity cost of time spend at school instead of in the labor market, health and nutrition benefits include the value of forgone time spent by females in taking their children to clinics and attending workshops, etc.

The savings component was recently introduced in Mexico. It consists of cash deposits to individual savings accounts in the banking system that can be accessed upon high school graduation. The funds can be used to finance higher education, for deposit as collateral in a financial institution to access a loan, for purchasing health insurance, or as down payment to purchase a house through a specific public housing program.

Finally, TCCTPs normally have impact evaluation and monitoring systems built in. These systems feed back into the operation of the program by identifying corrective measures to improve the operation, and for verifying the cost-effectiveness of each of the interventions.

As mentioned, Figure 6.1 describes a version of TCCTPs that is a prototype from several of the existing programs. In reality, there is no program with all the features described; all are variations around it. For instance, in Mexico, the *Oportunidades* program includes all the elements of direct support to households – with the school grants going all the way up to high school – but does not have mechanisms to strengthen the supply of education and health services.[13] Programs in Honduras and Nicaragua do include supply-side components.

Rawlings and Rubio (2003) provide a more detailed description of TCCTPs in Latin America, including Bolivia's *Beca Futuro* (BF), Brazil's *Bolsa Familia* (BF), Colombia's *Familias en Acción* (FA), Ecuador's *Bono de Desarrollo Humano* (BDH), Honduras' *Programa de Asignación Familiar* (PRAF), Jamaica's *Program of Advancement through Health and Education* (PATH), and Nicaragua's *Red de Protección Social* (RPS).[14]

The impact of TCCTPs

A key feature of many Targeted Conditional Cash Transfer Programs is their emphasis on impact evaluation through experimental and quasi experimental designs. There is now a solid literature showing the positive effects of TCCTPs on school attendance, progression rates, better health, and

[13]Originally created in 1997 under the name of *PROGRESA* (Programa de Educación, Salud y Alimentación), the program has been evolving through some changes in design – the savings component was included in 2003 – and a massive expansion of coverage, reaching around 5 million families. Rodríguez and Levy (2005) describe the design and implementation of the program.

[14]Other good reviews can be found in Coady and Morley (2004), Rawlings (2004), and Sedlacek *et al.* (2000). As noted by Rawlings (2004), there are other programs, such as the *Bolsa Escola* and the *Programa de Erradicacao do Trabalho Infantil* (PETI) in Brazil, and the *Agente Joven* in Chile, that only include educational support, and Brazil's *Bolsa Alimentacao* and *Cartao Alimentacao*, which include only health and nutritional components.

improved height and weight among previously undernourished children. The main feature of these outcomes is that they have permanent effects on beneficiaries. As already mentioned, one or more additional years of schooling are life-time irreversible assets and the same applies for health prevention and to nutritional support provided at early ages. These early interventions generate long-lasting consequences for cognitive ability, health, and productivity in general. The human capital assets acquired with the support of these interventions are what make them pro-growth.

Furthermore, since the programs entail cash transfers and other immediate in-kind benefits for households, they also have short-term effects on poverty. For instance, Székely and Rascón (2005) estimate that about one half of the seven percentage point poverty reduction in Mexico between the years 2000 and 2004 can be attributed to cash transfers from *Oportunidades*.[15]

As for the expected impact on human capital accumulation, perhaps the most solid evidence is from *Oportunidades*, which is the most evaluated of these programs. Evaluations for the first two years of operation by Behrman *et al.* (2001) show that the intervention considerably reduces drop-out rates and that it increases school progression especially between primary and secondary levels. The program also increased secondary attendance by 19 percent. There is also evidence that *Oportunidades* in its first phase increased secondary school enrollment rates for females by 7.2–9.3 percentage points and by 3.5–5.8 percentage points for males, in urban and rural areas, respectively. In another detailed analysis, Schultz (2001) shows that higher enrollment rates in the end result in higher education levels. In a two year period only, they generated an increase of two-thirds of a year of education among beneficiary children, and this reduces education inequality in the communities where the program operates.[16] Moreover, the increase of two-thirds of a year, projected to the future schooling progress of the average child, is estimated to augment future income flows permanently by 8 percent per year when children access the labor market. This is due to the higher productivity achieved through the additional education. Progressing through the program for a larger number of years is likely to generate even greater impacts.

Positive educational effects have also been found for the *FA* program in Colombia. A recent impact evaluation by Attanasio *et al.* (2005), shows that school attendance rates have increased by an average 5.5 percentage points among 14 to 17 year olds – with increases by 10.1 and 5.2 percentage

[15]Extreme poverty in Mexico declined from 24.2 to 17.3% between these years.
[16]The result is consistent with the findings in Behrman *et al.* (2001).

points in rural and urban areas respectively – and by 3 percentage points among 8 to 13 year olds after about one year of receiving conditional cash transfers.[17]

Maluccio and Flores (2005) also use experimental data to show that the *RPS* in Nicaragua has generated even greater effects on school enrollment, with increases of about 23 percentage points during the course of less than two years. In a similar study for Honduras, IFPRI (2003) finds that the *PRAF* program increased the originally very low primary completion rates by about 50 percent after only two years of operation, through cash transfers that represented increases of about 18 percent in household consumption.

The World Bank (2001a) reports positive educational effects from the *Bolsa Escola* program in Brazil. The report shows 5 percent reductions in drop out rates among beneficiaries, as well as greater grade-promotion rates – with differences of about 8 percentage points as compared to non beneficiaries. There is also considerable improvement in the proportion of children attending the grade that corresponds to their age.[18]

The experimental data collected during the operation of some of the TCCTPs also reveals considerable impacts on health outcomes. Gertler and Boyce (2001) find that in Mexico, the *Oportunidades* cash transfers – which on average increased household incomes by 20 percent – generated a 23 percent reduction in illnesses among children, while anemia declined by 18 percent among beneficiary children due to the support of the program.

For Colombia, Attanasio, Battistin, *et al.* (2005) find considerable increases in the use of preventive health facilities and services due to the support of *FA*, and a decline in diarrhea cases by more than 10 percent among young children. For Nicaragua, Maluccio and Flores (2005) register a 30 percent increase in growth monitoring by beneficiary families, and an increase of around 20 percent in child immunization, due to the intervention of the *RPS*.

There are also significant changes in consumption patterns derived from cash transfers, but also from the attendance of female household heads to workshops that provided with information on nutrition practices (which is one of the elements of conditionality). Hoddinot and Skoufias (2003) find important changes in consumption among beneficiary households in

[17]Impacts are lower at younger ages due to the initially higher school enrollment between 8 and 11 years of age.

[18]Positive education results have been also documented by Ahmed and del Ninno (2001) for the Food for Education Program in Bangladesh. According to the author's results, school attendance increased by 35%, while enrolment rates increased by 32.5%. Coady and Morley (2004) discuss some of the caveats of this particular study.

Mexico, which result in a 7.1 percent increase in caloric intake by family members, due to improved food selection, especially of vegetable and animal products. Attanasio, Fitzsimons, *et al.* (2005) find that the impact of the *FA* Program on household consumption is of 19.5 percent and 9.3 percent in rural and urban areas, respectively, and that most of the increase is due to more food consumption. Expenditures increase particularly in nutrient-rich food and in healthcare, education, footwear, and clothing for children. Maluccio and Flores (2005) find similar effects in Nicaragua.

The changes in consumption patterns combined with greater access to health services have strong implications for nutrition. The TCCTPs that have been scientifically evaluated also provide solid evidence in this respect. Behrman and Hoddinott (2001) find that in its first phase of its implementation *Oportunidades* increased children's height by an additional one-sixth of an inch per year due to the program, which yields an increase in lifetime earnings through productivity by 2.9 percent per year when children reach working age. According to Attanasio, Fitzsimons *et al.* (2005) the *FA* program has increased growth rates of around 0.5 cm among beneficiary children, while Maluccio and Flores (2005) register a 5 percent decline in child stunting due to the *RPS* – which is equivalent to a rate of decline that is 1.5 times faster than the improvement observed at the national level.

Although there are certainly challenges and scope for improvement – which will be discussed in the final section – the results so far support the view that TCCTPs are powerful mechanisms for improving human capital accumulation among the poor. Since they are financed through public spending, they entail a redistribution of wealth toward the poor, which increases the economic potential of this group of society in the short and long run.

Implementing TCCTPs: Challenging the status quo

As in the case of any new public intervention, TCCTPs are not implemented without their problems. Since they normally challenge the status quo in program design and operation, they face a number of obstacles at the initial stages of their introduction and also further along the way. The outcome of the debate on several crucial issues determines the success or failure of these interventions. This section discusses seven of the key aspects that the implementation of TCCTPs have faced (and continue to face) in the countries that have adopted them. These are: targeting vs universal benefits; building beneficiary registries; integrality; conditionality; cash vs in-kind benefits; evaluation; and continuity.

Targeted vs. universal benefits

One of the first hot debates triggered by the introduction of TCCTPs is the need for targeting due to the scarcity of resources.[19] As explained by Gelbach and Pritchett (2002), it is natural that if a particular public policy is financed through public resources, there will be political interest groups that will support the action or not, depending on whether they are able to reap some of the benefits. Therefore, a universal benefit will most likely be supported by the majority of voters, while at the other extreme, a finely targeted intervention for a small group will most likely be supported by that specific constituency, but may have much less support from the majority.

The fact that targeting inevitably leaves some groups of society "out" from receiving support of the kind that TCCTPs provide, added to the recent history of Latin America of a long tradition of universal benefits helps understand why this aspect of TCCTPs has generated such hot debates in several settings. An additional element is that in practice, targeting has not always been efficient and accurate in the region.[20]

One good example of these types of problems is the case of *Oportunidades*. Even though Skoufias *et al.* (2004) find that technically speaking targeting worked quite well in this program in terms of reducing under-coverage and leakage, Adato *et al.* (2000) present strong evidence that leaving out some families in the participating communities generated considerable distress and even opposition to the program from those left out. Paradoxically, this effect is precisely due to the success of the targeting process, since it reveals that families that were even marginally above the threshold for eligibility, were not included as beneficiaries.

---

[19]The concept of targeting is quite simple. It suggests that when budgets are limited the policy problem consists of identifying the poorest individuals or families to allocate the scarce means to them in order to obtain the largest possible poverty reduction per unit spent. To find the poor, one has to look for them, so, there has to be a balance between administrative costs that need to be incurred to find the target population, and the benefits of finding the poor. Under this framework, universal benefits incur in "leakage," since many of the non-poor, or the not so poor can benefit from resources that should perhaps be allocated only to the poorest of the poor. Most of the gains from targeting originate precisely in reducing leakage. However, this comes at a cost. Since finding all the poor would be too costly, almost inevitably, some of the poor will be "missed." Thus, the main challenge is to find a balance between administrative costs, leakage, and under-coverage. The papers by Ravi Kanbur (1985, 1987a, 1987b) are among the first to address the issue of targeting formally.

[20]Coady *et al.* (2004a, 2004b) provide what are perhaps the largest reviews of targeting methods and outcomes, and show that there has not been widespread success in terms of reaching the poor at low cost in developing countries. Coady and Morley (2004) also discuss targeting methods, and describe the procedures used by five TCCTPs.

There are several ways of ameliorating this kind of opposition to targeted programs. One alternative has been community-based targeting, where there is an open consultation to the community for identifying beneficiaries, or where the community is asked to validate the list of participating families. The main drawback of this method is that those selected might not be the same as those that would be chosen, say, through a means test to identify the neediest. Another method is to define a threshold in each community after which targeting is no longer applied, and full coverage is granted. Both of these options have in fact been used in Mexico, and they have been an escape valve for political opposition to the program at the local level.

Another problem that arises with targeting is that beneficiaries might change their behavior in order to be eligible for participation – for instance, not acquiring household appliances or not improving housing conditions in order to stay below the eligibility threshold. At an extreme targeting may introduce perverse incentives. For instance, those situated marginally around the threshold for eligibility may reduce labor supply and household income in order to become eligible. In the case of TCCTPs one advantage is that participation implies complying with conditionality, and as discussed later, this element reduces the risk of generating large undesirable changes in behavior. Although theoretically important, the available evidence shows that labor supply decisions by adults in the household have not been significantly modified by participation in programs in Mexico and Nicaragua.[21]

As for the direct costs of targeting, Caldés *et al.* (2004) have estimated that they initially represented on average, around 18 percent, 26 percent and 10 percent of total costs in Mexico, Honduras, and Nicaragua, respectively. However, as programs expand, there are significant economies of scale in this activity. For instance, in Mexico, after four years of operation targeting costs represent only 3 percent of total costs, while in Nicaragua they reached 1 percent after years.

So, the existing evidence on the cost and benefits of targeting in TCCTPs, suggests that it is possible to reduce political and monetary costs in identifying the neediest households in order to provide them with their benefits.

Building beneficiary registries

Universal interventions are by definition, open to the whole population and it is not necessarily crucial to know who exactly benefits from them, precisely because they are intended to have widespread coverage. TCCTPs

[21]See Parker and Skoufias (2000) for the case of Mexico, and Maluccio and Flores (2005) for Nicaragua. A theoretical analysis of labor supply responses to the introduction of welfare programs can be found in Kanbur *et al.* (1994).

modify the status quo in this respect because by their nature, they require a precise list of beneficiary families and individuals in order to verify conditionality compliance and for keeping systematic administrative controls of cash transfers.

The construction and update of a registry of beneficiaries commonly generates discussions in the implementation phase of TCCTPs mainly for two reasons. The first is that they make program operation transparent, as opposed to a situation where public funds are spent with no evidence or only scarce evidence of where they end up.[22]As explained by Székely (2006), social programs in Latin America have traditionally been prone to political manipulation and have been applied discretionally by public officials in many cases. With the introduction of a clear registry, these practices are discouraged.

The second reason is that registries indicate the exact benefits that each family or individual is entitled to receive, which leaves little room for political manipulation at the local level. Since TCCTPs do not require a large administrative apparatus to transfer cash – this is normally done through the banking system or specialized firms – they end up eliminating intermediaries between the government and each beneficiary. In a context where the tradition has been for local leaders and organizations to appropriate social programs, intermediaries and interest groups are usually an obstacle at the initial stages of the implementation. It is practically impossible to prevent local actors from reaping political benefits from cash transfers, but registries considerably reduce this possibility.

In spite of these difficulties, once registries start to be built and made public, in many cases there has been scope for using such registries as a policy tool for the design and planning of other interventions.[23]

Integrality

One of the most challenging issues in the implementation of TCCTPs, is the coordination across government ministries and entities. Coordination is needed since these programs entail a view of integrality – a combination of education, health, and nutrition benefits – that requires a clear mandate by a top level institution to guarantee that benefits are provided in a synchronized way and that the information flow on conditionality compliance flows harmonically. There is no question that investing in these three items

[22]As noted by Irarrázaval (2004) only six Latin American countries have more or less complete registries for social programs: Argentina, Brasil, Colombia, Costa Rica, Chile, and Mexico.

[23]For instance, in the case of Mexico, the *Oportunidades* registry has become the corner stone for providing the beneficiary population with other benefits, such as public services, credit, etc. They are also being used to tailor a package of other benefits for non-participating families.

simultaneously has important multiplicative effects – for instance, a child that is healthy and well fed will most likely have better possibilities of taking advantage from education services – but the problem is that Latin American governments are designed and organized on a sector basis that makes coordination difficult. Each sector has its own objectives and targets, which are not necessarily aligned to the operation of a TCCTP.

Usually, the solution to the synchronization problem has been to centralize coordination directly through the Presidential office, or to link it to budgetary decisions, but due to the limited degree of institutionalization of social policies across the region, these kinds of arrangements are not always solid enough to survive during political changes.

Conditionality

As mentioned earlier, the introduction of conditionality in the provision of cash transfers is perhaps the main innovation of TCCTPs. When conditionality is relaxed or is not verified these programs turn merely into cash grants similar to the more traditional social assistance interventions.

Even though it is quite clear that conditionality is the key for turning cash transfers into investments in human capital, imposing it is not without its problems. Apart from the operational complexities involved in their application, there has been more of an ideological discussion around how strict one should be in imposing it, and in several settings the question of introducing it at all has been hotly debated.[24] The main underlying argument against introducing conditionality and verifying it strictly, is that it is anti-ethical to condition support to the poor through a set of actions that impose direct and indirect costs for them. As is clearly discussed in Coady and Morley (2004), the compliance of conditionality often makes beneficiaries incur private costs such as time devoted to queuing for services, the opportunity costs and transportation for attending workshops, and even the opportunity and direct costs from obtaining certifications, among others. All these actions impose an additional burden on the poor.

However, there are two strong arguments in favor of conditionality, which lead to think that rather than discussing whether it should be introduced or not, the main question is how much of it should be imposed. The first argument, which has been already put forward, is that conditionality induces higher investment in human capital for the poor, than would be present without the program. Since the poor have higher propensity to consume, the relative prices that they face are artificially biased versus longer-term investments that may be much more rewarding than current consumption. Conditionality simply changes relative prices in favor of

[24]Two good examples of this are the cases of Mexico and Brazil.

human capital investment (lowering its cost through the cash transfer), at the cost of sacrificing potential current consumption.

There is also a political economy argument. It might be more difficult to achieve political support for a publicly funded cash transfer that only alleviates poverty in the short run, than for a publicly funded program that "helps the poor help themselves": the second generates a (human) capital stock that will generate returns in the future, and lower the need for future income transfers.[25]

A second argument in favor of imposing conditionality is that it is also a self-targeting device. Since conditionality imposes (opportunity and other) costs, only those that value the benefit more than the cost will actually participate. If better off individuals have higher opportunity cost for participating, then they will exclude themselves from the program.

Clearly, the main challenge is to design the conditionality in such a way that the marginal benefit of participating for the poor is higher than the marginal cost. As judged by the overwhelmingly high program take-up rates in Latin America, the benefits of participating in TCCTPs are higher than the costs imposed by the conditionality, but even so, the temptation for relaxing conditionality is still present in many countries. The problem is that eliminating or relaxing it may put the positive human capital gains at stake.

Cash vs in-kind benefits

Another of the elements of the status quo commonly challenged by TCCTPs in Latin America is the introduction of cash benefits. After a tradition of expanding in-kind subsidies for goods and services across the region for decades, it is not surprising that the use of cash transfers has also generated debate. Most of the debate has revolved around the question of whether cash will be spent on "adequate" goods or not. However, another important underlying issue is that many Latin American governments created large apparatuses – with their corresponding bureaucracies – for providing in-kind benefits, which are displaced by the simplicity of a cash transfer.

There are several theoretical arguments in the discussion of cash vs. in-kind transfers. The main economic argument in favor of cash transfers is that they provide beneficiaries with freedom of choice to satisfy what they

[25]The papers by Persson and Tabellini (1994) and Alesina and Rodrik (1994) are among the first to model the perverse effects of inequality on growth due to the pressure that inequality imposes on public spending. Following these models, one would expect the median voter to support social investments that lower the need for redistribution in the future, rather than supporting continuous flows of transfers that require permanently high taxation rates.

consider to be their most important needs – with the consequent increase in welfare. An in-kind transfer implies that the policy maker chooses for the beneficiaries, and even though the policy maker's choice may well coincide with that of the beneficiary, this is not necessarily the case in all situations.

Apart from the latter issue, there are other economic, administrative and political considerations in the cash vs in-kind debate. As explained by Tabor (2002) one of the main economic arguments is that since in-kind benefits distort relative prices in the markets where they intervene, they introduce inefficiencies in the economy by providing incentives for individuals and firms to consume or produce more of a particular good, respectively, than would be desired in a competitive market.[26] This reduces overall efficiency in the specific market where the intervention takes place, but it may also generate inefficiencies in the markets of complementary and substitute goods.

The administrative considerations mainly have to do with the cost of providing cash vs the cost of providing goods or services. While in-kind benefits have the advantage of not requiring targeting – beneficiaries self-target by demanding the good or service – their main drawback is the need of a (usually) costly apparatus to deliver the benefit, while cash can be provided under simple schemes that do not require large bureaucracies.[27] From the point of view of beneficiaries, an advantage of cash is that cash is fungible, while in-kind benefits are much less so.

The main political consideration seems to support in-kind vs. cash transfers. The argument is that in-kind benefits guarantee the financing of "desirable" goods or services, while cash can freely be spend by beneficiaries, even on "non-desirable" goods.

In practice, most TCCTPs have actually included a mix of cash (with conditionality) and in-kind benefits. As illustrated by the cases of Mexico and Nicaragua, there is even scope for complementarities between these kinds of benefits, and in fact, their combination has contributed to ameliorate the debate of whether one or the other should be preferred.

Evaluation

Serious impact evaluation is perhaps the best tool for a continued improvement in the operation of programs, it is certainly one of the most important inputs into the decision-making process for the distribution of public budgets, and it is one of the best ways for promoting

[26]See Blackorby and Donaldson (1998) for a detailed theoretical discussion of this aspect.

[27]Caldés *et al.* (2004) show that the cost of transfering cash in the *Oportunidades* (*PROGRESA*), PRAF and RPS programes in four years of operation averaged 22%, 10% and 6% of total costs, respectively.

accountability. However, evaluating the impact of poverty alleviation programs has *not* been a tradition in most developing countries, and it has certainly not been a tradition or a standard practice in Latin America. In fact, there seems to be an important evaluation gap in social development programs in general.[28] In the case of the large number of social programs that have proliferated across Latin America, and in particular, in the case of poverty alleviation programs, very few impact evaluations can be found.

There are several explanations for this gap. Some of them are purely economic and most of them are political. One economic argument is that since evaluations are a public good, there are few incentives for investing in it in each independent program. Furthermore, since impact evaluations require investing public resources, it is not clear whether the benefits of performing an evaluation will be greater than the benefit of supporting a larger number of families or individuals through the same budget.

As for the several political aspects, perhaps the most important are, first, that impact evaluations take time to generate results – in many cases they require several years – so it is not clear that the specific public official or agency that finances it, will be able to benefit from its results; second, some policy actors can preserve greater discretion when there is *less* knowledge to distinguish good programs from bad ones; third, the design and implementation of impact evaluations requires technical capacity, which is not always available in public institutions. But perhaps the main political argument, which is relevant for experimental or quasi-experimental evaluations, is that when an evaluation requires for the definition of control and treatment groups, a sub-group of the population will be excluded from the program arbitrarily.

The *PROGRESA* program (transformed later into *Oportunidades*) was a pioneer in implementing impact evaluations for poverty alleviation programs right at the start of its operation. The controversy around this decision was highly visible and hotly debated. Most of it revolved around

[28]This is shown at length in the document by Savedoff *et al.* (2006). For instance, these authors document that the ILO's *Universitas Programme* reviewed 127 studies, studying 258 community health schemes, and found that only 2 of these cases had internal validity, while several other reviews on community health schemes by Ekman (2004) Jakab *et al.* (2001) confirm the methodological weakness of the literature identified in the ILO Report. Similarly, systematic reviews of UNICEF projects by Victora (1995) find that only 15% of them included impact assessments, but many of these have serious methodological limitations. Informal surveys by the authors document that at the Inter-American Development Bank, merely 16% of all active projects by July 2004 collected data that allows for some kind of evaluation. Similarly, in 1998 the World Bank reported that only 5% of its projects had associated impact evaluations, while in 2000, this share increased to 10% (World Bank, 1999, 2001b).

the economic and the political arguments listed above. For instance, in the case of the economic costs of an evaluation, it was necessary to justify all costs in detail and to introduce aspects into the evaluation that would satisfy critics – such as the inclusion of family violence and other aspects that were not originally considered. The key element for making the evaluation possible was that the budget for this program was obtained by eliminating other interventions with dubious or unclear results – such as a tortilla subsidy program that had been in operation for several years with no evidence on its impact on poverty reduction – so the case could also be made that investing in generating knowledge about the effects of a cash transfer could also shed light on the pertinence of other public interventions (see Rodríguez and Levy, 2005).

The first stage of the evaluation of *PROGRESA* was clearly defined as 1997–2000, and more specifically, November 2000, which was the last month of the 1994–2000 administration. This definition assured program designers and operators that they would be able to reap the political benefits of the (presumably positive) results. This definition actually became central to the success of the program since it established a clear time line for improving the conditions of the poor. Actually, having positive impact evaluations results at this time was perhaps the most important reason why the following administration continued with it.

But implementing the evaluation was not without its problems. As mentioned before, it is common that evaluation is opposed mainly by the actors that have a stake in the program, since it imposes the risk of revealing inefficiencies in the operation. In the case of *PROGRESA-Oportunidades*, the implementation of the evaluation was taken and followed at the Presidential level, which left little scope for internal opposition. Additionally, even though technical capacity to design and carry out the evaluation was adequate, its operation was delegated to the International Food Policy Research Institute (IFPRI), an institution with proved technical capacity and experience to carry out the endeavor, and independence from the Administration implementing the program.

The success of the Mexican evaluation in terms of being a key factor for continuity from one Administration to the other (certainly a rare case in Mexico's history), for accessing larger budgets for its expansion, for improving the design of the program, and for accountability, lead the way to expand evaluation to all social programs in the country. Furthermore, similar evaluations have been applied in Honduras, Nicaragua, and Colombia (which we have referred to above) and have set a new standard for many other countries.

Continuity

As argued extensively in Székely (2006), social policies, and in particular, poverty alleviation policies in Latin America have been characterized by an extremely low level of continuity. Continuity is a crucial issue in the context of the discussion of pro-growth social policies. Due to their nature, TCCTPs are more pro-growth, the longer they are able to protect and support human capital investment. Perhaps the clearest case is education. Even though one extra year of schooling is beneficial for a poor family, it is well known that the returns to education are non-linear, and that the largest returns are obtained at the highest education levels. Furthermore, there are big increases in educational returns when completing an education level (i.e. the returns for an extra year in the early years of primary are much smaller than the returns from completing sixth grade). If human capital investment is truncated somewhere along the schooling system, the returns will be much lower.

An additional benefit from continuity is that it provides certainty to poor households, which are normally subject to *uncertainty* in their incomes. Having the guarantee of a continuous flow of monetary resources opens the possibility for other investments, it may open access to credit, and it might help smooth unexpected shocks.

Even though the virtues of continuity seem clear, the discussion about the pertinence of TCCTPs typically opens up again with political shifts. Perhaps documenting evidence on the virtuous effects of these programs in the longer run is the best antidote against this vulnerability.

Challenges for the future

TCCTPs are still rather new, and they face a series of challenges for their consolidation as growth-promoting policy mechanisms. Here we classify these challenges in two groups: program fine-tuning, and structural improvements.

Due to their novelty, it is quite reasonable to expect TCCTPs to fine-tune their design continuously. In fact, one of the main benefits of impact evaluations is precisely that they provide information for doing this. There are at least four areas where there is scope for fine-tuning. The first is targeting. Even though the available evidence points to rather successful results in this regard, the expansion of TCCTPs inevitably leads to leakage. Furthermore, since migration has increased importantly it is possible that socioeconomic conditions change more rapidly that they did in the past. Previously non-eligible households may become eligible due to changes in family composition or income flows associated with migration.

Another area with scope for fine-tuning is the definition of the amount of cash transferred for each of the items in the benefit package. For instance, changes in labor-market conditions might make the scholarships less attractive at a point in time, and this may reduce program uptake or compliance of the schooling conditionality. Additionally, with program expansion, it is desirable to tailor the benefits to the needs and conditions of new areas, population sub-groups, or even individual households.[29]

A related issue, brought up recently by de Janvry and Sadoulet (2006) is not only to review the size of cash transfers in different settings, but to analyze the optimal coverage in terms of schooling levels. These authors argue that in countries like Mexico, where primary attendance rates are already high, it might not be necessary to introduce scholarships for primary students. They suggest eliminating transfers in primary in order to increase post-primary transfers, where drop out rates are higher. Although this argument sounds reasonable, and should be analyzed in each particular setting, there are at least two counter arguments. One has to do with other research by the same authors (in Sadoulet *et al.* (2004)) where it is argued that TCCTPs have also been used as risk-coping mechanisms for poor families. If this is so, eliminating primary school scholarships may have effects well beyond primary attendance rates, especially, in terms of the ability of households to manage shocks. Still another argument, is that even though primary scholarships may not affect school attendance in the short run, they might have positive effects on cognitive capabilities (i.e. through better nutrition and health), which have impact on the longer-run ability to progress through the schooling system. This argument, however, is still to be verified.

Another area for fine-tuning, is evaluation. Since TCCTPs are still "young" it is reasonable to evaluate their short- and medium-term impacts, such as changes in school attendance, or child weight and height, etc. However, in the end, these programs are intended to increase productivity and income-earning capabilities after school age, which still needs to be verified. This will be possible when the first generation of fully covered individuals will reach working age and will reap the benefits of the human capital investment promoted by TCCTPs.

There is definitely also scope for fine tuning on the supply side in terms of the quality of education and health services. TCCTPs have now achieved their first objective of enabling poor households to use these services, but these services are generally prone to large improvements in quality.[30] Improving quality requires deep reforms in the education and health sectors, and this remains an outstanding issue across the Latin American region (Savedoff, 1998).

As for the structural challenges, there are at least three important issues. The first is that TCCTPs have been quite successful in defining eligibility

[29]For instance, Attanasio *et al.* (2004) show that scaling up the *Oportunidades* program to areas with different characteristics, generates lower impacts if the same incentive structure is provided to a different environment.

[30]See for instance Navarro (2003), Di Tella and Savedoff (2001).

criteria and developing mechanisms for targeting at the stage of incorporation of beneficiaries. However, most of these programs have no incentives to exit. Even though demographic changes within the family naturally modify the amount of cash and benefits that each household receives (for instance, scholarships are only provided until a certain age), these programs have not been able to build in "exit doors" or "graduation" mechanisms in their design so that families can evolve to other types of support once they have past the human capital accumulation phase. One first attempt has been the introduction of the savings fund in Mexico (the fourth component of the program), which is only accessed upon high school graduation, but still other mechanisms are needed to assure that TCCTPs will not become a "trap." Linkage to other programs where the accumulated human capital can be used to generate incomes might be a possibility.

Another challenge along the same lines is that TCCTPs were originally designed to combat structural poverty, but not to protect and benefit families that transit in and out of poverty at higher frequency. The main challenge in order to evolve from structural to dynamic poverty is to evolve into permanent and institutionalized safety nets. This requires linking beneficiary registries (which are now in place in the countries where these programs exist) with the tax records that allow identifying which households or individuals are in need at a point in time. The challenge problem is that most developing countries have very large informal sectors that are not linked to tax records. Tax systems would need to be considerably expanded before a safety net of this type is consolidated.

Finally, TCCTPs have set the conditions for a much more orderly and structured social policy in the countries where they have been implemented. Once beneficiary registries are in place, and evaluations have been assimilated into the operation of the programs, they have positive externalities on other programs. A next step is to consolidate registries for all poverty alleviation programs, so that TCCTPs can be complemented with other actions, such as housing support, credit for production, etc., and the population that is not eligible from the program can also participate through other interventions tailored to their needs. As for evaluation, once a greater stock of impact evaluations are in place, policy makers will be able to compare impacts across programs to ensure that each unit of public resources spend, has the greatest possible impact. Perhaps in the future it will be possible to assess which of the available poverty alleviation programs is more pro-growth. This would definitely be a great improvement with respect to the existing status quo.

References

Adato, M., D. Coady, and M. Ruel (2000) "Final report: an operation's evaluation of *Progresa* from the perspective of beneficiaries, promotors, school directors, and health staff," International Food Policy Research Institute, Washington, DC, August.

Aghion, P. and B. Armendáriz de Aghion (2004) "A new approach to poverty alleviation," Mimeo, Harvard University.

Aghion, P., E. Caroli, and C. García-Peñalosa (1999) "Inequality and economic growth: the perspective of the New Growth Theories," *Journal of Economic Literature*, 37(4), December.

Ahmed, A. and C. del Ninno (2001) "Food for education program in Bangladesh: an evaluation of its impact on educational attainment and food security," International Food Policy Research Center, Washington, DC.

Alesina, R. and D. Rodrik (1994) "Distributive politics and economic growth," *Quarterly Journal of Economics*, 108, pp. 465–90.

Attanasio, O., E. Fitzsimons, and A. Gómez (2005) "The impact of a conditional education subsidy on school enrolment in Colombia," Center for the Evaluation of Development Policies, Institute of Fiscal Studies, London, March.

Attanasio, O., E. Battistin, E. Fitzsimons, A. Mesnard, and M. Vera-Hernández (2005) "How effective are conditional cash transfers? Evidence from Colombia," *IFS Briefing Notes*, BN54, January.

Attanasio, O., C. Meghir and M. Székely (2004) "Using randomized experiments and structural models for 'scaling up': evidence from the *Progresa* evaluation," in F. Bourguignon and B. Pleskovic (eds), *Annual World Bank Conference in Development Economics*, Oxford University Press.

Attanasio, O. and M. Székely (2001) "Going beyond income: redefining poverty in Latin America," chapter 1, in O. Attanasio and M. Székely (eds), *Poverty and Assets in Latin America*, Johns Hopkins University Press.

Banerjee, A.V. and A.F. Newman (1993) "Occupational choice and the process of development," *Journal of Political Economy*, 101(2), pp. 274–98.

Behrman, J. and J. Hodinott (2001) "An evaluation of the impact of *Progresa* on preschool child height," *FCND Discussion Paper* no. 104, International Food Policy Research, Washington, DC.

Behrman, J., P. Segupta, and P. Todd (2001) "Progressing through *Progresa*: an impact assessment of a school subsidy experiment," *Pier Working Paper* no. 01–033, International Food Policy Research, Washington, DC.

Blackorby, C. and D. Donaldson (1998) "Cash versus in-kind, self selection, and efficient transfers," *American Economic Review*, 78(4), pp. 691–700.

Bourguignon, F. (2004) *The Poverty-Growth-Inequality Triangle*, The World Bank, Washington, DC.

Caldés, N., D. Coady, and J. Maluccio (2004) "The cost of poverty alleviation transfer programs: a comparative analysis of three programs in Latin America," Food Consumption and Nutrition Division, *FCND Discussion Paper* no. 174, International Food Policy Research, Washington, DC, April.

Coady, D. and S. Morley (2004) "From social assistance to social development: targeted education subsidies in developing countries," Center for Global Development, Washington, DC.

Coady, D., M. Grosh, and J. Hoddinott (2004a) "Targeting outcomes redux," *The World Bank Research Observer*, 19(1).

Coady, D., M. Grosh, and J. Hoddinott (2004b) "Targeting transfers in developing countries: review of lessons and experience," The World Bank, Washington, DC.

de Janvry, A. and E. Sadoulet (2006) "Making conditional cash transfer programs more efficient: designing for maximum effect of the conditionality," *The World Bank Economic Review*, February 1.

Di Tella, R. and W. Savedoff (2001) "Diagnosis corruption: fraud in Latin America's public hospitals," Johns Hopkins, Inter American Development Bank, Washington, DC.

Dollar, D. and A. Kraay (2002) "Growth is good for the poor," *Journal of Economic Growth*, 7(3), pp. 195–225.

Ekman, B. (2004) "Community-based health insurance in low-income countries: a systematic review of the evidence". *Health Policy and Planning*, 19, pp. 249–70.

Foster, J. and M. Székely (2000) "How good is growth?," *Asian Development Review*, 18(2), pp. 59–73.

Galor, O. and J. Zeira (1993) "Income distribution and macroeconomics," *Review of Economic Studies*, 60, pp. 35–52.

Gelbach, J.B. and L. Pritchett (2002) "Is more for the poor less for the poor? The politics of means-tested targeting," *Topics in Economic Analysis and Policy*, 2(1).

Gertler, P. and S. Boyce (2001) "An experiment in incentive-based welfare: the impact of *Progresa* on health in Mexico," Mimeo.

Hernández Licona, G. and M. Székely (2005) "Labor productivity: the link between economic growth and poverty in Mexico," in M.J. Bane and R. Zenteno (eds), *Poverty and Poverty Reduction Strategies: Lessons from Mexican and International Experience*, Harvard University Press, Cambridge, MA.

Hoddinot, J. and E. Skoufias (2003) "The impact of PROGRESA on food consumption," International Food Policy Research Institute (IFPRI) *Discussion Paper* no. 150, Washington, DC, May.

IFPRI (International Food Policy Research Institute) (2003) "Proyecto PRAF/BID: impacto condicional," Washington, DC.

Irarrázaval, I. (2004) "Sistemas únicos de información sobre beneficiarios en América Latina," Diálogo Regional de Política, Inter American Development Bank, Washington, DC.

Jakab, M., C. Krishnan, A. Preker, A. Gumber, A. Kelly, K. Ranson, P. Schneider, and S. Supakankunti (2001) "The impact of community financing on health, protection against impoverishment and social inclusion: what do household data tell us?," The World Bank HNP Discussion Paper submitted as a Background Report for the Commission on Macro-Economics and Health, Washington, DC.

Kakwani, N., B. Prakash, and H. Son (2000) "Growth, inequality and poverty: an introduction," *Asian Development Review*, 18(2), pp. 1–21.

Kanbur, R., M. Keen, and M. Tuomala (1994) "Labor supply and targeting in poverty alleviation programs," *The World Bank Economic Review* 8 (May), pp. 191–211.

Kanbur, R. (1987a) "Structural adjustment, macroeconomic adjustment and poverty: a methodology of analysis," *World Development*, 15(12), pp. 1515–26.

Kanbur, R. (1987b) "Measurement and alleviation of poverty," *IMF Staff Papers*, no. 34, pp. 60–85.

Kanbur, R. (1985) "Poverty: measurement, alleviation and the impact of macroeconomic adjustment," *University of Essex Discussion Paper* no. 125, Essex, England.

Machinea, J.L., A. Bárcena, and A. León (2005) *Objetivos de Desarrollo del Milenio: una mirada desde América Latina y el Caribe*, Economic Commission for Latin America and the Caribbean (ECLAC), Santiago de Chile.

Maluccio, J. and R. Flores (2005) "Impact evaluation of a conditional cash transfer program: the Nicaraguan Red de Protección Social," International Food Policy Research Institute (IFPRI), Washington, DC.

Navarro, J.C. (2003) "Who are the teachers? Teaching careers and incentives in Latin America," Johns Hopkins/Inter American Development Bank, Washington, DC.

Parker, S. and E. Skoufias (2000) "Final Report: the impact of PROGRESA on work, leisure, and time allocation," International Food Policy Research Institute, Washington, DC.

Persson, T. and G. Tabellini (1994) "Is inequality harmful for growth?," *American Economic Review*, 84, pp. 600–621.

Rawlings, L.B. (2004) "A new approach to social assistance: Latin America's experience with conditional cash transfer programs," *Social Protection Discussion Paper* no. 0416, The World Bank, Washington, DC.

Rawlings, L.B. and G. Rubio (2003) "Evaluating the impact of conditional cash transfer programs: lessons from Latin America," *The World Bank Policy Research Working Paper* no. 3119, The World Bank, Washington, DC.

Rodríguez, E. and S. Levy (2005) "El Programa de Educación, Salud y Alimentación, PROGRESA-Programa de Desarrollo Humano Oportunidades," chapter 4, in S. Levy, (ed.), *Ensayos sobre el Desarrollo Económico y Social de México*, Fondo de Cultura Económica, México, D.F.

Sadoulet, E., F. Finan, A. de Janvry, and R. Vakis (2004) "Can conditional cash transfer programs improve risk management?," *SP Discussion Paper* no. 0420, The World Bank, Washington, DC.

Savedoff, W. (1998) "Organization matters: education and health in Latin America," Johns Hopkins, Inter American Development Bank, Washington, DC.

Savedoff, W., R. Levine, and N. Birdsall (2006) "When will we ever learn? Recommendations to improve social development through enhanced impact evaluation," consultation draft of a Center for Global Development Working Group Report, Center for Global Development, Washington, DC.

Schultz, T.P. (2001) "School subsidies for the poor: evaluating a Mexican strategy for reducing poverty," International Food Policy Research, Washington, DC.

Sedlacek, G., N. Ilahi, and E. Gustafsson-Wright (2000) "Targeted conditional transfer programs in Latin America: an early survey," The World Bank, Washington, DC.

Skoufias, E., B. Davis, and J. Behrman (2004) "Final Report: an evaluation of the selection of beneficiary households in the Education, Health, and Nutrition Program (*PROGRESA*) of Mexico," International Food Policy Research Institute, Washington, DC.

Székely, M. (2006) "Midiendo el grado de institucionalidad de la política social en América Latina," Mimeo.

Székely, M. and E. Rascón (2005) "México 2000–2002: reducción de la pobreza con estabilidad y expansión de programas sociales," *Economía Mexicana*, 14(2).

Székely, M. (1998) *The Economics of Poverty, Inequality and Wealth Accumulation in Mexico*, MacMillan, Basingstoke.

Tabor, S. R. (2002) "Assisting the poor with cash: design and implementation of social transfer programs," *Social Safety Net Primer Series*, The World Bank Institute, The World Bank, Washington, DC.

Victora, C.G. (1995) "A systematic review of UNICEF-supported evaluations and studies, 1992–1993," no. 3, *UNICEF Evaluation & Research Working Paper Series*, New York.

World Bank (2001a) "Brazil, an assessment of the *Bolsa Escola* Program," Human Development Department, Latin American and the Caribbean Region, Washington, DC.

World Bank (2001b) *Poverty Reduction and the World Bank: Progress in Fiscal 2000*, Washington, DC.

World Bank (1999) *Poverty Reduction and the World Bank: Progress in Fiscal 1998*, Washington, DC.

Part III

Financial Market Development for Growth and the Capital Account

7

Financial Development, Growth and Equity in Brazil

Armando Castelar Pinheiro and Regis Bonelli

Introduction

Criticism of the Washington Consensus has increased in Latin America (LA) since the mid-1990s owing to the frustration with the region's slow GDP growth and the failure to promote equity. Although growth in the past decade accelerated *vis-à-vis* 1981–93, the gain was less than expected. The same applies to the comparison with the recent expansion of China and India, which have accomplished high growth while apparently disregarding – or even confronting – the Consensus's recommendations.

Inasmuch as the diagnosis that motivated first-generation reforms remains valid, it seems correct to blame the insufficient depth of reforms for at least part of the responsibility for LA's lackluster performance in the past decade. But this seems to be an insufficient explanation. Lindauer and Pritchett (2002) noted that reforms are rarely fully or perfectly implemented. This has reinforced the view that the insufficient breadth of reform has been another cause for the small growth gains with respect to output growth. Alternatively, critics blame the attempt to implement a single set of policies to all developing countries, disregarding their individual characteristics and stage of development, for the poor growth record and fear that institutional reforms are about to repeat the same mistake. Thus, each country should pursue its own development strategy, tailored to its own characteristics.

How does financial sector reform fit into this discussion? The literature stresses that financial development – broadly understood as improved access to finance – and growth are associated (Levine, 1997; Wachtel, 2003). It is also acknowledged that financial systems are not sufficiently developed in most countries of LA, partly on account of lack of reform, partly due to the absence or poor quality of supporting institutions, including the laws and organizations that regulate the financial system. A 'growth diagnosis' approach also indicates that financing constraints are a main impediment to growth. As advanced by Rodrik (2004, p. 11) in the case of Brazil:

> All the indications are that this [Brazil] is an economy that is bumping against a financing constraint. Real interest [rates] are extremely high despite a reasonable investment rate, and the current account balance is driven by the willingness of foreign creditors to lend ... Brazil, therefore, is a high-return country where the domestic financial system and external capital markets constrain the equilibrium level of investment. The solution therefore lies in improving financial intermediation and in increasing Brazil's external creditworthiness (in part by tight fiscal policies).

This is consistent with the view that the financial market has been one area in which reform progressed the least in Brazil – although the country's overall reform process was significant. With the country's high marginal productivity of capital, more and less expensive credit would help to spur growth. As noted by Wachtel (2003), however, "the observed association between financial sector deepening and growth does not" warrant ... "a simple prescription to encourage the unrestricted growth of financial intermediaries." Indeed, these expanded during the high inflation period without doing much financial intermediation or promoting growth or equity. What is needed, then, is to promote the "specific institutional characteristics and financial sector channels that contribute to growth" and equity. And these, as well as the barriers that prevent the expansion of credit and capital market activities in most of LA, are far from being perfectly understood.

This chapter examines the links between financial development, growth and equity focusing on the Brazilian case, with the objective of contributing to a broader discussion on the role of financial markets in fostering economic development in LA. The first section discusses Brazil's recent growth record and changes in financial intermediation in the region. The next section analyzes the growth–finance interface. This is followed by an evaluation of the issue of access to financial services, including mechanisms directed at small and medium enterprises (SME). The final section concludes on the impediments to financial deepening and inclusion drawn from the Brazilian experience.

Growth and financial depth in Brazil: Some stylized facts

In 1981–93 GDP growth rates in Brazil dropped to almost a fifth of those observed in 1946–80 (Table 7.1). This decline resulted essentially from: (1) a slowdown in the rate of capital accumulation; (2) a substantial drop in annual TFP growth, reflecting a decline in both labor and capital productivity;

Table 7.1 Brazil: GDP growth and the contributions of capital, labor and TFP, 1931–2004

Period	*A=B+C+D*	*Capital (B)*	*Labor (C)*	*Total Factor Productivity (D)*
1931–45	4.3	1.7	1.0	1.7
1946–80	7.4	4.6	1.4	1.4
1981–93	1.6	1.3	1.1	-0.7
1994–04[(a)]	2.7	1.0	0.6	1.1
Change from				
1981–93 to 1946–80	-5.8	-3.3	-0.3	-2.1
1981–93 to 1994–04	1.1	-0.3	-0.5	1.8

Sources: Pinheiro *et al.* (2001), updated using IBGE data using a typical Solow decomposition, with constant returns to scale and capital and labor output elasticities of 0.5.
Note: (a) For labor, average 1994–2003.

and (3) a slower expansion in employment, partly as a result of demographic transformations that are still unfolding. The reforms of the 1990s succeeded in accelerating GDP growth only modestly in the past decade. Moreover, all this acceleration resulted from a rise in TFP growth, whose contribution to output growth increased by 1.8 percentage point. The contributions of capital and labor, on the other hand, declined.

The slowdown in capital accumulation has not been the result of a decline in savings: the total savings rate, approximated by the gross capital formation rate, has remained relatively stable since the early 1990s (see Bacha and Bonelli, 2005). Total savings oscillated since price stabilization in 1994 in a range – 20–22 percent of GDP – that is above the mean threshold observed in the 1950–68 period and not that much lower than in the 1970s.

There have been, though, significant shifts in the composition of savings. Foreign savings, for instance, expanded after price stabilization in 1994. They fell in the aftermath of the 1999 macroeconomic policy mix change, with the floating of the Real and the significant adjustment in the primary fiscal accounts: in 2004 the current account surplus reached 2 percent of GDP.

The recovery in national savings in 1999–2004 (Giambiagi and Montero, 2005) highlights the almost one-to-one relation between the shifts in foreign and public savings in the past decade: in 1995–98, foreign savings increased by 3.9 percent of GDP, while public savings declined by 8.1 percent of GDP. In 1999–2004 the former dropped by 6.2 percent of GDP and the latter increased by 6.5 percent of GDP. Thus, contrary to the late 1960s and early 1970s, foreign savings crowded out public savings, rather than boosting investment. This suggests that in 1995–98 the financial system concentrated on transforming these additional funds into public debt.

To some, the recent upsurge in public savings may be enough to put Brazil back on a path of rapid sustained growth, once the country can again rely on positive foreign savings, thus reverting the current status as a capital exporter (Giambiagi and Montero, 2005). We have a less sanguine view, one that stresses the role of financial markets in funneling these savings into investment, rather than just substituting for public savings. Furthermore, the relative price of investment goods has risen substantially since the 1970s, so that the same pool of savings generates less real investment. Brazil's underdeveloped financial system can be blamed for part of this rise in investment goods prices: with little financial intermediation going on outside the acquisition of public bonds, firms and households have to rely on own generated funds to finance investment. This usually means that investment projects are implemented little by little, foregoing the gains from scale and specialization, and implying higher costs with unproductive capital due to longer implementation periods. Poor households and small business are more affected by these processes, because of their greater difficulty in accessing financial markets and self-accumulating resources – implying less equality in the access to finance than otherwise. Finally, the recent upturn in public savings was accomplished through a major rise in the tax burden, currently at 36 percent of GDP, well above the 1970s average of 25 percent of GDP. This too has important implications for the economy as a whole and the financial sector in particular.

In most dimensions, financial markets in LA are relatively underdeveloped, compared to both developed and Asian countries. Except for Chile, in most countries in the region the volume of bank credit to the private sector is low and has not increased in recent years. Brazil is no exception. At the end of 2004, bank credit to the private sector amounted to 24.4 percent of GDP, compared to multiples of that in developed and Asian countries. The bond market in LA (as in Brazil) is dominated by the public sector, which accounts for 81 percent of the total value, with financial institutions answering for another 14 percent. For the average of developed and emerging economies, the share of company bonds in the market is significantly higher, ranging around 14 percent. Although the stock of bonds issued by LA companies increased by 1 percent of GDP from 1995 to 2001 – from 0.5 percent to 1.5 percent of GDP – the volume of government bonds rose by 10 percent of GDP in the same period. The market capitalization of LA's main exchanges is also relatively small, compared to their counterparts in the US, Germany, and Asia. Chile and, to a lesser extent, Brazil are the exceptions. The number of listed companies and liquidity (measured by the turnover ratio) in LA also compare unfavorably to Asia, the US, and Germany. LA's exchanges are not, though, abnormally concentrated, regarding both market capitalization and traded volumes.

The market size for insurance in Brazil is relatively small as well. Per capita expenditures on insurance in Brazil are only a fraction of that in

OECD countries, notably the US and Japan, and lower than in other middle-income countries such as South Africa, Chile, and Mexico; but similar to that in Argentina, Uruguay, and Costa Rica. The Brazilian private pension fund industry, in turn, is reasonably large for developing country standards, with the assets of closed (individual company) pension funds alone mounting to 18.2 percent of GDP in 2003, up from 3.3 percent in 1990.[1]

Brazil has a well-developed financial infrastructure inherited from the high inflation period, when banks tried to maximize their floating income by speeding up financial transactions as much as possible. Since the 1970s it has also had relatively large public bond and stock markets, the latter mostly geared towards trading state-owned enterprises (SOE) shares. For these reasons, it was expected that with the lowering of inflation, the privatization of public banks, a jump in the market share of foreign financial institutions, improved prudential regulation, the enactment of a new bankruptcy law and other macro, structural and institutional reforms adopted since the mid-1990s, financial markets would experience a large expansion. This did not happen,[2] although there have been noteworthy changes in the financial system.

The large public sector deficits since 1995 have been one of the main reasons why low inflation and changed bank ownership failed to generate a greater expansion of the financial sector. This can be seen in Table 7.2, which shows the structure of the financial sector from the point of view of different sources of credit to the public and private sectors. The figures highlight that credit has expanded since the mid-1990s, but entirely on account of the rise in the public debt: the (net) domestic debt of the public sector more than doubled between 1994 and 2003. Private sector debt, on the other hand, rose after price stabilization, largely through increased foreign borrowing, but declined afterwards. The table also shows that:

1. The private sector relies relatively more on foreign creditors, although, like the public sector, its debt is mostly domestic. The importance of bank loans to the public sector declined after 1996, on account of both

[1]The open pension fund industry also expanded remarkably after stabilization. This expansion is closely linked to the various changes implemented in the second half of the 1990s in the social security systems of private and public sector workers, as well as the establishment of tax incentives for workers investing in those funds (through the postponement of tax payments until retirement).

[2]The adjustment processes associated to the end of high inflation partly explains this failure to expand the financial sector. In 1994–2002, 57 banks in distress were closed down and 46 sold to other institutions, including two of Brazil's top ten banks. Fearing a systemic crisis, the Central Bank launched the Program of Incentives for Restructuring and Strengthening the National Financial System (PROER). Similar programs were adopted to deal with the issue of state and federal banks in distress.

Table 7.2 Brazil: Sources of finance, 1994–2003 (selected years, end of period, % of GDP)

	1994	*1996*	*1998*	*2000*	*2002*	*2003*
Public sector (net)	*30.0*	*33.3*	*41.7*	*48.8*	*55.5*	*58.7*
Domestic (net)	21.3	29.4	35.5	39.1	41.2	46.7
NFS credits (gross)	5.5	5.5	2.3	1.1	0.9	1.0
Foreign (net)	8.7	3.9	6.2	9.6	14.3	12.0
Private sector (gross)	*44.4*	*42.2*	*50.0*	*53.3*	*50.2*	*45.0*
Domestic	38.4	33.1	32.2	30.6	27.4	28.9
Private bonds	2.0	2.1	2.5	2.6	3.1	2.8
Debentures	2.0	2.1	2.2	2.3	2.9	2.7
Promissory notes	0.0	0.1	0.3	0.3	0.1	0.0
Banks	30.9	25.5	27.4	26.9	23.4	25.1
Firms (Non-financial)	20.2	16.8	17.9	16.8	16.7	17.5
Non-directed loans		7.3	6.6	9.0	8.7	8.7
Directed loans				7.9	8.2	8.7
BNDES				4.9	5.3	5.8
Individuals	10.8	8.7	9.6	10.1	6.7	7.7
Non-directed loans		1.3	1.5	4.5	4.9	5.6
Directed loans				5.7	1.9	2.0
Foreign	6.0	9.1	17.8	22.7	22.8	16.1
Memo						
Total bank credit	36.4	31.0	29.7	28.0	24.3	26.1
Leasing				1.2	0.6	0.6
Federal government bonds	14.9	21.8	35.0	44.2	39.3	45.8
Bovespa's market capitalization		27.9	21.0	38.2	27.6	42.4
Primary stock issuance (Bovespa)		1.1	0.4	0.1	0.1	0.0
Exchange rate (R$/US$)	0.85	1.04	1.21	1.96	3.53	2.89

Sources: Central Bank, Cetip (Câmara de Custódia e Liquidação) and Rocca (2001).

Notes:
1. For 2000–3, ratios to GDP obtained directly from Central Bank. For 1994–9 these were derived using GDP figures inflated to end of December prices using the centered IGP-DI, as calculated by the Central Bank.
2. Total credit by the SFN to the private sector equals directed and non-directed credit plus leasing.
3. Assumes all loans by BNDES are awarded to firms.
4. Stock of Federal government bonds excludes those held by Central Bank.

the privatization of large SOEs, the sale and closing down of local state banks, and the measures taken to limit the indebtedness of the public sector as part of the fiscal adjustment process. Also important was the 'federalization' of state and municipal debts (some of which owed to financial institutions), which were transformed into public bonds.

2. The public sector borrows mostly by issuing bonds, whereas private bonds represent just about one-tenth of the domestic private debt. The importance of the latter increased after the Real Plan.
3. Roughly two-thirds of the bank loans to the private sector are granted to firms and one-third to individuals. For the former, about half consists of the so-called 'targeted' or 'directed' loans, that is, loans that are targeted to specific uses and/or funded with compulsory savings. Of these, the federal development bank, BNDES answers for over one half, accounting alone for about a third of all credit extended by banks to firms. The non-directed, or freely allocated loans have gained importance since 2000, partly on account of a decline in reserve requirements on sight deposits and a lowering of the IOF (*Imposto sobre Operações Financeiras*, a tax on financial transactions).

Finance and growth: The missing link

A recent survey by Wachtel (2003) states that "there is ample empirical evidence to make a convincing case that financial sector development promotes economic growth." But financial development cannot be simply equated to a large financial sector, as evidenced by the expansion in the number and size of financial institutions in LA during the high inflation period, despite a concomitant reduction in financial intermediation. It is the expansion and sophistication of growth-augmenting financial activities that matter.

There are two complementary approaches to analyze the financial sector institutions and channels that stimulate these growth-augmenting activities. The traditional approach stresses the role of financial systems in reducing information and transaction costs, and in that way fostering investment and productivity growth. Thus, Levine (1997) emphasizes five functions played by financial systems: "facilitate the trading, hedging, diversifying, and pooling of risk; allocate resources; monitor managers and exert corporate control; mobilize savings; and facilitate the exchange of goods and services." This approach is also adopted by Stiglitz (1994, p. 23), for whom "enforcing contracts; transferring, sharing and pooling risks; and recording transactions, [are] activities that make them [financial markets] the 'brain' of the entire economic system, the central locus of decision making."

Pagano (1993), in turn, adopts a production function approach to look at how the system affects capital productivity, the cost of financial intermediation and the savings rate. Financial development enhances capital productivity by: (1) fostering riskier, less liquid and larger investment projects, which also tend to be more productive; and (2) better screening projects and monitoring their implementation, thus alleviating problems of adverse selection and moral hazard. More developed financial systems also consume fewer resources to intermediate savings, and thus make a higher proportion of them available to investors. Finally, the financial system affects the savings rate, but the direction is ambiguous (Edwards, 1995; Loayza *et al.*, 2000): the greater availability of financial services helps mobilizing savings, because it allows savers to invest in more profitable and less risky projects; but to the extent that they are able to insure themselves in the financial market, their precautionary savings tend to decline. Moreover, an increase in the supply of credit to financially constrained agents, such as low-income consumers, should reduce savings, as they anticipate their consumption. On the other hand, greater investment lending, including greater access to housing finance, could help to boost savings, to the extent that it lowers the relative price of these assets (due to lower production costs).

The relatively small contribution of the Brazilian financial system to long-term growth can be examined using either approach. Of the functions highlighted by Levine, only the last one is reasonably well performed by financial institutions, thanks to the large and sophisticated logistics and physical infrastructure inherited from the high inflation period. In part, this follows from the limited role of financial institutions in mobilizing and allocating long-term savings.

The Brazilian financial system intermediates three types of savings: compulsory, contractual, and fully voluntary. The first consists of funds controlled by the government and financed by savings schemes to which workers and firms have to contribute compulsorily. These funds finance the operation of public federal banks engaged in supporting sector or regional development activities, and it is often the case that projects are selected and monitored with an eye on politics as much as on economic fundamentals. This is particularly serious because these are essentially the only domestic sources of long-term credit available to firms and housing finance.

Contractual savings include the funds held by pension funds and insurance companies. These institutions are in principle well placed to provide long-term and illiquid finance, since their liabilities are also long-term and predictable. But in Brazil they invest most of their assets in Treasury bonds.[3] Only closed pension funds have significant resources invested in stock (19 percent of total assets), part of which as partners in controlling blocks of large companies. But this is mostly the case of pension funds linked to SOEs, in which political interference is common, hampering their incentives to exert corporate control and improve the allocation of

[3]At the end of 2003, 95% of the reserves of insurance companies were invested in fixed income assets, mostly government bonds, against 57% in the case of closed pension funds and 91% for open pension funds.

resources. Thus, these institutions play a limited role in improving resource allocation through the screening and monitoring of investment projects.

Fully voluntary savings are sight and time deposits and investments in mutual funds, which are also managed by banks. Like other institutional investors, mutual funds concentrate their assets on Treasury bonds, playing an equally limited role in raising the economy's capital productivity. Part of the savings mobilized by banks as sight and time deposits is sterilized by the Central Bank as reserve requirements; part is compulsorily used to finance housing, rural and micro-credit activities; and the remainder is left for the banks to allocate as they wish. Together with part of the banks' own capital – the other part is largely invested in Treasury bonds – and funds borrowed abroad by banks, these resources are used to fund the so-called "freely allocated loans." At the end of 2004, loans to the private sector amounted to 24.4 percent of GDP, 60 percent of which are freely-allocated loans. It is through these loans that banks could in principle contribute more directly to improve resource allocation and monitor managers. But, in practice, these loans are geared mostly to finance household consumption and firms' working capital in approximately equal proportions, having maturities of less than ten and six months, respectively. Thus, the impact of financial intermediation on capital productivity is constrained, on the one hand, by public meddling with the funds channeled into investment finance, and on the other by the concentration of freely allocated loans on financing consumption and working capital.

Capital markets also play a limited role in investment finance: companies issued an average 1.4 percent of GDP in stocks and bonds in 1999–2003, and not all of these reached the market. Moreover, only a small number of large companies have access to finance at reasonable terms. Claessens *et al.* (2000) show that the proportion of funds external to the firm remained highly concentrated in the largest firms. Firms in the highest quintile obtain about 70 percent of all finance. Companies in the first three quintiles, in turn, secure less than 10 percent of total funds, depending mostly on retained earnings. Therefore, small firms and households rely almost entirely on internally

Table 7.3 Brazil: Interest rates and spreads on non-government-directed bank loans, 2001–04 (% p.a.)

	2001	*2002*	*2003*	*2004*
Bank's borrowing cost	7.2	1.1	6.4	5.0
Bank spreads				
Total	*27.0*	*30.0*	*31.9*	*28.1*
Firms	11.8	14.5	14.7	13.5
Individuals	48.9	51.4	55.6	46.5

Source: Central Bank.

generated funds to finance housing and commercial investments. Overall, more than two-thirds of firms' capital comes from retained profits.

A share of the savings that go into the financial system remain in the system in the form of bank spreads, fees and commissions paid to investment banks, security brokers and dealers, etc., paying for services provided, taxes, delinquency losses and, in some cases, abnormal profits. In Brazil, this share is relatively high: McKinsey (1998) estimates that just the waste caused by low productivity in the financial system subtracts 2 percent of GDP from the resources made available to investors. This helps to explain why in 2001–04 the interest rate spreads on freely allocated bank loans ranged between 27 percent and 32 percent, with averages of 51 percent and 16 percent on loans to individuals and firms, respectively (Table 7.3).[4] Transaction costs in stock markets are also significant: commissions are not high compared to other Latin American countries, but the spread is, as are the costs of underwriting and compliance with regulations applying to public companies (auditing, public notices, obligatory reports, etc.).

Bank spreads can be decomposed into net margin, administrative expenses, losses with default, and taxes/reserve requirements, with the actual breakdown being somewhat different for public and private banks: as expected, in the latter a lower proportion of the spreads is due to administrative costs and default losses, and proportionately more goes to profits. A cross-country comparison by Demirgüç-Kunt and Huizinga (1999) shows that Brazilian banks had the fifth largest net interest margin among banks of 76 countries, reflecting high ratios of overhead costs (the highest among the 76 countries), taxes (5th largest), loan loss provisions (13th largest) and net profits (24th highest) to total assets.

Insufficient bank competition is deemed a possible explanation for both high profits and low productivity – Demirgüç-Kunt *et al.* (2003) show, for instance, that bank margins tend to be associated with concentration. Belaisch (2003) shows that although concentration is not high – the largest 10 banks answer for 70 percent of total assets – rivalry among banks is not strong. Competition was expected to rise with increased openness of the financial market to foreign institutions in the second half of the 1990s, but although the quality of credit-granting analysis has improved, and administrative expenses fallen, net margins have stayed high by international standards (see Reis and Valadares, 2004).

Two tentative complementary explanations for the market power of financial institutions are a noncompetitive conduct (e.g., a tacit cartel), (tacitly) led public banks, whose costs are particularly high and lack a profit maximizing orientation (McKinsey, 1998); and the segmentation of credit

[4]Afanasieff *et al.* (2001) show that bank spreads in Brazil are among the highest in Latin America and are a multiple of those found in developed countries.

markets, that creates monopolistic banking relationships between banks and part of the borrowers. The problem is further composed by the lack of a clear mandate to the Brazilian Central Bank (BCB) and anti-trust agencies to foster competition in the sector. Competition is also weakened by financial regulations that raise the cost of migration from one bank to another.

High reserve requirements on sight and time deposits and income and transaction taxes on loans are another major component of interest rate spreads. According to Troster (n.d.), if no costs or any coverage for default are imputed to a loan, for every $100 of interest paid by a debtor, the saver is paid (net of taxes) $25.3, the bank profits $24.4, $0.8 is paid as deposit insurance premium and the government collects $49.5! Transaction taxes were also at some stage levied on stock market transactions, with significant negative consequences. Narita and Novaes (2003) estimate that the CPMF (a tax on checks and other withdrawals) levied on stock market transactions reduced the volume of transactions in the São Paulo Stock Exchange (Bovespa) by 19 percent.

The problems caused by the high tax burden on financial operations are compounded by the frequent change in tax rules, which raises risk substantially. This instability stems partly from a "cat and mouse" game between financial intermediaries and the tax authority: given the high tax burden, the former are especially motivated to find and explore loopholes, while the latter follows behind closing them. Constant changes in taxation contribute to shorten maturities and increase the preference for liquid assets.

High taxes, not necessarily on financial intermediation, also compromise financial intermediation by fostering informality and encouraging companies not to go public in order to keep murky accounts and in this way "lower" their tax burden – public companies have to abide to more stringent rules of disclosure. This happens in spite of the lower cost of capital faced by public companies. The impact of tax evasion on the quality of accounting information is particularly serious in the case of informal firms, whose access to financial markets is expensive and very limited. In particular non-transparent accounts make much of the relevant information on borrowers private to the bank with which companies keep a relationship, making borrowers "informationally" captured and allowing banks to extract monopoly rents (Pinheiro and Moura, 2003). For small and medium companies the opportunity cost of more transparent accounts seems a critical obstacle in the way of using external funds to finance investment, and most do not pass basic due diligence processes.

High default rates are another reason for high bank spreads in Brazil. In 2004 the average default rate on (freely allocated) loans to individuals was 13.2 percent, almost four times as much as that for firms (3.6 percent). These high delinquency rates are a result of high interest rates (a circular effect), the poor quality of information available to select borrowers, and weak creditor rights. The main complaint of creditors in Brazil is not the lack of legal protection, but its improper enforcement by the courts. The slowness of the judiciary is perceived to be the main problem not only for credit operations but also for the workings of justice in general (see Pinheiro, 2002). The World Bank's 2005 Doing Business survey also shows that collecting a debt in court or carrying out a bankruptcy process in Brazil take longer than on average in LA and in developing economies.

Furthermore, judicial decisions on credit disputes are perceived to be pro-debtor. This attitude is often the reflex of a certain degree of judicial activism that causes jurisprudence and patterns of judicial behaviour to play a role as, or more important than the law itself in regulating credit disputes. Therefore, creditors are usually unwilling to rely on legal instruments until there is a well-established jurisprudence. This explains why chattel mortgage (fiduciary alienation) is so well accepted for car financing but not house financing, while also making it very difficult to repossess most types of assets given as collateral, which then have a low impact in reducing risk and spreads.

The legal and judicial protection of minority shareholders is also perceived to be weak, which helps to depreciate share values and raise the cost of equity capital. Nenova (1999) estimates that weak property rights in Brazil lower company values by at least 20 percent. Shareholder rights are also weakened by the mismatch between cash flow and voting rights and the high ownership concentration of voting shares. Of a sample of 723 companies analyzed by Rocca (2001), only 11 percent did not issue preferential (non-voting) shares, against 27 percent that issued the limit two-thirds of total equity capital in preferential shares. On average, preferential shares made up 46 percent of the equity capital of those firms. For large companies, this proportion is even higher. The high concentration of ownership and voting rights is another problem. In two-thirds (67 percent) of the companies, the proportion of ordinary shares owned by the controlling shareholders with at least 5 percent of these shares is above 90 percent; with 16 percent in the 80–90 percent bracket. An indicator of weak minority shareholder rights is the high premium on voting rights. In Brazil, this premium is 23 percent (correcting for differences in liquidity, dividend policy, and share preference), compared to 18 percent in Germany, 9 percent in the UK, 3 percent in the US and 1 percent in Hong Kong. This high premium is associated with the high concentration of ownership in Brazil (Claessens *et al.*, 2000).

Judicial activism is part of what Arida *et al.* (2005) dubbed jurisdictional uncertainty, defined as the "risk of acts of the Prince changing the value of contracts before or at the moment of their execution," which, as is the case with court rulings, "manifests itself predominantly as an anti-saver and anti-creditor bias." Examples include the freezing of financial assets, the purging of price indices to lower monetary correction and the non-enforcement of dollar indexed leasing contracts by the Judiciary.

The poor quality of the information available to creditors and minority shareholders also discourages financial intermediation. The more and the better the credit information made available to lenders, the greater tends to be the access to credit (Galindo and Miller, 2001). In particular, firms in countries with better CIRs (Credit Information Registries) tend to rely more on debt than in those in which credit information is scarce and of poor quality.

Brazil has a large and well-established credit bureau industry, with private and public CIRs. These keep mostly black information on borrowers, which is used when deciding about small loans, usually to individuals or small businesses. They also function as enforcement mechanisms, since borrowers included in black lists are usually denied credit. But their use in larger and longer-term operations is much more limited, in which case creditors suffer with the poor quality of accounting and disclosure rules, which also affect minority shareholders. Only in the corporate segment, comprising large firms, several of which borrow or have their shares traded in foreign markets, is information deemed of relatively good quality. For small and medium firms, informality, as discussed above, is a major factor worsening the quality of financial information. According to Rocca (2001, p. 102), based on information collected from managers of private equity funds, 70 percent of the companies selected for investment are discarded at the due diligence stage, given the inconsistency of accounting registries and effective revenues and due to tax contingencies stemming from this. The poor quality of information disclosed to investors is also the result of the inadequate enforcement of disclosure norms, with a large proportion of listed companies failing to send the required information to CVM.

The above highlights as main barriers to financial deepening the distortions caused by the poor situation of the fiscal accounts and state interventions in mobilizing, draining, and allocating savings. A large part of the financial wealth in Brazil is held in short-term, highly liquid and well-remunerated public bonds, which crowd out private bonds and stocks. The difficulty faced by the government to elongate the maturities of its debt also limits the capacity of firms to issue long-term securities, making them unwilling to seek external finance. The high tax burden induces firms to become informal and mask their accounts and increases interest rate spreads, while at the same time making tax rules volatile and uncertain. Macroeconomic instability is also a hindrance to stretching maturities due to high market risk, as reflected in the high volatility of the stock market. Breaches of financial contracts involving the public sector are often motivated by the effort to prevent the public debt from entering into an explosive path.

Finance and equity: Too late, too little

Much of the criticism to first – and second-generation reforms in LA is linked to their apparent lack of impact on inequality. Can financial development improve equity in LA and, in particular, in Brazil? Our view is that it should help, although the link between finance and social conditions is more likely bi-directional than one way. Financial deepening should accelerate GDP growth. But the impact of growth on inequality and poverty is not uniform across countries, as it depends on the factor-intensity of growth and on who owns those factors. The factor of production owned by the poor is (unskilled) labor, and normally they lack, or have no access to, human, fixed (including land), and financial capital. This explains why policies aimed directly at alleviating poverty and improving the distribution of income that are not directly based on income transfers, which have limitations, usually focus on either redistributing capital or tilting the factor intensity of growth towards labor.

Financial development should benefit the poor more than proportionately because they are the ones who pay most for financial services and have least access to the system. A lower cost of consumption and investment finance will mean a direct income gain to the poor, and the opportunity to enhance physical and human capital accumulation, increasing their productivity and becoming better positioned to gain from growth. Better access to financial services should reduce their transaction costs, allow them to keep their savings at a safer and better-remunerated place, and even consume insurance and private social security services. Currently, outside the very expensive consumer loans extended by traditional financial institutions, their only option is the relatively small micro-credit segment.

Brazil offers a fertile environment for micro-finance – a large and entrepreneurial low-income population that lacks access to regular banking services and a favorable stance from public authorities – but despite registering some activity in this area since 1973, only in the past decade has the system of micro-credit started to receive some attention from the authorities. This occurred with the establishment of the "*Comunidade Solidária*" program, which allocated public funds to that end and encouraged the creation of new types of micro-finance institutions (1999) that gave the industry more flexibility regarding both funding and lending. Currently, different types of organizations provide micro-finance:[5]

1. *Non profit-seeking institutions*: Non-governmental organizations (NGOs), which are subject to the Usury Law; and public interest civil society

[5]The supply of micro credit in Brazil is made through a diversity of institutions under different regimes Micro credit can be assessed by formal and informal entrepreneurs. Typical loan values amount up to R$ 5,000 (approximately US$2,000) and interest rates charged reach approximately 4–4.5% per month (yearly consumer price inflation in Brazil is currently around 5.5%). Requirements include a clean record (at least one year) and a guarantor. Alternative mechanisms are joint guarantees and credit cooperatives (Expósito da Silva, 2003, pp. 100–2).

organizations (Oscip), registered with the Ministry of Justice, and which are not subject to the Usury Law; and

2. *Profit-seeking institutions*: Credit society for micro-entrepreneurs (SCM), which needs to be authorized by the BCB and may be controlled by any individual or organization, including private financial institutions or Oscip; and any conventional financial institution.[6]

Despite expanding considerably over the past decade, micro-finance in Brazil has flourished less than in other Latin American countries (World Bank, 2004b). Moreover, it remains highly dependent on the public sector, either directly, as with Banco do Nordeste's "*Credi Amigo*" program, or indirectly, by way of financial support from BNDES to NGOs providing micro-finance. Autonomous micro-finance institutions (such as ABN-Amro's "*Real Micro-Crédito*") are few and small.

Brazil also has a large credit cooperative industry that operates in a loan range similar to that of the micro-finance institutions. It is, though, more skewed towards individuals and less active in the informal business segment, which is the prime target of micro-finance. Credit cooperatives, which have existed in Brazil for over a century, account for a larger volume of credit, are less dependent on public support and have expanded more rapidly than the micro-finance institutions. Their share in total lending by the banking system more than doubled between 1977 and 2002. The number of SCM also expanded vigorously since they were allowed to operate in 1999, but these are still very few when compared to the cooperatives: their total lending at the end of 2002 amounted to just 0.0007 percent of GDP. Moreover, they account for a small share of the micro-finance industry in Brazil, which is dominated by the Oscip and NGO. As noted by the World Bank (2004b, p. 52):

> Many microfinance institutions are largely beyond the purview of formal financial system supervision, but estimates suggest that the total number of clients served increased from around 3,000 in 1995 to around 160,000 by end-2001, while the active loan portfolio grew to some R$140 million. This is small compared to the credit cooperative system, and also small compared to other countries in the region, once adjusted for country size. Peru and Bolivia had estimated microfinance clienteles of around 185,000 and 380,000 at end 2001, respectively, while small countries such as Nicaragua and El Salvador also had over 80,000 microfinance clients.

[6]For a detailed account of micro-finance and credit cooperatives in Brazil see World Bank (2004b) and Banco Central do Brasil (2003a and 2003b). According to Darcy and Soares (n.d.), 47% of the micro-finance institutions are OSCIP, 31% NGO, 12% SCM and 10% funds.

The poor should also benefit from financial development if the access of SMEs to finance increases. Because SMEs are more labor intensive than large firms, a large expansion in SMEs output should make growth more labor intensive. Moreover, SME could possibly play a larger role in enhancing entrepreneurship and alleviating poverty, thereby potentially contributing to reduce inequality. Small firms have a much more limited access to credit and finance than medium firms – despite the fact that the size limits of medium firms are flexible, depending on the investigator (usually up to 50 employees is small; from 50 to 5000, medium-sized). But, however defined, SMEs represent a sizeable proportion of firms, employment, and output in both developing and, especially, in the developed countries. In LA they represent 50 percent of formal employment in Mexico, almost 60 percent in Ecuador and Brazil, around 70 percent in Argentina, Colombia, Panama and Peru. In a sample of developed countries the figures are: 60 percent in Germany and the United Kingdom, 70 percent in France and 80 percent in Italy and Spain (BID, 2005, p. 195).

Lack of access to credit is an important obstacle to the development of SMEs.[7] Only 28.8 percent of the small firms have access to bank credit, compared to 42.8 percent for medium and 54.5 percent for large firms. Financing restrictions to small and medium firms in LA have four main causes: (1) fixed costs of loans (related to evaluation, supervision, and repayment of loans, which increase the cost of loans to small borrowers; micro credit is not a solution here because the amounts are likely to be large); (2) difficulty to repossess collateral; (3) bankruptcy costs; and (4) asymmetric information, which causes moral hazard and adverse selection problems.

An empirical analysis of financing constraints found that the main restrictions faced by firms are due to: (1) difficulties in the enforcement of credit contracts (effective compliance reduces financing restrictions perceived by firms); (2) lack of proper credit information registry (private registry has a positive impact; public registry has no impact); (3) the existence of dislocation, or crowding out effect (high public domestic debt increases financing restrictions and reduces access to bank credit); (4) high bank concentration and bank ownership (high concentration increases financing restrictions to SMEs; there is some evidence that state property reduces restrictions to SMEs; the presence of foreign banks reduces restrictions overall, and not just to SMEs); and (5) GDP volatility (BID, 2005).

Financial development also lowers the cost of financial capital and physical investment in the economy as a whole. This will raise investment and

[7]The data mentioned in the text come from the World Bank's *World Business Environment Survey* (WBES), which covers approximately 10,000 firms in 81 countries (20 in LA and 2,000 firms) in 1999–2000. See BID (2005).

labor productivity, lifting wages of employed workers. On the other hand, higher labor productivity would have a negative impact on employment, unless output is to expand sufficiently. In particular, there is a risk that the less skilled workers suffer most, if they are the ones capital can most easily substitute for. This stresses the importance of financial reform accelerating growth for its social impacts to be positive. To the extent that growth is indeed constrained by the lack of investment finance, the benefits to the poor are uncontroversial. But this could not be the case in countries in which other factors constrain growth.

Inasmuch as different market segments and/or participants are unequally affected by the disincentives provided by weak creditor protection, reforms in this area could have particularly important implications regarding the access of certain economic agents to credit. That is, the rationing of credit resulting from debtor-oriented laws can disproportionately affect certain types of borrowers, restricting their access to credit or penalizing them with especially large spreads. This point is illustrated by the results of Gropp *et al.* (1997), who find that in American states with debtor-oriented bankruptcy laws, credit tends to be channeled to high-asset households, with a reduction in the availability and amount of credit extended to low-asset households. Moreover, they find evidence that low-asset households are charged higher interest rates on automobile loans in high bankruptcy exemption states. Pinheiro (2002) shows that in Brazil small borrowers are especially harmed by the difficulty of creditors to enforce loan contracts through collateral repossession or other types of judicial collection.

Thus, financial reform will also contribute to reduce inequality for it will require solving problems that affect the poor and small businesses disproportionately: for instance, better defined property rights, less informality, more macroeconomic stability and competition. Informality is one of the main areas in which the needs of financial reform and social policies coincide. Alongside the relative scarcity of jobs in the corporate sector, particularly "formal" jobs, since the early 1990s new employment opportunities in LA countries have been concentrated in largely informal small business, cooperatives and self-employment, posing powerful barriers to economic growth and productivity change. A recent study argues forcefully that informality explains the large inter-firm productivity gaps observed in Brazil and is also a powerful obstacle to productivity growth (McKinsey & Company, 2004).[8] Informal firms invest little in physical and in human

[8]The productivity gap between informal and formal firms in Brazil is estimated at about 50%. This is due to the difficulty to access financial market mechanisms, reduced access to judiciary in order to enforce contracts, disincentive to grow due to fears of being caught by government agencies in charge of enforcing tax and other legal norms and procedures, and insertion in productive chains formed by informal firms as well.

capital, have a more difficult access to credit, and have no incentive to grow, for they would become more visible to the authorities. Their commercial relationships tend to be with other informal firms (World Bank, 2004a).

Finally, financial reform can improve income distribution if it entails making the distribution of financial incentives less skewed towards large farms and firms and more pro-poor. The Brazilian financial system is also a means to transfer subsidies to specific sectors, firms, and social groups. Agriculture is the most conspicuous case, but other sectors also benefit. Farmers benefit from targeted credit, which is channeled mainly through three federal banks (notably Banco do Brasil). Funding for rural credit comes mainly from mandated credit and compulsory savings funds.[9] A relatively high proportion of its population still lives in rural areas. Therefore, the potential clientele for rural credit mounts to approximately 35 million people and an estimated 4.8 million rural establishments, or farm units. But land distribution is highly skewed, with the wealthiest 1 percent of farmers accounting for 45 percent of landholdings and the poorest 50 percent of farmers holding just 2 percent of agricultural land. And it is the wealthiest farmers who benefit the most from government subsidies, in this way emptying any distributive goals of such programs, while at the same time bringing into question the need of subsidies due to market failures – large farmers have various means to deal with risk and other problems inherent to rural production. Thus, as noted in World Bank (2004b, p. 192):

> [A] large part of this directed credit fails to meet intended targets, however, with better-off farmers, for example, capturing much of the subsidies, rather than the poorer groups for whom the subsidies are intended. In agriculture the largest 2% of the borrowers receive 57% of the loans, while the smallest 75% of borrowers receive only 6% of credit."

As in agriculture, it is the large firms in industry and other sectors that receive most of the subsidies intermediated by public banks and regional development funds. Historically, the better-off segments of the population also benefited the most from housing finance subsidies.

---

[9]First, there is a 25% reserve requirement on sight deposits in the banking system, which can either be deposited with the Central Bank without remuneration or used for lending to agriculture at controlled interest rates. This answers for over half of the rural credit funds. Second, there is an array of off-budget taxes, compulsory savings, and constitutional funds, managed by public banks. These also have exclusive access to the "equalization of interest rates" instrument, which supports the "Programa Nacional de Agricultura Familiar" (Pronaf, a credit program aimed at rural households).

Final remarks

Market reforms in Brazil came later and were implemented more gradually and flexibly than in other LA countries, but eventually they caught up with the regional average and even surpassed it: in 1999 Brazil's overall index of structural reform matched Chile's. And, after a difficult start, with a contraction of GDP in 1990–92, reforms seemed to have enhanced growth, with the economy expanding vigorously in 1993–95, with further rapid growth expected for the rest of the decade. Actually, Brazil grew on average only 2.4 percent per year in 1995–2004. Moreover, after a substantial decline in poverty with the end of high inflation, in 1994, little progress was accomplished in reducing the country's severe social inequalities.

The reforms of the 1990s succeeded in raising productivity growth, but not investment rates: capital accumulation proceeded even more slowly in 1994–2004 than in the so-called "lost decade." The high cost of investing is one of the underlying causes, and lack of proper finance is one of the factors that pushes investment cost up. Long-term finance to private investors on adequate terms is scarce, other than that provided by public banks. Given Brazil's high marginal productivity of capital, facilitating the access to finance and lowering its costs is a sure way to accelerate growth.

The financial sector is one of the areas in which reform was most intensive in LA, but also the one in which Brazil lagged most behind. Recent initiatives aimed at improving the sector's institutional framework include the creation of a new public CIR at the BCB, the enactment of legislation allowing for salary-backed loans, and the reforms in the bankruptcy and corporate laws. The results so far have not been noticeable: the cost of capital remains extremely high, there is little financial intermediation taking place, and external finance reaches only a limited number of large firms.

In this context, our analysis has stressed the importance of reforms geared to improving the quality of information and strengthening the rights of creditors and minority shareholders. It also examined explanations for the relatively small contribution the Brazilian financial system has had towards promoting growth and equity. Four are worth summarizing.

First and foremost is the incomplete macroeconomic adjustment of the economy – and, in particular the existence of a large public debt – which leads to high interest rates, market volatility, and a preference of savers for liquid, short-term financial investments. By giving savers the alternative to invest in highly paid, low risk, highly liquid public bonds, the public sector sets a hard-to-meet benchmark for private investors, while downplaying the role of the financial sector in selecting and monitoring investment projects. This is the case of institutional investors, which control large sums of financial saving, largely invested in Treasury bonds. Fiscal imbalances also explain the relatively high reserve requirements on sight and term deposits, reducing the pool of savings that banks can draw on to finance firms and households.

Second, the high tax burden (35.9 percent of GDP in 2004) and the associated high degree of informality and fiddling with company accounts, which lower the quality of the information disclosed to financial institutions and minority shareholders. This lowers the supply of external finance and makes it more expensive. But most companies prefer to pay this price to give up the opportunity to partly evade taxes. Financial intermediation per se is also subject to high taxes, enlarging the wedge between the cost of capital to investors and the return obtained by savers. These enhance the importance of retained profits as a source of investment finance, notably in the case of small and medium companies, being another factor contributing to financial disintermediation.

Third, the central role of the state in mobilizing and allocating savings, largely an inheritance of the pre-1990s development model, which dampens the impact of financial intermediation on capital productivity. Virtually all long-term credit in Brazil is funded through compulsory savings and the mandatory use of a part of sight and term deposits to finance selected activities. These resources amount to 40 percent of all credit available to the private sector and are mostly intermediated by public banks. Both the loss of flexibility and political interference in the allocation of credit by public banks reduce the impact of financial intermediation on capital productivity.

Fourth, the low protection of minority shareholders and especially creditors against expropriation by the state and private parties creates a highly uncertain and risky environment that raises the cost of capital, discourages financial intermediation and raises the preference for short-term and liquid financial assets. This low protection of rights reflects a number of factors – judicial activism, high volatility of tax rules, contract breaches by the government, and the slow enforcement of laws and regulations – including an overall bias against financial investors in the executive, legislative and judicial branches of government.

Some of these problems are even more acute in the so-called retail segment, which covers individuals and small businesses. Financial institutions operating in this segment tend to direct loans to consumers, rather than producers; prefer to operate with the rich, rather than the poor; and essentially supply only short-term loans. Default rates are higher than the average, and so are interest rate spreads. This is the targeted clientele of micro-credit institutions, which have expanded their activities in recent years, but from a very low base. Their activities are hampered by the same kind of legal and informational problems that complicate traditional institutions: lack of valuable, well titled, executable collateral; severe problems of asymmetric information; and, in the case of small businesses, a high mortality rate.

Emerging economies with relevant capital markets have low inflation and a relatively low public debt. Thus, considering the issue of sequencing, Novaes (2005) shows that the transition to such a macroeconomic environment, allowing for a decline in interest rates, has preceded a discrete improvement in financial market development, confirming our assessment that furthering the fiscal adjustment process and lowering the public debt to GDP ratio are pre-requisites not only for lowering the tax burden and jurisdictional uncertainty, but ultimately to allowing for financial development in Brazil.

Pronounced market instability, high real interest rates, large public deficits, high taxes, high reserve requirements on sight deposits, poor borrower screening, and insufficient creditor protection are factors that add up to make finance scarce and expensive to firms and individuals. The combined effects of these problems are financial disintermediation and a preference for liquid, short-term financial assets. Savers also tend to either reinvest their savings or keep them abroad in safer jurisdictions. The end result is a financial system that, although counting on a sophisticated infrastructure, plays a very limited role in fostering growth and equity.

References

Afanasieff, T., P. Lhacer, and M. Nakane (2001) *The Determinants of Bank Interest Spreads in Brazil*, BCB, Brasilia, D.F.

Arida, P., E.L. Bacha, and A. Lara-Resende (2005) "Credit, interest, and jurisdictional uncertainty: conjectures on the case of Brazil," in F. Guavas, I. Goldman and S. Herrera (eds), *Inflation Targeting, Debt, and the Brazilian Experience, 1999 to 2003*, MIT Press, Cambridge, MA.

Bacha, E.L. and Bonelli, R. (2005) "Uma interpretação das causas da desaceleração econômica do Brasil," *Revista de Economia Política*, 25(3), July–September, Editora 34, São Paulo, SP.

Banco Central do Brasil (2003a) *Evolução do sistema financeiro: Relatório 2002*, BCB, Brasilia, DF.

Banco Central do Brasil (2003b) *Cooperativas de crédito: História da evolução normativa no Brasil*, BCB, Brasilia, DF.

Banco Interamericano de Desenvolvimento (BID) (2005) *Libertar o Crédito-Como Aprofundar e Estabilizar o Financiamento Bancário*, Campus Elsevier, Rio de Janeiro.

Belaisch, A. (2003) "Do Brazilian banks compete?," International Monetary Fund, *IMF Working Paper*, no. 03/113, May.

Claessens, S., D. Klingebiel, and M. Lubrano (2000) "Corporate governance reform issues in the Brazilian equity market," World Bank.

Darcy, S. and M. Soares (n.d.) "Democratização do crédito no Brasil: atuação do Banco Central," BCB.

Demirgüç-Kunt, A., L. Laeven, and R. Levine (2003) "Regulations, market structure, institutions and the cost of financial intermediation," *National Bureau of Economic Research, Working Paper* no. 9890.

Demirgüç-Kunt, A. and H. Huizinga (1999) "Determinants of commercial bank interest margins and profitability: some international evidence," *World Bank Economic Review*, 13(2).

Edwards, S. (1995) "Why are saving rates so different across countries? An international comparative analysis," *National Bureau of Economic Research, Working Paper* no. 5097.

Expósito da Silva, A.F.R. (2003) "Micro-empreendimentos na região metropolitana do Rio de Janeiro: diagnóstico e políticas de apoio," Master's Dissertation, Coppe/UFRJ. Rio de Janeiro, RJ.

Galindo, A. and M. Miller (2001) "Can credit registries reduce credit constraints? Empirical evidence on the role of credit registries in firm investment decisions," IDB.

Giambiagi, F. and F. Montero (2005) "O ajuste da poupança doméstica no Brasil: 1999/2004" ("*The adjustment of domestic savings in Brazil: 1999/2004*"), (processed) Discussion Paper no. 1119, IPEA, Rio de Janeiro.

Gropp, R., J. Scholz, and M. White (1997) "Personal bankruptcy and credit supply and demand," *Quarterly Journal of Economics*, 12(1).

Levine, R. (1997) "Financial development and economic growth: views and agenda," *Journal of Economic Literature*, 35(2), June.

Lindauer, D. and L. Pritchett (2002) "What's the big idea? The third generation of policies for economic growth," *Economía*, 3(1).

Loayza, N., K. Schmidt-Hebbel, and L. Servén (2000) "Saving in developing countries: an overview," *The World Bank Economic Review*, 14(3).

McKinsey&Company (2004) *Eliminado as Barreiras ao Crescimento Econômico e à Economia Formal no Brasil*, São Paulo, SP, Brazil, June.

McKinsey Global Institute (1998) *Productivity: The Key to Accelerated Growth in Brazil*, São Paulo and Washington, DC.

Narita, R and W. Novaes (2003) *A CPMF e o mercado acionário brasileiro: efeitos sobre governança corporativa e estilos de investimento*, Departamento de Economia, PUC-Rio de Janeiro.

Nenova, T. (1999) "The value of corporate votes and control benefits: a cross-country analysis," NBER.

Novaes, A. (2005) "Mercado de capitais: lições da experiência internacional," in E.L. Bacha and L. Chrysóstomo de Oliveira (eds), *Mercado de Capitais e Crescimento Econômico*, Rio de Janeiro, Contracapa, ANBID-IEPE/CdG Symposium.

Pagano, M. (1993) "Financial markets and growth: an overview," *European Economic Review*, 37(2–3).

Pinheiro, A.C., and A. Moura (2003) "Segmentation and the use of information in Brazilian credit markets," in M. Miller (ed.), *Credit Reporting Systems and the International Economy*, MIT Press, Cambridge, MA.

Pinheiro, A.C. (2002) *Creditor Rights, Enforcement and the Access to Credit*, Rio de Janeiro.

Pinheiro, A.C., I. Gill, L. Severn, and M. Thomas (2001) "Brazilian economic growth in 1900–2000: lessons and policy implications," paper prepared for the Global Development Network Third Annual Conference, Rio de Janeiro, Brazil.

Reis, J.G.A. and S.M. Valadares (2004) "Reforma do sistema financeiro do Brasil: implementação recente e perspectivas", Inter American Development Bank, *Economic and Social Studies Series*, RE1–04–003, March.

Rocca, C.A. (ed.) (2001) *Soluções para o Desenvolvimento do Mercado de Capitais Brasileiro*, IBMEC, José Olympio Editora.

Rodrik, D. (2004) "Rethinking growth policies in the developing world," draft of the *Luca d'Agliano Lecture in Development Economics*.

Stiglitz, J.E. (1994) "The role of the state in financial markets," *Proceedings of the World Bank Annual Conference on Development Economics 1993*, pp. 351–66.

Troster, R. (n.d.) *Spread bancário no Brasil*, Febraban, Rio de Janeiro.

Wachtel, P. (2003) "How much do we really know about growth and finance?," *Federal Reserve Bank of Atlanta Economic Review*, First Quarter.

World Bank (2004a) *Doing Business in 2005: Removing Obstacles to Growth*, World Bank, IFC and Oxford University Press, Washington, DC.

World Bank (2004b) *Brazil – Access to Financial Services*, Report no. 27773–BR.

8
Financial Globalization: From Crises-Prone to Development-Friendly?

Ricardo Ffrench-Davis[1]

Introduction

Opening of the capital account has been one of the strongest policy recipes of mainstream economics since the 1980s. The recipe has been implemented vigorously in Latin America, encompassing a wide variety of flows including acquisitions of public and private firms, bonds, equity stock and derivatives.[2] After significant innovations in international capital markets in the 1990s, private flows flowed abundantly into Latin America, particularly, in 1990–97. Liberalization has also included flows of domestic capital, seeking the full integration of local financial markets to international markets.

The incidence of private capital flows on domestic economic activity has been an outstanding feature of Latin American economies (LACs) during the past quarter of a century. Actually, on frequent occasions, capital surges have been associated to financial crises rather than to vigorous capital formation and sustainable GDP growth. This fact highlights the central role played by the transmission of boom–bust cycles in international capital markets into the host markets, and the vulnerabilities and hysteresis effects that pro-cyclicality tends to generate on diverse emerging economies

---

[1]This chapter is partly based on Ffrench-Davis (2005, Chapter VI) and on output of a research project of ECLAC, with support of the Ford Foundation (see Ffrench-Davis, 2006, Chapter I). I appreciate the comments of Augusto de la Torre, Claudio Loser, José Luis Machinea, Roberto Zahler, and colleagues at ECLAC. I appreciate the research assistance of Heriberto Tapia and Rodrigo Heresi.

[2]See ECLAC (2002a, Chapters 2 and 5); Morley *et al.* (1999); Stallings and Studart (2006); Williamson (2003).

(EEs).[3] Financial volatility has been one significant variable underlying the poor growth performance: (1) in 1990–2005, annual GDP per capita grew merely 1 percent, *vis-à-vis* the world and the USA averaging 1.2 percent and 1.8 percent, respectively; (2) output per member of the labor force stagnated between 1990 and 2005; and (3) the investment ratio remained notably depressed notwithstanding intense "market reforms" and a recovery of capital inflows.

Significant shifts in expectations, usually reinforced by subsequent risk-rating changes, lead to sharp pro-cyclical adjustments in the availability of financing, maturities, and spreads. The most damaging, as argued below, rather than very short-term volatility, are the medium-term fluctuations: several years of over-optimism and abundant financing (i.e. 1991–94 and mid-1995–97), followed by several years of over-pessimism and dryness (1998–2003). The outcome of that pro-cyclical environment includes several years with recessive output-gaps, depressed actual productivity (TFP), and lowered investment ratios. Given a natural asymmetry in macroeconomic performance (economic activity cannot exceed persistently full employment but can stay for long significantly below), average actual TFP, investment ratios, employment and social equity, and GDP growth are severely affected by instability.

In this chapter I analyze how and why the transmission of financial volatility into LACs has been one determinant variable behind the poor economic and social performance of the region since the early 1990s. In the first section, after summarizing the two more traditional arguments in favor of capital account opening by developing economies, two newer arguments are analyzed. In the second section it is argued why recessions leave significant long-lasting economic and social costs. Even the better-behaved recoveries usually end in a GDP plateau notoriously below the pre-crisis plateau. In the third section, it is analyzed how and why, repeatedly, crises are built in boom periods. The role of *short-termist agents* and *processes* of persistent positive shifts of the supply of funding during the boom stage are stressed. The final section, concludes with some lessons for providing a market environment actually "friendly" to labor and capital that are the producers of economic growth.

---

[3]Marfán (2005) shows that pro-cyclicality has been located in private flows. Actually, public funding has tended to behave counter-cyclically (see ECLAC, 2002b). Ffrench-Davis (2006) presents a comparative analysis of macroeconomic policies of selected Asian, African and Latin American economies. Ffrench-Davis (2005) analyzes trade, financial and macroeconomic reforms in Latin America under the aegis of the Washington Consensus, and offers ingredients for an alternative analytical framework. Several assertions in this chapter have their statistical or econometric support in the latter book. See complementary analyses in Agosin (2006); Frenkel (2004); Griffith-Jones (1998) and Ocampo (2006).

Newer arguments for liberalizing capital flows

Flows from capital-rich to capital-scarce economies and flows compensating external shocks are the two most classic arguments in favor of capital flows to LDCs. Real returns on marginal investment in capital-rich countries are expected to be systematically lower than those in "soundly" managed capital-scarce countries like the EEs. Indeed, net inflows of external savings can supplement national savings, raise productive investment and, thus, boost growth. In turn, expansion of aggregate income can further increase domestic savings and investment, thereby creating a virtuous circle that contributes to the convergence of levels of economic development.

Given the large gap between the stock of capital per worker in Latin America and in developed nations such as the US (a relation 1 to 5 in 2003), there is broad space during a long span of time, for equilibrating flows from capital-abundant to capital-scarce economies.

This traditional framework has powerful policy implications: (1) capital inflows should consistently finance productive investment; that is, crowding-out of national savings should be avoided; (2) investment must be allocated efficiently (requiring the supply of the other ingredients of the production function, and a real macroeconomic environment suitable for productive investment); (3) the country must invest intensively in tradables in order to generate a trade surplus large enough to transform domestic savings into foreign currency, to service external liabilities; and (4) creditors must be willing to provide stable and predictable flows of finance on reasonable terms. Particularly, it should perform a counter-cyclical role by balancing

Table 8.1 Latin America (19): Composition of capital flows, 1977–2004
(percentage of trend GDP, %)

	1977–81	*1982–90*	*1991*	*1992–94*	*1995*	*1996–97*	*1998–2003*	*2004*
1 Current Account (2+3+4)	-3.9	-1.3	-1.4	-3.1	-2.4	-3.0	-2.3	1.0
2 Trade Balance	-1.5	2.4	0.4	-1.5	-0.8	-1.2	-0.7	2.3
3 Rents	-2.6	-4.2	-2.6	-2.4	-2.6	-2.7	-2.9	-3.5
4 Unrequited transfers	0.2	0.5	0.8	0.9	1.0	0.9	1.3	2.2
5 Net Capital Inflows (6+10+11+12)	4.6	1.3	2.9	4.3	3.2	4.2	2.4	0.2
6 Net FDI (7+8–9)	0.8	0.6	0.9	1.1	1.6	2.9	3.2	2.4
7 M&A inflows			0.2	0.4	0.5	1.5	1.8	1.1
8 Greenfield FDI inflows			0.8	0.9	1.4	1.6	1.8	2.0
9 Outflows			0.1	0.2	0.3	0.3	0.4	0.7
10 Portfolio	0.2	0.0	1.4	4.0	0.1	1.9	0.1	-0.6
11 Other Capital	3.5	-2.2	-0.3	-1.1	-0.5	-0.4	-1.6	-2.2
12 Special Flows	0.1	2.8	1.0	0.3	2.0	-0.2	0.6	0.5
13 Reserves Accumulation (5+1)	0.7	0.0	1.5	1.2	0.8	1.2	0.1	1.1
14 Net Transfer of Funds (5+3)	2.0	-2.9	0.3	1.9	0.7	1.5	-0.5	-3.4

Source: Ffrench-Davis (2006, Table VI.1). Trend GDP was calculated by filtering nominal GDP in US dollars (Hodrick-Prescott filter, lambda = 100). Portfolio flows include bonds and stock purchases (ADRs among them). Other capital includes, among others, bank loans and errors and omissions. Special flows include use of IMF credits and exceptional financing.

transitory differences between output and expenditure, or between import and export prices, or spreading out over time the adjustment to permanent changes in relative prices; thus, it would allow a stabilizing intertemporal adjustment of consumption and investment. Given the smallness of EEs markets, *vis-à-vis* international financial markets, a stabilizing behavior of the supply is potentially feasible. In average, capital has tended to flow in the expected direction, but frequently several or all those requirements have not been fulfilled.

In boom periods, positive net inflows and positive net transfers have eliminated any binding external constraint; however, in recessive periods negative net transfers have prevailed, actually imposing a binding external constraint in two long periods (see 1982–89 and 1998–2003 periods in Table 8.1).[4]

Crowding-out of national savings and a variant of the "Dutch" disease have been frequent during booms. Flows have compensated terms of trade shocks systematically only during periods of generalized abundant supply. For instance, in 1991–97, agents that were affected by a falling export price usually could borrow abroad rather easily. On the contrary, in cases of weak finance supply, a worsening of the terms of trade has led to sharper dryness or to a consolidation of a binding external restriction; the outcome tends to be a private capital account contributing to a destabilizing intertemporal adjustment.[5] Indeed, financial markets, systematically, have pressed EEs authorities to face the negative external shocks with a pro-cyclical recessive policy. The sexennium 1998–2003 offers an outstanding case of recessive pro-cyclicality in South America, as discussed in the next sections.

But newer arguments have been brought on by promoters of capital account liberalization. We now discuss two of them.

Flows diversifying risk

The argument is that capital mobility would allow individuals to satisfy their risk preferences more fully through greater asset diversification. This microeconomic argument has been used widely for justifying a full opening of the capital account, particularly including the opening to outflows of domestic funds.

There are several ways to diversify risk or insure against diverse types of risk. For instance, by trade diversification and stabilization funds (including international reserves policy) to face exports and imports instability as a

[4]Capital flows minus interest and profit payments became negative in both periods, in amounts equivalent to 2.9 percent and 0.5 percent of GDP, respectively.

[5]Prasad *et al.* (2003, Section I.c and Table 4), conclude that "procyclical access to international capital markets appears to have had a perverse effect on the relative volatility of consumption for financially integrated developing economies."

prudential macroeconomic policy; at the micro-level, with sectoral and geographical diversification by the firm, and by producers of goods and services[6] and of creditors/debtors by operating with derivatives markets.[7] These forms of diversification or direct insurance should foster development of new techniques and products with probably higher though uncertain returns for the suppliers of funding.

But, a quite different matter is a capital account opening to diversify the financial assets and equity stock portfolio of residents. There are some interesting analytical pieces in the literature supporting this risk diversification argument. For instance, Obstfeld (1998) develops a model based on the hypothesis that global financial integration implies a portfolio shift from low-risk-low-returns capital to high-risk-high-returns capital, with an increase in global productivity. From an EE view, there are three qualifications I would like to pose:

1. There is an overlapping of the risk diversification argument with that of flows from capital-rich to capital-scarce markets in response to differential returns; there is need of distinguishing between higher world productivity due to resources being reallocated from capital-abundant to capital-scarce economies, and a reallocation from low risk to high risk projects encouraged by output and geographical diversification.[8]
2. Actually, what we do observe are cross-border flows tending to move into better-known and non-high risk assets in the recipient economies; a look at stocks (for instance, ADRs) and bonds of EEs transacted internationally, documents it sharply: they usually correspond to large, mature, and better graded domestic firms. In particular, the same happens with financial investment abroad of EEs residents. An important exception is in the case of the bubbles, in which investors likely do not reveal an appetite-for-risk, but rather an assumption away of risk during the contagion of over-optimism.
3. It is assumed that financial investment rapidly transfers into productive investment (capital formation), what has frequently not occurred, as exposed in the second section.

[6]It is assumed that the trade cycles of the new products or destinations are not synchronized, and that they do reduce average fluctuations.

[7]The accelerated growth of derivatives markets contributed to soften "micro-instability," but has tended to increase "macro-instability" and to reduce transparency. See Dodd (2003) for an analysis of the channels by which stability and instability are transmitted.

[8]There is a natural association between financial returns and the value of marginal productivity of capital, within each economy, but during the cycle large divergences use to appear between the two. These divergences are at the core of financial crises, with a corresponding collapse of asset prices, exchange rate depreciation and interest rate hike.

It is quite relevant that, for a given EE, financial opening for the implementation of financial risk diversification implies liberalizing outflows by residents. Usually, closeness has been tougher on outflows by residents than on inflows from foreigners. Consequently, most probably, full liberalization would tend to imply net outflows from –the more incomplete, smaller, less liquid and less deep– emerging markets, rather than the opposite.[9] Evidently, these net outflows may diversify risk for domestic financial investors and agents. However, most likely, it does not contribute to diversify risk on returns to domestic producers, what actually does tend to be achieved with output and geographical diversification of sales. Additionally, while those outflows may reduce savings available domestically and the financing for productive investment and, I suspect, tend to foster a short-term bias in domestic financial markets.[10]

The fact is that international financial diversification is presently being given evident priority in policy-making; for instance, when eliminating capital gains taxes on cross-border operations and in the encouragement that a liberalization process grants to intermediaries of financial investment in offshore markets. But, the fact is that both activities are quite isolated from the sources of systemic competitivity and productive development. In brief, there appears to be no well-documented connection of this form of risk diversification with the sources of domestic productivity increases and growth convergence. On the contrary, that sort of priority tends to concentrate energy of economic agents in purely financial activities; this implies a *neo-rent-seeking* attitude: to make short-term profits at the expense of other agents, instead of profits derived from increased productivity. The policy challenge is one of a rebalance in favor of "productivism" and longer-term horizons.

Capital account opening and macroeconomic discipline

This is the newest argument in favor of capital account liberalization. It states that the dependency from capital inflows can make a significant contribution to deter political authorities from adopting irresponsible and populist macroeconomic policies. It is argued that, consequently, fully opening the capital account would encourage "sound macroeconomic fundamen-

---

[9]In Mahani *et al.* (2006) it is documented that Korea and Malaysia – the two fastest recovering EEs after the Asian crisis – kept restrictions on outflows by residents as a countercyclical macroeconomic device. See Zahler (2006) for an analysis on outflows by private pension funds in Chile.

[10]Bhagwati (2004) argues convincingly that financial volatility has been detrimental for trade, discouraging its liberalization.

tals."[11] In the case of irresponsible, weak, or divided governments, it may be true for *domestic* sources of instability, i.e., large fiscal deficits, permissive monetary policy, and populist exchange-rate overvaluation. Indeed, the menace of sudden private capital outflows can become a powerful deterrent for those forms of populism. However, in the case of responsible authorities, it is a redundant tool on that side of the coin. On the other hand, during capital surges, it has been observed that lax demand policies or exchange-rate overvaluation have tended to be fostered, rather than discouraged, by financial markets (in periods of over-optimism of financial agents); praises from financial markets for inflation drops – that were led by a mix of large capital inflows, exchange rate appreciation, and rising external deficits – have been quite common during boom periods in the last quarter of a century. That is, it is the financial market itself which, during the booms, has generated incentives for EEs to enter *vulnerability zones* (see the third section). The perverse outcome during booms is duplicated during the contractive stage that usually follows the boom, when excessive punishment by those same markets has tended to force national authorities to adopt overly contractionary policies. The consequence is a straightforward pro-cyclicality.

In fact, the implications for macroeconomic policies appear to be particularly significant during the recessive stages. The recent six year recessive gap in Latin America – in 1998–2003 – had an evident macroeconomic origin. In all those years there was a significant output gap (an actual GDP below potential output). The 5.1 percent average growth recorded in 2004–05 as compared to 1.2 percent in 1998–2003 (see Table 8.2), without any significant change in capital formation, reveals that the output gap was in fact significant. It is interesting that the output gap and its changes are mostly located in the non-exportable component of GDP; this is the part of GDP more dependent on domestic macroeconomic management.[12] As

[11]A recent working paper of the IMF (Tytell and Wei, 2004) examines the "discipline effect" of financial globalization on macroeconomic balances, focusing on the two pillars in fashion – low inflation and fiscal balances – disregarding the other components of a comprehensive set of real macroeconomic balances. Particularly, they find that the "discipline effect" was effective in reducing inflation. However, we should consider the control of inflation not an end, but an input for improving market information and the allocation of human and physical resources. Research examining why success by LACs in reducing inflation has come together with failure in both growth and equity is quite scarce.

[12]The bulk of the changes in GDP growth between expansive periods (1990–97 and 2004–05) and recessive periods (1982–89 and 1998–2003) are located in the non-exported component of GDP. That is, GDP has fluctuated more due to instability in non-exports than in exports. The former instability is associated to the pro-cyclical nature, from the perspective of the real economy, of macroeconomic policies implemented under the Washington Consensus. See Ffrench-Davis (2005, Chapter 2 and Table 5.2).

Table 8.2 Latin America (19): Growth of exports and non-exported GDP, 1990–2005 (annual average growth rates, %)

	GDP	*Exports*	*Non-exports*
1990–97	3.2	8.3	2.5
		(1.0)	(2.2)
1998–2003	1.2	5.4	0.5
		(0.8)	(0.4)
2004–05	5.1	9.2	4.2
		(1.7)	(3.4)
1990–2005	2.7	7.3	1.9
		(1.0)	(1.7)

Source: Based on official figures from ECLAC for 19 countries. Figures into brackets are estimates of points of GDP growth contributed by exports and non-exports (rest of GDP), respectively. The direct contribution of exports to GDP is the domestic value-added component of gross exports of goods and services. Export value-added was estimated by discounting from gross exports their imported content. The imported content was assumed to be equal to the share of non-consumer imports in total GDP; for Mexican maquila, actual figures of value-added were used.

Table 8.2 shows, in 1998–2003 the by-far-larger drop in GDP corresponded to non-exports, and in 2004–05 the by-far-larger share of the recovery of GDP growth also corresponded to non-exports resulting from a sharp fall in the respective output gap. A binding external constraint was determinant of that gap. The restriction was dominated by private capital flows during most part of the period. The proper technical response – for a growth-friendly outcome– would have been a sharp reactivating policy with effective switching policies. However, most countries pursued recessive policies that determined the actual poor GDP performance.[13] Even Chile followed a rather similar behavior, recording a 2.7 percent growth in 1998–2003 *vis-à-vis* 7.1 percent in 1990–97 and 6.1 percent in 2004–05.[14] The fact is that LACs gained "credibility," in financial markets and with international financial institutions, at the expense of recording a poor growth performance.

Beyond the macroeconomic implications, as well there are implications for democracy in EEs. One, most worrisome, implication is that national

[13]Two notable exceptions are the reactivating macroeconomic shock therapy adopted, with variants, by Korea and Malaysia in 1998 (see Mahani *et al.* (2006). Their actions show that there was an alternative to the passive approach adopted by LACs that waited until 2004 for recovery to be led by external positive shocks. Also show that there are diverse alternatives for a recovery based on domestic policy-led shocks, as the different sets of common and diverse features in Korea and Malaysia depict.

[14]The rather better performance of Chile (2.7 percent versus the 1.3 percent average of the region) is partly associated with the innovative structural fiscal balance approach adopted by the government in 2001, which allowed avoiding a pro-cyclical fiscal policy during the recessive years 2001–03.

political authorities may lose the capacity to pursue the legitimate policy proposals for which they were elected by the democratic electorate. There are mesoeconomic implications, such as on tax policy, giving way to a relaxation of the tax burden on capital and on higher income sectors, at the expense of labor and mid/low income brackets.

Actually, there is a growing duality, reflecting a counter-democratic trend, in the constituencies taken into account by authorities in EEs. A dilemma for decision makers arises between pleasing financial agents or the domestic agents in the "real" economy (workers and firms) bearing the consequences. An outcome of the specific road taken by globalization has been that experts in financial intermediation – a microeconomic training– have become determinant, in too many cases, for the evolution of the domestic macroeconomic balances and their volatility. Central banks and ministries of finance frequently, in their own wording, have been following the "advise of markets," by which it is implied a group of influential agents in financial markets, which are merely a small fraction of private markets and of the generation of GDP.

It is "irrational," and evidently inefficient from the perspective of resource allocation and total factor productivity, if the decisions of authorities, which should obviously be taken with a long-term horizon, seeking sustainable growth with equity, become entrapped with the lobbying and policy recipes of experts in short-term and liquid flows.

Elusive growth and equity: the role of financial inflows

A dominant feature of the "new generation" of business cycles in EEs are the sharp fluctuations in domestic private spending and balance sheets, associated to boom–bust cycles in external financing. As stated earlier, these swings in economic activity have mid-term persistence. The corresponding deviations from a stable trend tend to be biased against SMEs and less-trained labor. Incompleteness in labor and financial markets (see Bourguignon and Walton, this volume), and the quite diverse mobility and time horizons of "producers" and "financiers" are at the core of the inequitability biases of instability.

The rise of external financing in the 1990s contained a significant exogenous or push origin (Broner and Rigobon, 2006; Calvo, 1998); but actual inflows tend to produce policy changes, which then introduce pull or endogenous factors. It can be interpreted that the former effect is the primary dominant one when a growing deficit on current account and appreciating exchange rates coexist with the accumulation of international reserves. That happened in most LACs in 1990–97.

External shocks, both positive and negative, are multiplied domestically if exchange rate and monetary policies are pro-cyclical, as it actually has been encouraged by financial market agents and multilateral financial

Figure 8.1 Latin America: Net capital inflows and RER, 1987–2005 (% of GDP, indice 1997=100)

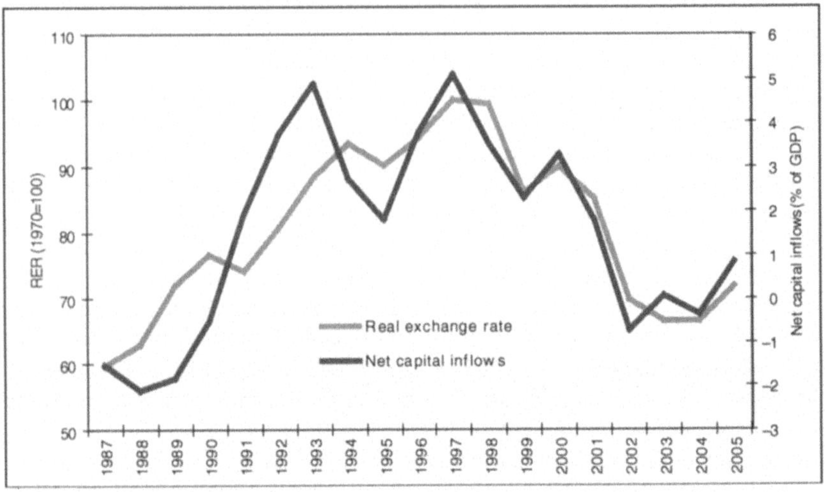

Source: Ffrench-Davis (2005, Figure 6.2), based on ECLAC figures. Real exchange rate defined in terms of dollars per unit of local currency. Preliminary figures for 2005.

agencies.[15] As a consequence of a pro-cyclical behavior, during the capital surges we have observed that EEs have, frequently, penetrated in *vulnerability zones*, during expansive *adjustment processes* including some combination of: (1) rising external liabilities, with a large liquid or short-term share (IMF, 1998; Rodrik and Velasco, 2000); (2) large current account external deficits; (3) appreciated exchange rates; (4) currency and maturity mismatches; (5) high price/earnings ratios of domestic financial assets; and (6) high prices of real estate. Bust in EEs, usually has come after a boom in capital inflows, which have been generating all these destabilizing market signals (Ffrench-Davis, 2005, chapters VI–VII).

Figure 8.1 illustrates the incidence of capital flows on the foreign exchange rate. The impact is so strong that a weighted average of LACs

[15]The mainstream fiscal recipe differs during the boom and recession; particularly under advice by the IMF, tends to behave counter-cyclically during the boom and pro-cyclically during recession. However, data show that the effects of capital inflows during booms are overwhelmingly larger than counter-cyclical fiscal restraint during financial surges. Even in the case of Chile, in 1996–97, fiscal policy moderation generated the largest public surplus of the 1990s (over 2 percent of GDP), but expansive exchange rate and monetary policies, led by capital inflows, implied a duplication of the deficit on current account in comparison to 1990–95 (see Ffrench-Davis, 2002, p. 21).

shows a high correlation between net capital inflows and the average real exchange rate of the region in the nearly two decades period covered. These flows have shown to be a dominant force on the exchange rate behavior over that of trade in goods and services in the short to mid-term. Afterward, when real external disequilibria become unsustainable, an abrupt correction frequently takes place with a recessive adjustment;[16] usually this reversion has been led by financial outflows.

The longer and deeper the economy's penetration into those *vulnerability zones*, the more severe the *financieristic trap* in which authorities tend to get caught, and the lower the probability of leaving it without undergoing a crisis and long-lasting economic and social costs. The absence or weakness of policies moderating the boom – lack of adequate breaks during the process toward overheating – inhibits the feasibility of adopting a strong reactivating (counter-cyclical) policy under a recessive environment after the bust.

In fact, in this sort of crises, a downward adjustment of aggregate demand takes place after the drying-up of supply. The negative financial shock underlying the Asian crisis was compounded by a concomitant terms of trade worsening; it is evident that there were no spontaneous capital flows compensating the terms of trade negative shocks. Usually, there has been an "automatic" component in the domestic adjustment, associated to a significant loss of international reserves, complemented with diverse doses of either automatic or policy-increased interest rates, currency depreciation, and fiscal contraction. Naturally, the drop in domestic demand (or of its rate of growth) tends to correct the external deficit, and consequently that source of the demand for foreign currency. In these sharp processes of adjustment, frequently a drop in GDP (or rate of GDP growth) follows,[17] which tends to make necessary a subsequent additional fall in aggregate demand. Obviously, the larger the cumulative drop in GDP, the heavier the economic and social costs of adjustment and the foregone welfare. Most of the drop in GDP does

[16]Rodrik, in this volume, stresses the crucial role that the exchange rate has come to play, after trade liberalization and restrictions from the WTO, on the use of productive development policies by EEs.

[17]Large deficits on current account (duly controlled by the terms of trade fluctuations) make unavoidable a reduction in aggregate demand; but a drop in GDP is neither necessary nor convenient. With an efficient combination of demand-reducing and switching policies there should be no large output loss associated to the downward adjustment of aggregate demand. The actual huge GDP losses with respect to the previous growth trend, clearly signal that the economies we are dealing with are too inflexible *vis-à-vis* sharp negative shocks, and that switching policies are not efficient or have become less efficient given the loss of tools, or that the recipes in fashion impose a pro-cyclical or, at best, neutral policy. Particularly, an over-killing demand-reduction tends to predominate.

Figure 8.2 Chile and Korea: GDP and aggregate demand, 1987–2005

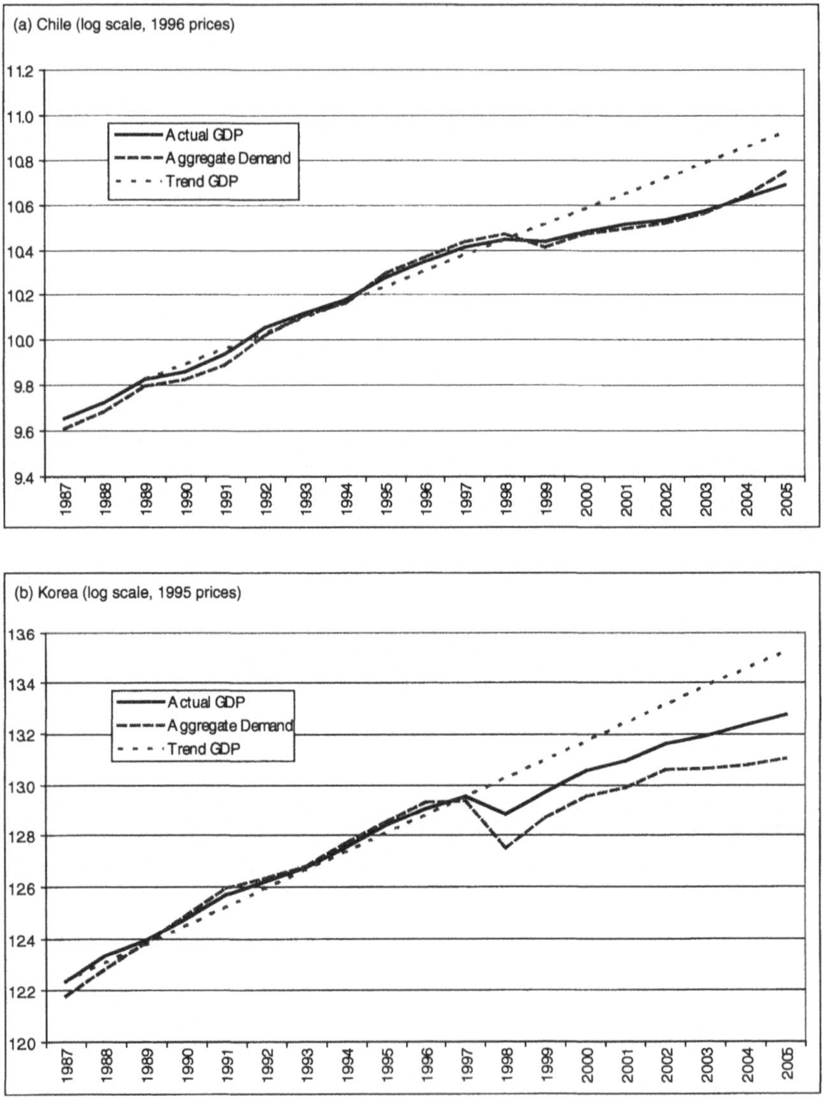

Source: Author's calculations based on data from the Central Bank of Chile and the Asian Development Bank. Trend GDP was calculated for periods in which potential and actual GDP were rather close: 1989–98 in Chile, and 1987–97 in Korea. Preliminary figures for 2005.

not imply, necessarily, destroyed capacity but a transitory underutilization, an *output gap* (potential GDP larger than actual GDP). That is a *recessive gap*. A positive implication, nonetheless, is that the resulting output gap provides room for a subsequent recovery. Indeed in all moderately or well-managed economies, a recovery usually follows the fall in activity.[18]

However, even in the outstanding cases of fast recovery – the so-called v-shaped recoveries – significant costs have been observed.[19] Generally, countries are pushed into a lower GDP path. Figure 8.2 depicts the cases of Korea and Chile. Before the crisis, both were in a growth trend in the order of 7 percent per year, considered sustainable by most observers; actually, both economies had been growing somewhat faster than 7 percent. Even these two outstanding economies, after 1998, remain notoriously below the previous trend.

These economic and social costs are associated with three particularly relevant dynamic medium-term effects on GDP. One is a usual sharp reduction of productive investment during the crisis, which naturally deteriorates the future path of potential GDP; for instance, the already mediocre investment ratios in LACs fell 1.5 points of GDP between the averages of 1992–99 and 2000–2003. The drop in capital formation is associated to a persistent output gap, unemployment, and generalized uncertainty and pessimism with the bust. The rising output gap implies a depressed actual total factor productivity.[20] Second, due to the worsening of balance sheets (Krugman, 2000), financial system loans become tighter, usually with significant liquidity restraints for SMEs; frequently, also the public budget worsens and investment is postponed (Easterly and Servén, 2003). Third, a

[18]In more naive econometrics it is interpreted that total factor productivity (TFP) rises with recovery. What actually happens, to a large degree, is that underutilized factors become employed. We have shown that control by the output gap corrects downward standard estimates for the contribution of TFP to Latin American GDP growth, and corrects upward that of capital formation. See Ffrench-Davis (2005, Chapter III).

[19]As said, there is a significant asymmetry in the behavior of the output gap. Actual GDP can drop significantly below potential GDP, while it cannot exceed it by much. In Ffrench-Davis (2002, Chapter I.2 and Appendix) we estimated the non-sustainable share of actual GDP in the diverse boom periods experienced by Chile. This asymmetry contributes to explain the regressive bias of instability. During recession, the drop usually is deeper for SMEs; even if in the expansive stage the recovery in SMEs were stronger than in large and modern firms, the average output gap would remain larger for SMEs, given the asymmetry.

[20]Here we are referring only to a drop in TFP due to underutilization of installed productive capacity. In recessive gaps it is likely that some few firms might increase innovation to survive, and some absorb and renovate failing firms that they acquire, but it is also likely that uncertainty and capital markets incompleteness discourage most firms to innovate, especially innovation associated with capital formation.

growing body of evidence documents that boom–bust cycles has ratchet effects on social variables (Rodrik, 2001; Tokman, 2004; World Bank, 2003). The deterioration of the labor market (open unemployment, a worsening in the quality of jobs or in real wages, and rising informality) is generally very rapid, whereas the recovery is slow and incomplete. This is reflected, for instance, in the long-lasting worsening of real wages in Mexico after the Tequila crisis (Frenkel and Ros, 2004); two crucial variables behind this outcome are that: (1) labor supply keeps rising, while capital formation experiences a sharp drop and the average rate of use of the stock of capital is reduced; and (2) SMEs and informal sectors, both labor-intensive, tend to be more affected by instability. It is relevant, for equity and average growth performance, that the upward process usually tends to be more gradual or slower than the downward adjustment, which tends to be abrupt.

These three problems signal policy priorities during the crises: sustaining public investment, encouraging private investment; contributing to reschedule liabilities, and assisting in solving currency and maturity mismatches; reinforcing a social network that uses the opportunity to improve the productivity of temporarily underutilized factors, and the need to enforce an active counter-cyclical macroeconomic approach.

Pro-cyclical financial flows that destabilize macroeconomic balances

An outstanding feature of "modern" currency and financial crises is that they have been suffered by EEs that usually were considered to be highly "successful" by IFIs and financial agents; actually, EEs were awarded with growingly improving grades from international risk rating agencies and falling spreads, in parallel with rising stocks of external liabilities (Frenkel, 2004; Reisen, 2003; Williamson, 2003).

It is analytically interesting to explain why private funds do continue to flow, notwithstanding that disequilibria is being built.

Diversification toward volatility

International financial flows since the early 1990s became notably more diversified than in the 1970s. One comparatively stable flow is that of FDI,[21] which after the Tequila crisis rose sharply: from about 1 percent of GDP in the early 1990s to about 3 percent since the mid-1990s. However, in that last period only one-half of those inflows corresponded to

[21]Prasad *et al.* (2003, Table 1 and Figure 3) report data on volatility of total (greenfield plus M&A) inward FDI, bank loans and portofolio investment. They confirm the conclusion from other abundant research that FDI is less volatile.

greenfield FDI, while acquisitions did multiply by nine between both periods (see Ffrench-Davis, 2005, Table VI.1; UNCTAD, 2005). During expansive periods, the financial counterpart of acquisitions tends to stay in the host country, while during depressive situations tends to outflow instantaneously. Its behavior is straightforwardly pro-cyclical. The outcome with the new diversified set of financial flows is potentially unstable, since: (1) the trend has been a shift toward a set of short-term and liquid *reversible sources of funding*[22] (equity portfolio flows, liquid bonds, medium-and short-term bank financing; short-term time deposits; acquisitions of domestic firms by foreign investors); and (2) most share synchronized contagions of over-optimism and of over-pessimism. The macroeconomic implications of the reversibility of flows are not observed during the expansive–boom stage of the cycles, but its pervasiveness, for real macroeconomic stability, explodes abruptly with the negative change of mood of markets. Additionally, it is noteworthy that a significant proportion of short-term and liquid inflows as well as the mounting mergers and acquisitions are delinked with the direct generation of productive capacity.

The fact is that change in the volume and composition of international supply in combination with capital accounts opening by LACs, implied that several economies moved into *vulnerability zones* (we repeat the signals: some combination of large external liabilities, with a high short-term or liquid share; currency and maturity mismatches; a significant external deficit; an appreciated exchange-rate; high price/earnings ratios in the stock market, plus low domestic investment ratios). In parallel, as said, agents specialized in microeconomic aspects of finance, placed in the short-term or liquid segments of capital markets, acquired a dominant voice in the generation of macroeconomic expectations.

Pro-cyclical risk-rating and spreads

There is an extremely relevant literature on the causes of financial market failures: the asymmetries of information between creditors and debtors, and the lack of adequate internalization of the negative externalities that each agent generates (through growing vulnerability), that underlie the cycles of abundance and shortage of external financing (Krugman, 2000; Stiglitz, 2000). Beyond those issues, as stressed by Heymann (2000) and Ocampo (2003), finance deals with the future, and evidently concrete "information" about the future is unavailable. Consequently, the tendency

[22] Persaud (2003), argues that modern risk-management by investment funds and banks, based on value-at-risk measured daily, works pro-cyclically in the boom and bust. A complementary argument by Calvo and Mendoza (2000) examines how globalization may promote contagion by discouraging the gathering of information and by strengthening incentives for imitating market portfolio.

to equate opinions and expectations with "information" contribute to herd behavior and multiple equilibria.

Actually, we have observed a notorious contagion, first of over-optimism, and then of over-pessimism in many of the financial crises experienced by EEs in the past three decades. In all three significant surges of the past quarter century, loan spreads underwent, in a *process*, a continued decline, notwithstanding that the stock of liabilities was rising sharply: spreads fell for 5–6 years in the 1970s; over 4 years before the Tequila crisis, and nearly 3 years before the arrival of the Asian crises (see Ffrench-Davis, 2006, Figure I.2).

This behavior of spreads has implied, during the expansive side of the cycle, a sort of downward sloping medium-run supply curve; which is a highly destabilizing feature. During all three expansive processes there has been an evident contagion of over-optimism among creditors but, rather than appetite for risk, there prevails an underestimation or assuming away of risk on the part of creditors.

The literature emphasizes the role of moral hazard, resulting from implicit or explicit public insurance and the like. However, in the frequent booms we have observed, many creditors behave pro-cyclically, in an honest and transparent over-optimistic attitude. That signals the need for a prudential regulation and supervision that incorporates also effective counter-cyclical microeconomic mechanisms. But, beyond that, it is counter-cyclical macroeconomic policies that ought to hold the major responsibility.

With respect to debtors, the evidence for periods of over-optimism is that most of them do not borrow thinking of default and expecting to be rescued or to benefit from a moratoria. Contrariwise, expectations of high yields tend to prevail: borrowers are also victims of the syndrome of financial euphoria during the boom periods.

The dominant role of short-termist agents

Over and above these variables, there are two additional features of the creditor side that are crucially important. One feature is the particular *nature of the leading agents* acting on the supply side. There are natural asymmetries in the behavior and objectives of different economic agents. The agents predominant in the financial markets are specialized in short-term liquid investment, operate within short-term horizons, and naturally are highly sensitive to changes in variables that affect returns in the short-run. The second feature is the gradual spread of information, among prospective agents, on investment opportunities in EEs. This feature is present not only in the "initial" capital account opening, but also in the subsequent renewal of inflows following each associated crisis.

In fact, agents from different segments of the financial markets become gradually drawn into new international destinations as they take notice of the profitable opportunities offered by emerging economies previously unknown to them or abandoned during a crisis. This explains, from the supply-side, why the surges of flows to emerging economies – in the 1970s and 1990s – have been *processes* that went on for several years rather than one-shot changes in supply.

In this sense, it is relevant for policy design to stress the distinction between two different types of volatility of capital flows, short term ups-and-downs, and the medium term instability that leads several variables – such as the stock market, real estate prices, and the exchange rate – to move persistently in a given direction for several years. The expectation of persistent changes provides "wrong certainties" to the financial markets, encouraging capital inflows *seeking economic rents* rather than differences in real productivity.

For instance, increased supply in all three recent financial booms has generated a process of exchange-rate appreciation in most LACs; the expectations of continued, persistent, appreciation encouraged additional inflows from dealers operating with maturity horizons located within the expected appreciation of the domestic currency.[23] For allocative efficiency and for export-oriented development strategies, a macroprice – as significant as the exchange rate, particularly after trade liberalization–led by capital flows conducted by short-termist agents reveals a severe policy inconsistency.[24] The increase in aggregate demand, pushed up by financial and terms-of-trade inflows and appreciation, expands "artificially" the absorptive capacity and the demand for foreign savings, and leads to a rising share of the domestic demand for tradables. Thus, exogenous changes abroad in international capital markets, as said, are then converted into an endogenous process, leading to domestic vulnerability given the potential reversibility of flows.

In brief, the interaction between the two sets of factors – *the nature of agents and a process of adjustment* – explains the dynamics of capital flows over time: why suppliers keep pouring-in funds while real macroeconomic

[23]For short-termist agents the actual and expected profitability increased with the appreciation process. That same process, if perceived as persistent, would tend to discourage investment in the production of tradables intensive in domestic inputs. Therefore, it is most relevant, because of its policy implications, what happens with the behavior of exchange rates during the expansive or boom stage. It is mainly then when external imbalances and currency and maturity mismatches are, inadvertently, being generated.

[24]During the 2004–06 economic recovery, LACs have again been experiencing appreciation, on this occasion associated with improved terms of trade rather than with capital inflows.

fundamentals worsen. When creditors *discover* an emerging market, their initial exposure is low or non-existent. Then they generate a series of consecutive flows, which result in increasing stocks of financial assets in the EE; actually, too rapid and/or large for an efficient domestic absorption. Frequently, the absorption is artificially increased by exchange rate appreciation, and a rising real aggregate demand, resulting in an enlarged external deficit and a crowding-out of domestic savings.

"Rational" short-termist agents, "irrational" macroeconomics

The creditor's sensitivity to negative news, at some point, is likely to, suddenly, increase remarkably when the country has reached diverse *vulnerability zones*; then, the creditors take notice of: (1) the rising level of the stock of their assets held in a country (or region); (2) the degree of dependence of the debtor market on additional flows, which is associated with the magnitude of the current-account deficit; (3) the extent of appreciation; (4) the need of refinancing of maturing liabilities; and (5) the amount of liquid liabilities likely to flow out in face of a crisis. Therefore, it should not be surprising that, after penetrating deeply in those vulnerability zones, the sensitivity to adverse political or economic news and the probability of reversal of expectations grows steeply (Rodrik, 1998). The intensity of the change in the availability of financing tends to be enhanced with the liberalization of outflows of domestic savings.

The accumulation overseas of stocks of assets by financial suppliers until the boom stage of the cycle is well advanced, and, then, a subsequent sudden reversal of flows, can *both* be considered to be *rational* responses on the part of individual agents with short-term horizons. This is because it is of little concern to this sort of investor whether (long-term) fundamentals are being improved or worsened while they continue to bring inflows. Indeed, for the most influential financial operators (that particular segment of "the market"), the more relevant variables are not related to the long-term fundamentals but to short-term profitability. What is relevant to these financial investors is that the crucial indicators from their point of view – prices of real estate, bonds and stock, and exchange rates – can continue providing them with profits in the near term and, obviously, that liquid markets allow them, if needed, to reverse decisions timely; thus, they will continue to supply net inflows until expectations of an imminent near reversal build up. This explains why they may suddenly display a radical change of opinion about the economic situation of a country whose fundamentals, other than liquidity in foreign currency, remain rather unchanged during a shift from *over-optimism* to *over-pessimism*.

Naturally, the opposite process tends to take place when the debtor markets have adjusted downward "sufficiently." Then, the inverse process makes its appearance and can be sustained for some years, like in 1991–94 or 1995–97, or short-lived like in late 1999 and 2000.

Concluding remarks

Given the volatility of international financial markets, the opening of the capital account has frequently led EEs to import external financial instability, with capital inflows engendering a worsening in macroeconomic fundamentals. Indeed, those flows have induced deviations of macro variables and ratios from sustainable levels: during booms, the financial market itself has generated incentives for EEs to enter *vulnerability zones*.

Economic agents specialized in the allocation of financial funding, who may be highly efficient in their field but operate with short-horizons "by training and by reward," have come to play a leading role in determining macroeconomic conditions and policy design in EEs. It implies that a "financieristic" approach becomes predominant rather than a "productivistic" approach. In contrast, growth with equity requires improving the rewards for productivity enhancement rather than *financial rent-seeking* searching for capital gains. There is a need to rebalance priorities and voices.

Toward development-friendly macroeconomics

The approach that has been in fashion in the mainstream academic world and IFIs in recent years (or neo-liberal or Washington Consensus approaches), emphasizes macroeconomic balances of two pillars: low inflation and fiscal balances, with a clear disregard for the overall macroeconomic environment for producers. This environment includes, besides the two pillars, other most influential variables: aggregate demand and macroprices such as interest and exchange rates. Additionally, a frequent assertion in the more recent conventional literature is that an open capital account imposes macroeconomic discipline on EEs. Indeed, this approach assumes that full opening of the capital account would contribute to balance the external sector and automatically generate an aggregate demand consistent with productive capacity: It is well documented that that is not the usual experience in the frequent cases of external, positive and negative, financial shocks experienced by EEs (Ffrench-Davis and Ocampo, 2001).

In fact, several LACs fulfilled the main requirements of neo-liberal macroeconomic balances. However, economic activity was notably unstable, in the period covered in this chapter. Overall changes in GDP were led by ups-and-downs in aggregate demand, with an effective demand that has deviated sharply from the production frontier and with "wrong" or outlier macroprices and ratios. Frequently, these prices and aggregate demand have been out of equilibria, as reflected in economies working either below potential GDP or at full capacity but with a large external deficit. They tend to miss the intermediate area where, precisely, mid-term equilibrium values are usually found. These features have responded mostly to shifts in net capital flows, and domestic monetary adjustments have been associated with changes in international reserves rather than with changes in domestic credit by the Central Bank (Ffrench-Davis, 2005, Chapter VII and Figure I.2).

The behavior of aggregate demand, at levels consistent with potential GDP and well-aligned macroprices (such as interest and exchange rates) are a crucial part of a third pillar of real macroeconomic balances. Empirical work shows that strong increases in investment are associated with a macroeconomic environment that is able to place effective demand at a level consistent with potential output, with "right" exchange and interest rates, and that situation is expected by private investors to be sustainable (see Ffrench-Davis, 2005, Chapter III).

In boom periods, when the degrees of freedom to choose policies are broader, authorities should accumulate resources in stabilization funds, improve fiscal balances, increase international reserves, prepay external debt, avoid exchange rate appreciation, and regulate capital inflows. In recessive periods, it should imply, for instance, (1) continued implementation of a structural fiscal balance (recognizing that during recession tax proceeds are abnormally low and that, in those circumstances, public expenditure should not follow taxes in their descending runaway, and viceversa during the boom!!), and (2) a strong encouragement to effective demand, with effective switching policies whenever domestic activity is clearly below productive capacity. A severe obstacle to a counter-cyclical policy has been the policy in fashion of full, across-the-board, opening of the capital account during booms. There is need to reform domestic capital account and financial reforms, and to reform the actual international financial architecture (Bhattacharya and Griffith-Jones, 2004).

Financial globalization and governance

Certainly, the degrees of freedom for efficient domestic policies in an increasingly (but also incompletely and inequitably) globalized economy are more limited than before, but there is still space to choose among a wide variety of alternative paths to *make* globalization, and effectively capturing net benefit with it.

Prudential domestic policies, such as the selective capital controls established in Chile in the 1990s, can reduce the external vulnerability and allow for counter-cyclical exchange rate and monetary policies during the bust. Furthermore, even once a crisis has taken place, domestic policies are also crucial to minimize its negative effects and accelerate economic recovery. Korea and Malaysia, two countries that performed comparatively quite well after their severe crises, followed different policy approaches but both developed active and consistent counter-cyclical macroeconomic policies, in contrast with most EEs, particularly LACs.

The integration of capital markets has remarkable implications on governance, room for domestic policies, and on the constituencies to which national governments respond. In fact, many leaders in EEs are living a deep duality: on the one hand, political authorities are elected by their countries' voters, and promise to implement a platform designed before their election, but on the other hand they also seek, after being democratically elected, the support of those who "vote" for their financial investments (not necessarily productive investments or even at the expense of productive investment). Recent cycles in financial markets have revealed a significant contradiction between the two, in a negative-sum game, with large output gaps and discouraged capital formation.

Thus, economic authorities should undertake the responsibility of making real macro-fundamentals prevail (sustainable external deficit; moderate stock of external liabilities, with a low liquid share; reasonable matching of terms and currencies; crowding-in of domestic savings; limited real exchange rate appreciation; effective demand consistent with the production frontier), in order to achieve macroeconomic balances that are both sustainable and functional for long-term growth. That requires them to avoid entering *vulnerability zones* during economic booms-cum-capital surges; during recessive periods they must be able to make intensive use of counter-cyclical devices, resting on the strengths developed in the expansive years. If those strengths are insufficient, support from IFIs and private financial markets under reformed counter-cyclical conditionality would be welcome.

References

Agosin, M. (2006) "Capital flows and macroeconomic policy in emerging economies", in J. Stiglitz, R. Ffrench-Davis and D. Nayyar (eds), *Macroeconomic Policies*, Oxford University Press, London and New York.

Bhagwati, J. (2004) *In Defense of Globalization*, Oxford University Press, New York.

Bhattacharya, A. and S. Griffith-Jones (2004) "The search for a stable and equitable global financial system," in J.J. Teunissen (ed.), *Diversity in Development: Reconsidering the Washington Consensus*, FONDAD, The Hague.

Broner, F. and R. Rigobon (2006) "Why are capital flows so much volatile in emerging than in developed countries?", in R. Caballero, C. Calderón and L.F. Céspedes (eds), *External Vulnerability and Preventive Policies*, Central Bank of Chile, Santiago.

Calvo, G. (1998) "Varieties of capital-market crises," in G. Calvo and M. King (eds), *The Debt Burden and its Consequences for Monetary Policy*, Macmillan, Basingstoke.

Calvo, G. and E.G. Mendoza (2000) "Rational contagion and the globalization of securities markets," in *Journal of International Economics*, 51.

Dodd, R. (2003) "Derivatives, the shape of international capital flows and the virtues of prudential regulation," in R. Ffrench-Davis and S. Griffith-Jones (eds), *From Capital Surges to Drought*, Palgrave Macmillan/WIDER, Basingstoke.

Easterly, W. and L. Servén (eds) (2003) *The Limits of Stabilization*, Stanford University Press, Palo Alto, California.

ECLAC (Economic Commission for Latin America and the Caribbean) (2002a) *Globalization and Development*, United Nations, Santiago. An abridged version, edited by J.A. Ocampo and J. Martín, was published by Stanford University Press, 2003.

ECLAC (2002b) *Growth with Stability: Financing for Development in the New International Context*, ECLAC Books, no. 67, Santiago.

Ffrench-Davis, R. (ed.) (2006) *Seeking Growth under Financial Volatility*, Palgrave Macmillan/ECLAC, Basingstoke.

Ffrench-Davis, R. (2005) *Reforming Latin America's Economies: After Market Fundamentalism*, Palgrave Macmillan, Basingstoke.

Ffrench-Davis, R. (2002) *Economic Reforms in Chile: From Dictatorship to Democracy*, University of Michigan Press, Ann Arbor.

Ffrench-Davis, R. and J.A. Ocampo (2001) "The globalization of financial volatility," in R. Ffrench-Davis (ed.), *Financial Crises in 'Successful' Emerging Economies*, Brookings Institution, Washington, DC.

Frenkel, R. (2004) "From the boom in capital inflows to financial traps", prepared for the Capital Account Liberalization Task Force, IPD, Columbia University, online at: (http://www.gsb.columbia.edu/ipd/pub/Frenkel5_3_04.pdf)

Frenkel, R. and J. Ros (2004) "Macroeconomic policies and the labor market in Argentina and Mexico," Working Paper of ECLAC project on *Management of Volatility, Financial Globalization and Growth in Emerging Economies.*

Griffith-Jones, S. (1998) *Global Capital Flows, Should They Be Regulated?*, Macmillan, Basingstoke.

Heymann, D. (2000) "Major macroeconomic upsets, expectations and policy responses", *CEPAL Review*, no. 70, Santiago, April.

IMF (International Monetary Fund) (1998) *World Economic Outlook, 1998. Financial Crises: Characteristics and Indicators of Vulnerability*, chapter VII, Washington DC, May.

Krugman, P. (2000) "Crises: The price of globalization?", Federal Reserve Bank of Kansas City, *Symposium on Global Economic Integration: Opportunities and Challenges*, Jackson Hole, Wyoming.

Mahani, Z.-A., K. Shin and Y. Wang (2006) "Macroeconomic adjustment and the real economy in Korea and Malaysia since 1997", in Ffrench-Davis (2006).

Marfán, M. (2005) "Fiscal policy efficacy and private deficits: a macroeconomic approach", in J.A. Ocampo (ed.), *Rethinking Development Challenges*, Stanford University Press, Palo Alto, California.

Morley, S.A., R. Machado and S. Pettinato (1999) "Indexes of structural reform in Latin America", ECLAC, Santiago.

Obstfeld, M. (1998) "The global capital market: benefactor or menace?," *Journal of Economic Perspectives*, 12(Fall).

Ocampo, J.A. (2006) "Overcoming Latin America's growth frustrations: the macro and mesoeconomic links", in Ffrench-Davis (2006).

Ocampo, J.A. (2003) "Developing countries' anti-cyclical policies in a globalized world", in A. Dutt and J. Ros (eds), *Development Economics and Structuralist Macroeconomics: Essays in Honor of Lance Taylor*, Edward Elgar, Aldershot, UK.

Persaud, A. (2003) "Liquidity black holes," in R. Ffrench-Davis and S. Griffith-Jones (eds), *From Capital Surges to Drought*, Palgrave Macmillan/WIDER, Basingstoke.

Prasad, E.S., K. Rogoff, S.-J. Wei, and M. Ayan Kose (2003) "Effects of financial globalization on developing countries: some empirical evidence," *IMF Occasional Paper*, no. 220, September.

Reisen, H. (2003) "Ratings since the Asian crisis," in R. Ffrench-Davis and S. Griffith-Jones (eds), *From Capital Surges to Drought,* Palgrave Macmillan/WIDER, Basingstoke.

Rodrik, D. (2001) "Why is there so much economic insecurity in Latin America?," *CEPAL Review*, 73, Santiago, April.

Rodrik, D. and A. Velasco (2000) "Short-term capital flows," *Annual World Bank Conference on Development Economics 1999*, The World Bank, Washington, DC

Rodrik, D. (1998) "Who needs capital account convertibility?," in P. Kenen (ed.), *Should the IMF Pursue Capital Account Convertibility?, Princeton Essays in International Finance*, No. 207.

Stallings, B. and R. Studart (2006) *Finance for Development: Latin America's Banks and Capital Markets after Liberalization*, Brookings Institution, Washington, DC.

Stiglitz, J. (2000) "Capital market liberalization, economic growth and instability," *World Development*, 28 (6), June.

Tokman, V. (2004) *Una voz en el camino*, Fondo de Cultura Económica, Santiago.

Tytell, I. and S.-J. Wei (2004) "Does financial globalization induce better macroeconomic policies?," *Working Paper*, WP/04/84, International Monetary Fund, Washington, DC.

UNCTAD (2005) *Foreign Investment Report 2005*, United Nations, Geneva.

Williamson, J. (2003) "Overview: an agenda for restarting growth and reform," in P. Kuczynski and J. Williamson (eds), *After the Washington Consensus: Restarting Growth in Latin America*, Institute for International Economics, Washington, DC

World Bank (2003) *Inequality in Latin America and the Caribbean: Breaking with History?*, chapter 8, Washington, DC.

Zahler, R. (2006) "Macroeconomic stability and investment allocation by domestic pension funds in emerging economies: the case of Chile," in Ffrench-Davis (2006).

Part IV

Trade for Growth

9

Trade and Growth: Why Asia Grows Faster than Latin America

Manuel R. Agosin[1]

Introduction

It is already an accepted stylized fact of international development that Latin American countries (LACs) grow at more modest rates than the Asian exporters of manufactures. It is also true that the latter countries made a transition to export-oriented growth well before LACs; moreover, they have been considerably more successful in encouraging export growth and in diversifying their output and export mix.

This chapter explores the connection between export expansion and GDP growth, with special reference to the differences observed between both regions. It will not attempt another go at the controversy of whether openness is positively associated with economic growth, a topic that has been dealt with exhaustively in the literature (see Rodríguez and Rodrik, 2000). By now, the issue seems to have been settled: many countries (Korea and Taiwan being the paradigms) were able to grow rapidly while maintaining high import barriers and relaxing them once export-oriented development had been consolidated; at the other extreme, others, among which there are several LACs, opened up their economies with much more modest effects either on exports or economic growth.

We are interested in the issue of whether export growth is associated with overall economic growth. In a statistical sense, the relation must hold, since exports are a part of GDP. Here the focus will be on whether there is a particular kind of export growth that can result in sustained growth both in exports and GDP. We posit that countries with diversified export structures are able to record consistently higher export growth than countries where

[1]I am grateful for the able research assistance of Alfie Ulloa and Alejandro Támola. I acknowledge the useful comments made by Robert Devlin and Roberto Bouzas. Ricardo Ffrench-Davis read the manuscript thoroughly and made suggestions that lead to significant improvements.

exports are concentrated in a few products. Moreover, in economies with diversified export structures, export growth has more positive effects on the economy as a whole and, therefore, translates into higher rates of economic growth than in economies where exports are concentrated in a few products.

The first section presents some analytical considerations of why output and export diversification (OED) should be positive for growth. After looking at the export and growth experience for Latin America and Asia, we show that, indeed, there seems to be a negative association between export concentration and growth through the effect of concentration on export and output volatility. Then we show that OED, as proxied by an export diversification index, is a strong explanatory variable in a simple empirical growth model estimated with cross section data for 1980–2003, the period for which the data on export composition is available. The coefficients yielded by the empirical model are used to estimate the contribution of different factors to growth in a sample of Asian and Latin American countries. The final section recapitulates.

Some analytical considerations

Why would export diversification be beneficial for growth? There are potentially two different types of effects:

1. *The portfolio effect*: The greater the degree of diversification the less volatile will be export earnings. Less volatile export growth is likely to be associated with lower variance of GDP growth. This is, in itself, a positive aspect of diversification, since countries with imperfect (or no) access to world financial markets will not be able to smooth consumption in the face of large fluctuations in exports and output. In addition, the variance and the mean of the growth rate may be negatively correlated. This adverse effect of volatility on average growth could result from hysteresis. Periods of contraction lead to the destruction of installed capacity and to deskilling of the labor force, both of which cannot be easily undone during the next boom. Also, countries whose exports are highly dependent on one or a few products tend to have more volatile real exchange rates than countries with diversified export structures, and real exchange rate volatility discourages investment in tradable goods or services.
2. *Dynamic benefits of diversification*: One of the single most important characteristics of countries with low per capita income is the fact that they have a comparative advantage in a very limited range of goods. In other words, because of the paucity of skills or lack of complementary inputs (some non-traded), these countries are unable to apply knowledge about production that exists elsewhere in the world. As a country develops, it becomes increasingly able to produce an ever wider range of goods and

> can begin to compete in international markets in them. While not the only one, the ability to export certainly can be judged to be an appropriate indicator of international competitiveness. Countries that are able to diversify their exports are also those that have been able to expand their range of comparative advantage. And a broad range of comparative advantages is synonymous with development.

In a sense, OED is only a proximate cause of growth and is itself a result of several phenomena associated with development and which have been highlighted in the endogenous growth literature. These include the accumulation of skills, learning by doing, positive pecuniary externalities that stem from the production of key non-traded inputs (e.g., infrastructure services), positive technological externalities associated with skill creation, and technological innovation. Here we will take OED to represent one of the visible symptoms that those phenomena have been at work in the economy.

The accumulation of skills is not a totally exogenous phenomenon. Sometimes it may be the result of deliberate policies; in other cases it may be interdependent with the establishment of plants producing new export goods. For example, the establishment of Intel in Costa Rica to produce micro chips for foreign markets led to an increase in computer programming education (in part subsidized by Intel itself). That education benefits not only Intel but has positive spillovers on related sectors (software, for example) and even on other unrelated sectors that can raise their productivity through investments in information technology.

Learning by doing lowers the costs of production to the firm where it is taking place. But it could also have externalities for other firms in the sector or even for producers in other sectors. In a low-skill economy, the very fact that a new good is being produced may have positive technological externalities for other firms in the sector (through the building up of industry-specific skills) or even for firms in totally unrelated sectors (through the creation of non-specific skills that are essential for modern production in general).

Learning by doing can also have pecuniary externalities by lowering the costs of production of firms using inputs newly produced in the economy. Perhaps transport costs are too high for importing the input. As domestic production increases and costs are lowered, this may render competitive sectors that use the product as an input.

One might object that the hypothesis that export diversification leads to faster growth on the grounds that it flies in the face of international trade theory, be it Ricardian, Hecksher–Ohlin, or Krugman–Helpmann. Traditional trade theory stresses the comparative-advantage benefits of specialization, which presumably increases welfare and real incomes. The new trade theories, by emphasizing economies of scale, would also appear to favor specialization, at least on an intra-industry basis. It should be noted, though, that all highly specialized economies are poor. On the other hand, all developed economies are highly diversified, both in their production and export structures.

Is OED another aspect of long-term growth that occurs spontaneously as a result of market forces? Can it be induced as a deliberate objective of development policy? All developed economies exhibit OED, and in this sense OED may be the result of a long process of market-driven development. This was the case with the transformation of the Scandinavian countries from natural resource exporters to producers and exporters of a wide array of manufactures goods (see Meller and Blomstrom, 1991). For developing countries that have succeeded in growing rapidly in the post-war period, OED was the explicit policy of governments intent on rapid industrialization. The best-known examples are Korea and Taiwan.[2] There are other less spectacular examples. In spite of its reputation for market-oriented reforms, Chile's success in diversifying its exports away from copper were partly the result of deliberate policies of promoting production of new goods for international markets (Agosin, 1999).

Is import substitution industrialization (ISI) a necessary first stage of OED? Many countries began diversifying their production structures through ISI. This is true both of countries that were very successful and of those that did less well (like some LACs). The Asian exporters of manufactures began their industrialization drive with protectionism; later, when new manufacturing sectors had emerged under the shelter of ISI, they switched to export promotion (EP). The skills acquired during ISI were essential for the success of EP. In a sense, this was also true of the larger LACs (especially Brazil), although the path they followed was considerably rockier.

Several studies address the question of whether firms become more competitive by exporting or those who export do so because they have lower costs or higher productivity in the first place. The question appears to have been settled in favor of a self-selection view in which firms that succeed in export markets have superior technologies, are able to produce quality products profitably, or employ higher-skilled workers.[3] Many studies conclude that learning by exporting is not an important factor explaining

---

[2]The classic chronicles are Amsden's (1989) account of Korean industrialization and the description of Taiwan's experience by Wade (1990). See also Rodrik (1995). Interestingly, a recent paper by Jäntti *et al.* (2005) shows that, during the postwar period, Finland followed a model that had much in common with that of Korea.

[3]There is an extensive literature on this subject. For an analysis of Chilean industry, see Alvarez and López (2004). Evidence from Morocco, Mexico, and Colombia can be found in Clerides *et al.* (1998). Roberts and Tybout (1997) present further evidence for Colombia.

permanence in international markets. This would seem to favor the hypothesis that firms learn by producing for the domestic market and then attempt to break into international markets.

However, studies using a different methodology and a production-function approach yield exactly the opposite result. In a recent paper, Herzer and Nowak-Lehmann (2004) estimate a production function with a VAR technology using time series for Chilean macroeconomic variables over the period 1963–2001. In this model, the number of exported goods and the share of industrial goods in total exports are treated as proxies for the accumulation of knowledge, the presence of positive knowledge spillover effects, and learning by exporting. Using a different methodology but still within a time-series, macroeconomic framework, Amin Gutiérrez de Piñeres and Ferrantino (2000) also find that, in the long-run, export diversification and growth are positively correlated in Chile (Chapter 4) and Colombia (Chapter 5).

It would seem that an ISI stage is not the only way of achieving OED. Some countries have diversified their production mix directly by exporting, especially when the first firms are fully or partly foreign-owned. This has been the experience of Chile, a country that has based its export diversification on new goods.[4] China's export oriented growth of recent decades seems to have also followed this pattern, since the goods produced owe little to previous industrialization. The importance of foreign direct investment has been paramount, but multinational firms have been required to enter into joint ventures with national firms, first state-owned but increasingly private (Rodrik, 2006).

Subcontracting arrangements have also been used as a way around the need to incur in large sunk costs in marketing and product design. The recent Chinese export boom seems to have relied heavily on these two mechanisms. Much of what is exported is produced directly for foreign markets and consumed in relatively small amounts or not at all in the domestic market. In this way, China has gone from being a relatively closed economy with an import-to-GDP ratio of less than 10 percent in the early 1980s to about 35 percent at present.

So, in a sense, the issue of whether ISI or EP is to be preferred as a development strategy is a straw man. There are many paths to Rome. The correct strategy is contingent on the characteristics of the country applying it. Since economies of scale are very important in manufacturing (and even in

[4]However successful, the experience of Chile has had some unfortunate characteristics. Much of the skills developed during the ISI period (1940s through 1973) were destroyed during the import liberalization period (1973–79). Agosin and Ffrench-Davis (1995) argue that more pragmatic policies similar to those followed by Korea may have allowed firms to survive and orient their output to foreign markets.

most modern services), large countries are more likely to benefit from protection than very small economies. ISI was successful in creating entrepreneurial and worker skills in countries with a minimum market size, but was much less so, and exhausted its potential much faster, in smaller countries.

The real capabilities of a country to absorb or adapt a foreign technology in a relative short period of time, together with the speed at which the technology is changing in the leading countries, is another element to be taken into account. The Brazilian informatics policy of the 1980s, consisting in protecting the domestic market for information technology products and requiring foreign investors to form joint ventures with domestic interests, proved to be an expensive failure, because Brazil, at the time, did not have the capability to catch up quickly with Silicon Valley and the technology was itself evolving rapidly. India's more selective approach of fostering software development has been much more successful.

We will present evidence in favor of the hypothesis that export diversification is positively associated with growth. We posit that export diversification, coupled with high export growth rates, has been a trait of recent growth success. High rates of export growth do not guarantee high economic growth: they must be accompanied by export diversification. Undoubtedly, there are other factors behind successful growth experiences, but this chapter will not deal with them in detail.

Export diversification is not necessarily the same thing as exports of manufactures. Some countries whose exports are heavily concentrated on primary commodities may diversify into other natural-resource-based industries rather than into manufactures. Conversely, export concentration is not synonymous with primary commodity exports. However, historically export concentration has tended to be associated with concentration in one or a few primary commodities. Heavy export concentration in one or a few manufactures is an anomaly.[5] And diversification has been associated always with the production and export of goods with higher-skill and higher-knowledge intensity.

What does the literature tell us? All recent papers find that diversification is good for growth. However, none is able to distinguish between the portfolio effects and the dynamic benefits of OED on growth. In fact, these are difficult if not impossible to disentangle. Lederman and Maloney (2003) calculate a Hirschman–Herfindahl index (HHI) of export concentration at the four digit SITC level and, together with other variables of trade structure (the share of natural resources in total exports and the Grubel–Lloyd index of intra-industry trade), plug it into an empirical model of growth.

[5]The only examples that come to mind are clothing exports from Central American export processing zones and heavy concentration on micro chips in Costa Rica since the establishment of an Intel plant in the late 1990s.

The results are consistent with the hypothesis that is at the core of the current chapter. The objective of the LM paper is to show that natural resource abundance is beneficial to growth and not inimical to it, as some authors have claimed (for example, Sachs and Warner, 1995). The HHI is used mainly as a control variable. However, their results with regard to export concentration are not robust to model specification, a problem that they share with those obtained by Amin Gutiérrez de Piñeres and Ferrantino (2000, Chapter 7).

Trade and growth in Latin America and Asia, 1980–2003

As shown in Table 9.1 and Figure 9.1, the Asian exporters of manufactures grew much faster during 1980–2003 than LACs. Asian output and exports grew more than twice as fast as Latin America's. Even if one excludes the 1980s, the "lost decade" in Latin America, these differences also apply to the period since 1990, although the Asian average rates of growth of output and exports are somewhat lower than twice the ones recorded by LACs. However, even during the period 1990–2003, the country with the highest rate of growth of GDP in Latin America (Chile) was surpassed by five of the ten Asian countries included in the sample.

What is interesting about these figures is that the Asian countries consistently grew faster than LACs, both with regard to GDP *and* to exports. In fact, the ratio of GDP growth to export growth is practically identical in the two regions for the two periods shown.

Table 9.1 GDP and export growth in Latin America and Asia, 1980–2003 (percentage annual change in GDP and real exports of goods and services)

	1980–2003		*1990–2003*	
	GDP	*Exports*	*GDP*	*Exports*
Growth rates				
Latin America	2.4	5.3	3.0	6.2
Asia	5.9	11.1	5.5	11.7
GDP-export elasticity				
Latin America	0.49		0.45	
Asia	0.47		0.53	

Source: Author's calculations, based on World Bank, *World Development Indicators*.

Notes: Exports refer to real exports of goods and services (nominal values deflated by the GDP deflator of exports of goods and services). Countries included are, in Latin America, Argentina, Bolivia, Brazil, Chile, Colombia, Costa Rica, Dominican Republic, Ecuador, El Salvador, Guatemala, Honduras, Mexico, Nicaragua, Panama, Paraguay, Peru, Uruguay, Venezuela; in Asia, Bangladesh, China, Hong Kong, India, Indonesia, Korea, Malaysia, Philippines, Thailand, and Vietnam.

Figure 9.1 Latin America and Asia: Growth of GDP and of exports of goods and services, 1990–2003 (average annual rates of growth)

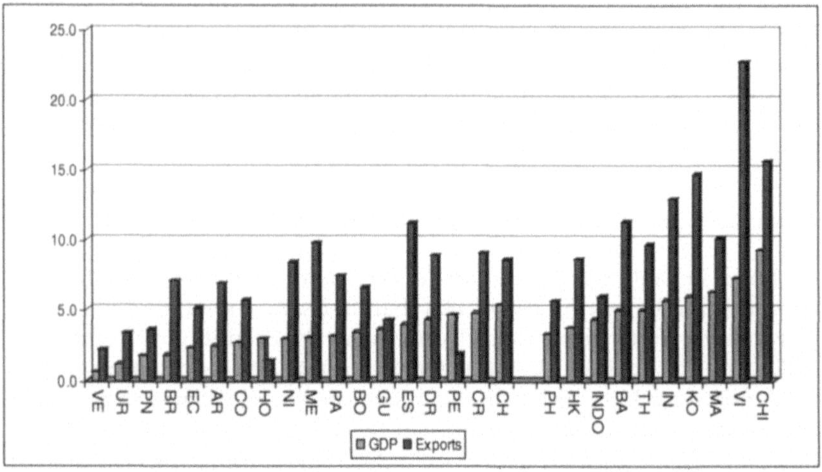

Source: World Bank, *World Development Indicators*.

Note: Country abbreviations are as follows: in Latin America, Argentina (AR), Bolivia (BO), Chile (CH), Colombia (CO), Costa Rica (CR), Dominican Republic (DR), Ecuador (EC), El Salvador (ES), Guatemala (GU), Honduras (HO), Mexico (ME), Nicaragua (NI), Panama (PN), Paraguay (PA), Peru (PE), Uruguay (UR), and Venezuela (VE); in Asia, Bangladesh (BA), China (CHI), Hong Kong (HK), India (IN), Indonesia (INDO), Korea (KO), Malaysia (MA), Philippines (PH), and Vietnam (VI).

Of course, this does not mean that faster export growth is the key to the success of the Asian countries relative to their Latin American counterparts, since there are many other differences between them, but faster export growth, and the factors that underlie it, do appear to have played a role.

There is evidence that OED has been a trait in the development pattern of Asia. The proxy for OED that we use here is the HHI,[6] taken from UNCTAD's *Handbook of Trade and Development Statistics* and measured at the three-digit SITC level. This indicator is detailed enough to capture, however imperfectly, both vertical and horizontal diversification. By vertical diversification is meant the shift from exporting, say, primary commodities to exporting manufactures. Horizontal diversification refers to the broadening of the export basket by diversifying into goods within the same

[6]The HHI for country j is defined in the following manner: $\sum\left(\frac{x_{ij}}{x_j}\right)^2$, where x_{ij} is the value of exports of good i by country j and x_j represents the value of total exports of country j.

Table 9.2 Selected Latin American countries and Asian exporters of manufactures: Hirschman-Herfindahl export concentration index, 1980–2002

	1980	*1986*	*1992*	*1998*	*2002*
Latin America[a]	0.36	0.40	0.30	0.26	0.25
Argentina	0.15	0.17	0.15	0.13	0.14
Brazil	0.15	0.12	0.09	0.09	0.09
Bolivia	0.39	0.52	0.32	0.20	0.25
Chile	0.41	0.37	0.31	0.28	0.27
Colombia	0.58	0.58	0.24	0.25	0.22
Costa Rica	0.32	0.39	0.30	0.19	0.21
Ecuador	0.55	0.45	0.47	0.35	0.39
El Salvador	0.38	0.71	0.24	0.24	0.13
Guatemala	0.31	0.47	0.22	0.24	0.19
Honduras	0.37	0.50	0.46	0.44	0.20
Mexico	0.48	0.27	0.15	0.11	0.13
Nicaragua	0.37	0.52	0.29	0.32	0.18
Panama	0.26	0.37	0.45	0.30	0.31
Paraguay	0.28	0.40	0.36	0.43	0.38
Peru	0.26	0.25	0.27	0.22	0.25
Uruguay	0.24	0.20	0.18	0.17	0.19
Venezuela	0.67	0.57	0.56	0.49	0.75
Asia[a]	0.22	0.17	0.13	0.14	0.14
China.	0.17	0.08	0.07	0.09	
Hong Kong	0.16	0.16	0.15	0.18	0.12
Taiwan	0.12	0.10	0.09	0.14	0.15
India	0.11	0.16	0.14	0.14	0.13
Indonesia	0.53	0.34	0.19	0.16	0.12
Korea, Republic of	0.09	0.10	0.11	0.15	0.15
Malaysia	0.30	0.23	0.16	0.20	0.22
Thailand	0.20	0.14	0.09	0.11	–

Source: UNCTAD, *Handbook of Trade and Development Statistics*, Geneva.

Note: [a]Unweighted average of countries shown.

broad category of goods; for example, from grapes with seeds to seedless grapes, or from coffee for the mass market to gourmet coffee.

As can be seen from Table 9.2, in 1980 Asian countries, on average, had much lower HHI than LACs; during the period up to 2002 the index declined consistently in all Asian countries, with the exception (surprisingly) of Taiwan. However, in 2002 even this latter economy exhibited a lower HHI than most LACs. Indonesia, a country whose exports were heavily concentrated on oil in 1980, had a dramatic fall in its HHI over the 1980–2002 period, from 0.53 to 0.12. China, also, while starting with a relatively low HHI in 1986, experienced an important decrease to less than 0.10, which is a level observed in most developed countries. Most of the

Asian exporters of manufactures are rapidly approaching HHI's that are very similar to those of developed countries.

Several LACs have been going through a diversification of their exports. Particularly impressive has been the decline in the HHI of Mexico, Colombia, and, to a lesser extent, Chile. However, their exports remain more concentrated than those of the Asian exporters of manufactures.

Practically the same picture emerges if one looks at the number of goods exported, also at the three-digit level. The maximum number of positions in the SITC classification of international trade at three digits is 239. Practically all Asian countries are fast approaching that number. While an increase in the number of goods exported can also be seen in Latin America, that increase has been more modest, so that the average number of goods exported remains at about one-half the maximum.

Figure 9.2 The portfolio effect of export diversification on growth in 1980–2003: a simple flow chart

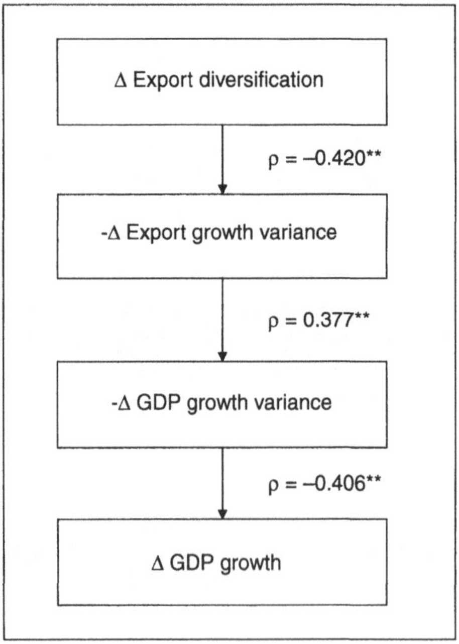

Source: World Bank, *World Development Indicators*; and UNCTAD, *Handbook of Trade and Development Statistics*. Export growth refers to goods and services in 2000 US dollars. GDP growth data are in 2000 US dollars.

Notes: The values of ρ represent the correlation coefficients between the variables in the two adjacent boxes measured without the Δs. All of them are significant at the 1% level. The data used are for 106 countries over the 1980–2003 period.

Evidence in favor of the portfolio effect

The portfolio effect of OED on growth claims that export diversification should be associated with faster growth. The causal relationships are summarized with the aid of a simple flow chart in Figure 9.2. Export diversification is related positively to growth through its effects on reducing the variance of export and GDP growth. As already stated, less GDP growth volatility should have a positive effect on GDP growth.

These hypotheses are not falsified by the data available for the period 1980–2003. The flow chart above would lead one to expect a negative correlation between export diversification and the variance of export growth, a positive correlation between the variance of export growth and the variance of GDP growth, and a negative correlation between the variance of GDP growth and the rate of GDP growth.

This is precisely what the data show (see correlation coefficients in Figure 9.2). All correlation coefficients are of the expected sign and are significantly different from zero at the 1 percent level. Export diversification is measured as *DIV* = 1 – *HHI*. Increases in *DIV* are highly correlated with declines in the variance of export growth. In turn, a lower variance of export growth is highly correlated with a lower variance of GDP growth. Finally, a lower variance in GDP growth is strongly associated with higher GDP growth.

Of course, many things other than export growth and export diversification affect the growth rate of GDP. But the data do not allow one to reject the hypotheses that export diversification, through its impact on reduced instability of exports and output, leads to higher growth.

Growth empirics: Does export diversification add anything?

In this section, we explore whether export diversification has any explanatory power in a standard empirical model of growth. Two different variables were used. One was *DIV* by itself, a second *DIV* interacted with export growth (*RX*DIV*). As will be noted below, while DIV has the correct sign and is highly significant, it is the interactive variable that has the most explanatory power. The intuition behind the inclusion of this interactive variable is that diversification is more powerful when a country's exports are growing rapidly than just by itself. Note the difference between Colombia and Malaysia: both wind up in 2002 with a *DIV* of 0.78 (*HHI* of 0.22), but Malaysia's exports grew at a rate of 10.7 percent in the period 1980–2003, while Colombia's grew only at an average rate of 5.7 percent. GDP growth in Malaysia averaged 6.4 percent, while it only reached 3.1 percent in Colombia.

The estimation strategy is to add *DIV* and *RX*DIV* to an otherwise standard empirical growth model. The variables considered were initial GDP

Figure 9.3 GDP growth, openness, and export diversification, 1980–2003

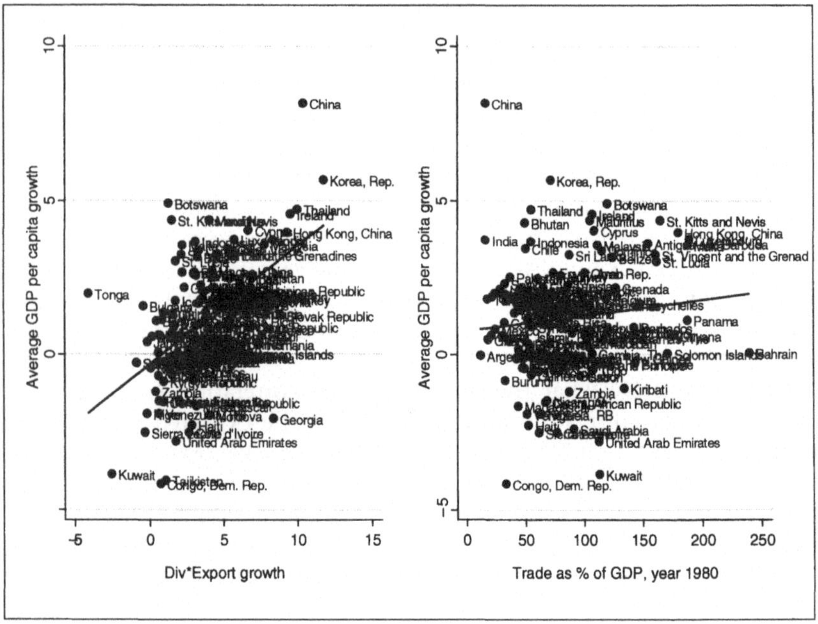

Source: Author's calculations, based on World Bank, *World Development Indicators*; and UNCTAD, *Handbook of Trade and Development Statistics*.

per capita, initial openness (trade as a percentage of GDP), average fixed capital formation during the period, and the rule of law index (developed by Kaufmann *et al.* 2005).[7]

For starters, the interaction between export growth and diversification appears to be a more appropriate proxy for growth-enhancing participation in the international economy than the degree of openness measured by exports plus imports as a share of GDP. As can be seen in Figure 9.3, which plots the rate of growth of GDP per capita in 1980–2003 against openness and against *RX*DIV*, this latter variable appears to be more correlated with growth than the degree of openness.

The results of the exercise are shown in Table 9.3. When one controls only for initial GDP per capita and openness, *DIV* and *RX*DIV* are of the correct sign and highly significant when they are entered individually into the regression, as in equations (1) and (2). But they both affect the

[7]A host of different controls were also used, including the average years of schooling in the population aged 15 through 64, but they were not found to add anything to the equation.

Table 9.3 An empirical model of growth of GDP per capita (dependent variable: average annual rate of growth of GDP per capita, 1980–2003)

Explanatory variables	*(1)*	*(2)*	*(3)*	*(4)*	*(5)*	*(6)*
log YPC80	–0.210*	.007	–0.006	0.247***	–0.596***	–0.593***
	(–1.72)	(0.08)	(–0.06)	(–2.64)	(–5.16)	(–4.96)
TRADE80	0.012***	0.013***	0.013***	–0.008*	0.005*	0.004
	(2.95)	(4.16)	(4.07)	(–2.07)	(1.66)	(1.61)
I	0.213***	0.149***	0.149***			
	(7.95)	(6.05)	(5.97)			
RL	0.633***	1.104***	1.108***			
	(3.25)	(5.87)	(5.79)			
DIV	4.846***		0.221	2.757***		–0.090
	(5.68)		(0.24	(3.47)		(–0.12)
RX*DIV		0.526***	0.515***		0.315***	0.319***
		(9.58)	(7.28)		(6.39)	(5.23)
Adj. R2	0.215	0.474	0.455	0.530	0.707	0.704
No. of obs.	119	115	115	109	106	106

Sources: All data are from World Bank, *World Development Indicators*, except for HHI, which is from UNCTAD, *Handbook of Trade and Development Statistics*. Underlying GDP and export data are in constant 2000 US dollars. Exports refer to goods and services. The rule of law index is from Kaufman *et al.* (2005) and is measured in 1996.

Notes: Method of estimation: OLS
Constant not shown; t ratios in parenthesis.
* Significantly different from zero at the 10% level.
** Significantly different from zero at the 5% level.
*** Significantly different from zero at the 1% level.

Definition of variables:
YPC80 = GDP per capita in 1980
TRADE80 = exports plus imports divided by GDP in 1980
I = gross fixed capital formation (average for the period), as a share of GDP
RL = rule of law index (1996)
DIV = export diversification index (1 – *HHI*)
RX*DIV = rate of growth of exports multiplied by *DIV*

significance of initial GDP. Openness, so far, appears to be significantly correlated with growth of income per capita. The inclusion of both *DIV* and *RX*DIV*, in equation (3) renders *DIV* not significantly different from zero, while the coefficient associated with *RX*DIV* remains almost unchanged and is still highly significant. In addition, *RX*DIV* has a much greater explanatory power (the R squared jumps significantly when this latter variable replaces *DIV*). Thus *RX*DIV* would appear to be our preferred variable. It is also quite robust to changes in specification.

Next, we introduce *DIV* and *RX*DIV* into a more completely specified model, one that includes gross fixed investment and the rule of law index.

This is done in equations (4) and (5). It can be seen that this parsimonious model is quite powerful. Initial GDP per capita becomes highly significant, the significance of the openness variables diminishes considerably (which suggests that openness is a stand-in for other effects), and investment and the rule of law are both of the correct sign and also highly significant. These results confirm the finding in the literature that growth is positively related to investment, a hypothesis that goes back to the Harrod–Domar model and is corroborated in some of the more recent endogenous growth literature. The results also lend credence to the more recent emphasis on institutions as important determinants of growth. Other things being equal, countries where the government is perceived as working for the good of society as a whole experience higher economic growth than those where this is not the case.

When the two variables associated with OED are introduced into this model, the interaction of export growth and export diversification (*RX*DIV*) turns out to be highly significant and of the correct sign, whether the diversification index by itself is entered into the equation as an additional variable or is left out. Moreover, the value of the coefficient of RX*DIV is very robust to changes in the specification of the model.

The incidence of crises

The 1980s were marked by external and domestic financial crises in Latin America. These crises were protracted and affected most countries in the region. The external debt crises was in many cases accompanied by bank failures, falling GDP, and surging unemployment. It was, indeed, a "lost decade." On the other hand, during the late 1990s several rapidly growing exporters of manufactures in Asia experienced similar crises, albeit shorter-lived than those of LACs in the 1990s. From 1998 to 2002, partly as a consequence of contagion from the Asian and Russian financial crises, several LACs again suffered either a contraction of output or a sharp deceleration in their rates of growth. Mexico, the Central American countries, and those in the Caribbean were severely affected by the slowdown in the United States in 2000–02. These factors certainly have had an impact on long-term growth, but are not reflected in the model presented above.

In this section, we incorporate into the model two crisis variables, which turn out to be very significant; they both improve the explanatory power of the model. One is derived from the database of Caprio and Klingebiel (2003) for banking crises. This variable (*CK*) is the proportion of the 24 years in the sample (1980–2003) during which countries were affected by banking crises. The alternative crisis variable (*CRISIS*) is the proportion of years during which each country had growth rates that were lower than the sample average minus 1.5 times the standard deviation of growth in 1980–2003.

Both variables yield similar results (Table 9.4). The diversification variable used in these regressions (*RX*DIV*) again proves to be very robust to the inclusion of the crises variables. All other control variables are also robust and extremely significant, with the exception of the ratio of trade to GDP, which even switches signs when the definition of crisis is changed.

Table 9.4 Introducing crises (dependent variable: average rate of growth of per capita GDP, 1980–2003)

Explanatory variables	*(1)*	*(2)*
log YPC80	–0.711***	0.522***
	(–5.91)	(–4.55)
TRADE80	–0.006*	0.005*
	(–1.75)	(1.77)
I	0.206***	0.139***
	(8.20)	(5.74)
RL	1.247***	0.875***
	(5.80)	(4.41)
RX*DIV	0.104***	0.312***
	(3.82)	(6.47)
CK	–0.012**	
	(–2.05)	
CRISIS		–6.162**
		(–2.85)
Adj. R2	0.809	0.727
No. of observations	75	106

Sources: All data are from World Bank, *World Development Indicators*, except for HHI, which is from UNCTAD, *Handbook of Trade and Development Statistics*. Underlying GDP and export data are in constant 2000 US dollars. Exports refer to goods and services. The rule of law index is from Kaufman *et al.* (2005) and is measured in 1996. The banking crisis data are from Caprio and Klingebiel (2003).

Notes: Method of estimation: OLS

Constant not shown; t ratios in parenthesis.

* Significantly different from zero at the 10% level.

** Significantly different from zero at the 5% level.

*** Significantly different from zero at the 1% level.

Definition of variables:

YPC80	= GDP per capita in 1980
TRADE80	= exports plus imports divided by GDP in 1980
I	= gross fixed capital formation (average for the period), as a share of GDP
RL	= rule of law index (1996)
RX*DIV	= rate of growth of exports multiplied by DIV
CK	= proportion of years in which a country experienced a banking crisis
CRISIS	= proportion of years in which a country's growth rate was below the sample average growth rate minus 1.5 times the sample's standard deviation

Even though the equation incorporating the variable derived from Caprio and Klingebiel has somewhat greater explanatory power, we prefer the one using the alternative measure. Falling GDP or growth slowdowns happen for a variety of reasons, and not all of them are due to banking crises. In addition, the second crisis variable allows us to use the entire database, while use of the variable derived from Caprio and Klingebiel shrinks the sample from 106 to 75.

Table 9.5 Contributions to growth of GDP per capita, 1980–2003 (percentage annual growth rates and participation in growth rates)

			Contribution of			
Country	*Observed growth*	*Predicted growth*	*Diversification*	*Investment*	*Rule of law*	*Crises*
Latin America						
Argentina	0.1	–0.7	1.4	2.5	0.2	-1.0
Bolivia	–0.3	–0.2	0.9	2.2	–0.6	0.0
Brazil	0.6	1.1	2.4	2.9	–0.2	–0.5
Chile	3.5	2.4	1.7	3.3	1.1	–0.3
Colombia	1.0	0.4	1.1	2.6	–0.4	0.0
Costa Rica	1.2	1.9	1.7	3.1	0.6	–0.3
Ecuador	0.1	0.5	0.9	2.9	–0.3	–0.3
El Salvador	0.0	–0.9	0.8	2.1	–0.4	–0.5
Guatemala	–0.1	-1.0	0.4	2.1	–0.6	0.0
Honduras	–0.2	0.5	0.2	3.5	–0.7	0.0
Mexico	0.8	1.4	2.5	3.1	–0.1	–0.5
Nicaragua	-1.3	0.7	0.6	3.5	–0.6	–0.3
Panama	1.2	0.6	0.3	3.1	0.2	–0.5
Paraguay	0.1	0.7	1.0	3.3	–0.4	–0.3
Peru	0.0	–0.1	0.9	3.1	–0.3	–0.8
Uruguay	0.4	–0.8	1.0	2.0	0.5	–0.8
Venezuela	-1.9	-2.1	0.2	2.6	–0.6	–0.8
Asia						
Bangladesh	2.0	2.0	2.1	2.6	–0.6	0.0
China	8.2	6.2	3.2	5.2	–0.4	0.0
Hong Kong	3.9	4.8	2.9	3.9	1.5	–0.3
India	3.7	3.7	2.6	3.1	0.0	0.0
Indonesia	3.6	2.0	1.0	3.6	–0.3	–0.3
Korea	5.6	5.1	3.7	4.4	0.7	–0.5
Malaysia	3.6	4.5	2.4	4.3	0.7	–0.3
Philippines	0.4	1.3	1.5	3.1	–0.1	–0.5
Thailand	4.7	5.2	3.1	4.4	0.4	–0.3

Source: Author's calculations, based on equation (2) in Table 9.4. Data are as described in Table 9.4.

How important are different factors in explaining growth?

The contributions to growth of the various factors identified in the preceding sections can be estimated multiplying the coefficients of equation (2) in Table 9.4 by the observed values of the explanatory variables and expressing the results as a share of the observed rate of growth of per capita GDP. Interest centers on the export diversification variable, investment, the rule of law, and crises.

As can be seen in Table 9.5, the higher growth rates of Asian countries appear to be explained by a larger contribution of export diversification and investment. These two variables together pretty much explain the differences in growth performance. The rule of law variables makes a less negative contribution in Asia than in Latin America; crises have been significantly less prevalent in Asia, subtracting less from the contribution to growth of the positive factors than in Latin America.

It should be noted that all the contributions identified in Table 9.5 exceed the observed growth rates. This is because some factors have been omitted (conspicuously, the role of conditional convergence, as measured by initial per capita GDP) and because the equation yields a large and negative constant (–3.2), indicating the probable presence of unexplained factors.

Conclusions

This chapter has shown that export growth can be important to overall economic growth, and that the key to success is not export growth per se but export growth together with diversification. The channels through which diversified export growth stimulates output growth appear to be two. One of them we have called the portfolio effect. Diversification of exports leads to less export volatility, which in turn results in lowered output volatility. Countries with highly unstable economies grow more slowly than countries that exhibit more dampened cyclical fluctuations. The data do not contradict this chain of causation.

The second effect is associated with the fact that export diversification is likely to be a proxy for the widening of comparative advantages that come with a more diversified economy. OED is associated with knowledge acquisition and spillovers, enhanced abilities to carry out research, on-the-job training that has positive externalities, etc. Once a critical level is reached, OED may acquire a self-sustaining character, with further OED occurring spontaneously.

The empirical results are congruent with this model. In a cross-country econometric model of growth, the proxy for OED used (the interaction between export growth and export diversification) is highly significant and makes an important contribution to explaining variations in growth rates across countries.

The empirical model shows that variables other than export diversification also play a role in explaining differences in economic growth between countries. Investment certainly takes pride of place. It has already been noted that the dynamic Asian economies have rates of investment that are quite higher than those of the Latin American countries. The strength of investment could well be associated with export growth and export diversification.[8] If export growth is sustained over long periods of time, as has been the case in Asia, fast export growth could well be a powerful stimulus to investment. Export diversification is also likely to be beneficial to investment, since the more diversified exports are the stronger will be the linkages between some exporting activities and the rest of the economy.

References

Agosin, M.R. (1999) "Trade and growth in Chile," *CEPAL Review*, 68, pp. 79–100.

Agosin, M.R. and R. Ffrench-Davis (1995) "Trade liberalization and growth: recent experiences in Latin America," *Journal of Interamerican Studies and World Affairs*, 37, pp. 9–58.

Álvarez, R. and R.A. López (2004) "Orientación exportadora y productividad en la industria manufacturera chilena," *Cuadernos de Economía*, 41, Santiago, pp. 315–43.

Amin Gutiérrez de Piñeres, S. and M.J Ferrantino (2000) *Export Dynamics and Economic Growth in Latin America*, Ashgate, Aldershot, England.

Amsden, A. (1989) *Asia's Next Giant: South Korea and Late Industrialization*, Oxford University Press, New York.

Caprio, G. and D. Klingebiel (2003) "Episodes of systemic and borderline financial crises," Database, World Bank, online at: http://econ.worldbank.org/WBSITE/EXTERNAL/EXTDEC/EXTRESEARCH/0,,contentMDK:20349050~pagePK:64165401~piPK:64165026~theSitePK:469382,00.html

Clerides, S.K., S. Lach, and J.R. Tybout (1998) "Is learning by exporting important? Micro-dynamic evidence from Colombia, Mexico, and Morocco," *Quarterly Journal of Economics*, 113, pp. 903–47.

Herzer, D. and F. Nowak-Lehmann (2004) "Export diversification, externalities and growth", Discussion Paper No. 99, Ibero-America Institute for Economic Research, Georg-August-Universität Göttingen, Göttingen, Germany, August, online at: http://www.iai.wiwi.uni-goettingen.de/content/pdf/DB99.pdf

Jäntti, M., J. Saari, and J. Vartiainen (2005) "Country case study: Finland. Combining growth with equity," paper presented at the WIDER Jubilee Conference, June 16–17, 2005, Helsinki, online at: http://www.wider.unu.edu/conference/conference-2005-3/conference-2005-3.htm

Kaufmann, D., A. Kraay, and M. Mastruzzi (2005) "Governance matters IV: governance indicators for 1996–2002," *World Bank Policy Working Paper*, 3630, Washington, DC, June.

[8]However, investment and export diversification are not so highly correlated that their joint inclusion in the econometric model renders one of them not significant. In fact, the coefficient of the diversification variable is quite robust to the introduction of investment

Lederman, D. and W.F. Maloney (2003) "Trade structure and growth," *World Bank Policy Research Working Paper*, no. 3025. Washington, DC, April.

Meller, P. and M. Blomstrom (1991) *Diverging Paths. A Century of Latin American and Scandinavian Economic Development*, The Johns Hopkins University Press for the Inter-American Development Bank, Washington, DC.

Roberts, M.J. and J.R. Tybout (1997) "The decision to export in Colombia: an empirical model of entry with sunk costs," *American Economic Review* 87, pp. 545–64.

Rodríguez, F. and D. Rodrik (2000) "Trade policy and economic growth: a skeptics guide to the cross-national evidence," *NBER Macroeconomic Annual 2000*, 15, 261–325.

Rodrik, D. (2006) "What's so special about China's exports?," Harvard University, unpublished.

Rodrik, D. (1995) "Getting interventions right: how South Korea and Taiwan grew rich," *Economic Policy*, 20, pp. 55–107.

Sachs, J. and A. Warner (1995) "Economic reform in the process of global integration," *Brookings Papers on Economic Activity*, 1, pp. 1–118.

Wade, R. (1990) *Governing the Market: Economic Theory and the Role of Government in East Asian Industrialization*, Princeton University Press, Princeton, NJ.

10

Trade and Growth: Past Experience and Perspectives for Latin America

Marcelo de Paiva Abreu[1]

Introduction

The collapse of the gold exchange standard in the late 1920s led Latin American countries (LACs) to seek new growth strategies as natural answers to specific developments rather than as conscious strategies resulting from public debate. In the largest economies, this followed a well-known pattern. First, there was a deepening of import substitution industrialization in the wake of the balance of payments shock. In some of them, such as Brazil and Mexico, this was only a new step in a process with roots before the turn of the twentieth century.

After a golden age lasting until the 1960s, import substitution came to be combined in the late 1960s and 1970s with limited liberalizing reforms and the extension of pick-the-winner policies to encompass export promotion. This new model was based on selective export subsidies and the attraction of foreign direct investment based on export performance criteria. Especially in the larger economies, FDI was mostly attracted by a combination of high tariffs (or effective non-tariff barriers), subsidies in various forms, and limitations to the right of establishment of competitors. Liberalization of access of imports to domestic markets proceeded at a much slower pace. Growth performance in some LACs was still rather good in the 1970s, but less so than in the period before the oil shock of 1973–74.

In the 1980s, as financial crisis and recession hit Latin America, new growth strategies began to take shape in most economies based on a comprehensive set of domestic economic reforms, which included improved access of imports to domestic markets and privatization of public assets. The comprehensiveness of such reforms of course varied very considerably depending on the economy. They went much further in economies such as

[1]I thank Roberto Bouzas, Robert Devlin and Ricardo Ffrench-Davis for their comments, even if they were not always incorporated into the final text.

Chile and Costa Rica, were less extensive in economies as Argentina and Mexico, and even less so in Brazil. In some of the smaller Latin American economies fully-fledged export platforms were created, generally in the form of *maquiladoras* targeting the United States market for clothing products. The results in terms of GDP growth performance tended to be disappointing for the region as a whole.

The generally mediocre growth performance of Latin America in the recent period contrasts very sharply with the growth performance of many East Asian economies, and especially so with that of China since 1980. As this growth performance has been accompanied by a very fast expansion of trade, there has been an increasing interest in the links between trade and growth, and especially between exports and growth. There has also been a resurgence of interest in policies aiming at improving supply-related responses, seeking inspiration in policies adopted by China.

Improved export growth performance also depends on improved market access, and this has been stimulating a large number of initiatives that involve trade liberalization. The interest of specific Latin American economies in different formats and sequencing of trade liberalization measures is bound to vary very considerably depending on their characteristics. It is important to keep this in mind when assessing developments of bilateral, subregional, regional and multilateral trade negotiations.

The first section considers how import trade liberalization efforts affected domestic markets in different Latin American economies, how the process can be deepened and which are the obstacles faced. The next section analyzes the links between exports and growth and how Latin America has been performing recently. This is followed by a discussion on the diversity of the export composition of different Latin American economies. The possible role of supply-response policies is considered in the next section. There is an attempt to establish a taxonomy of Latin American interests in market access negotiations, based on different export structures and trade geographic orientation. Developments in the main subregional, regional and multilateral negotiations are considered. Conclusion are then drawn.

Imports and growth

To the extent that, besides the level of domestic economic activity, tariffs and non-tariff barriers are the main variables to explain imports they are the crucial variables to consider when links between imports and growth are analyzed. There is much work trying to relate low tariffs with high growth, a view widely held by policy-makers, especially in multilateral organizations. But the subject has been surrounded by deep controversy, both in the long-term and for more recent periods. Work by O'Rourke (2000) and Clemens and Williamson (2001), for instance, suggested a positive correlation between import tariffs and economic growth across countries from

1875 to 1914. This has been criticized by Irwin (2002) on several grounds, including the weight of land-abundant outliers that used tariffs as a source of revenue. For the more recent period, there is also deep controversy. Several studies, such as Sachs and Warner (1995), have suggested that openness is correlated with higher economic growth in the post-war period. Frankel and Romer (1999) overcame the simultaneity problem and found that more trade is related to higher income. But Rodríguez and Rodrik (2001) have found little evidence that lower tariff and non-tariff barriers to trade are significantly associated with growth.

Pre-great depression experience in Latin America indeed suggests a positive link between tariffs and growth, but this is at least partly related to the market power of some of the bigger economies in specific commodity markets, such as coffee and copper. More recent experience indicates that trade liberalization might be a necessary rather than a sufficient condition for higher growth. While it is true many Latin American economies that engaged in deep trade liberalization did not reap the expected growth performance, it is also true that no economy that has been laggard in its trade liberalization since the 1980s is among the economies with a good growth record.

Average tariffs for 1985–2002 and GDP per capita PPP growth since 1990 are presented in Table 10.1 for selected LACs. Beware that MFN tariffs are a good indication of protection in some economies but in other economies, as for instance in Chile, Costa Rica, and Mexico, they are not as much of the trade is conducted with partners in FTAs. Argentina, and especially Brazil and Colombia, are examples of a relatively high tariff – in spite of a

Table 10.1 Latin American selected economies: GDP-PPP 1990–2003 per capita growth rate and unweighted average tariff rates, 1985–2002, (%)

	GDP-PPP per capita growth rate 1990–2003	*Average unweighted tariff rates*			
		1985	*1990*	*1995*	*2002*
Argentina	1.9	22.8	18.2	13.9	13.2
Brazil	1.0	51.3	30.5	12.8	12.3
Chile	4.0	26.0	15.0	11.0	7.0
Colombia	0.5	46.4	34.1	13.3	11.7
Costa Rica	2.7	22.3*	16.8**	11.7	6.0
Dominican Republic	3.6	n.a.	n.a.	17.8***	10.1+
Mexico	1.1	22.6	13.1	13.0	16.4
Peru	1.7	63	26	16++	13.5+++
Venezuela	−1.7	32*	15	12***	12.2

Sources: World Development Indicators, Abreu (2004b), World Trade Organization (1994), (1995), (1996a), (1996b) and (2001), FTAA data base.
* 1986. ** 1989 *** 1994 +2001 ++1993 +++2000.

rapid pace of liberalization until the mid-1990s – and a mediocre growth performance. In a polar position are the low tariff-high growth basket cases: Chile, Costa Rica and the Dominican Republic. Mexico is perhaps the best example of a low protection and low growth experience.

In some of the larger economies, with significant sectors producing capital goods, the costs of maintaining high protection in terms of foregone growth have been substantial. Smaller economies have been able to reap the benefits of unhindered access to the international market buying capital goods that are cheaper and state of the art. In Brazil's high protection closed access to the international markets and high inflation stimulated demand for real assets. Between 1970 and 1990, prices of capital goods doubled in relation to the GDP deflator. Since 1990, trade liberalization has reversed this trend and may have answered for some 0.8 percent of GDP yearly growth. The mediocre growth performance might have been even worse without trade liberalization, even if import tariffs on most capital goods are still around 20 percent.[2]

Export performance and growth

The historical evidence on the geographical distribution of world exports makes clear the shrinking importance of Latin America since 1928 for most economies (see Table 10.2). Market shares of Argentina and Uruguay fell to one-eight and one-tenth of their level in 1928. Some economies, especially those exporting coffee, however, were able to increase their market share between 1928 and 1950. This was due to significant increases in world coffee prices in the immediate post World War II period.

Many of the comments made on the links between protection and growth can be repeated in relation to export performance and growth, although in this case the long-term bad performance affects practically all Latin American economies, with the exception of Mexico, even if its share in 1928 was artificially low given the economic difficulties since the early 1910s and its share in 2003 reflected the effects of NAFTA. While in mature economies it is to be expected that exports increase at lower rates than world exports (especially if they are not involved in significant integration initiatives),[3] in developing economies this is an indication of lack of competitiveness as the structure of world exports shift from commodities to manufactures. The relevant measuring rods for Latin America are China and the rest of Asia (excluding Japan and the Middle East).[4] Since 1928

[2]See Abreu (2004b, pp. 17–19).

[3]It should be noted that data in Table 10.2 refer to national economies. In particular, the European Union is not treated as a single economy. This is why the European share of world exports remains relatively stable over time.

[4]West Asia is mainly the Middle East.

Table 10.2 Latin America: Shares of world exports, 1928–2003, (%)

	1928	*1950*	*1980*	*2003*
Latin America	9.32	12.35	5.47	5.03
MERCOSUR	4.93	4.61	1.45	1.42
Argentina	3.12	1.92	0.39	0.39
Brazil	1.45	2.22	0.99	0.98
Paraguay	0.05	0.05	0.02	0.02
Uruguay	0.31	0.42	0.05	0.03
Chile	0.72	0.47	0.23	0.28
Mexico	0.74	0.86	0.89	2.22
Andean Community	1.25	3.11	1.50	0.73
Bolivia	0.13	0.12	0.05	0.02
Colombia	0.39	0.65	0.19	0.17
Ecuador	0.06	0.12	0.12	0.08
Peru	0.38	0.31	0.19	0.12
Venezuela	0.35	1.91	0.95	0.34
CACM	0.32	0.48	0.23	0.16
CARICOM	0.26	0.40	0.57	0.12
Cuba	0.85	1.10	0.27	0.02
Other Latin America*	0.40	1.32	0.33	0.06
United States	15.42	16.72	11.03	9.72
Europe	47.68	40.00	39.80	46.28
United Kingdom	10.74	10.03	5.50	4.09
Japan	2.72	1.35	6.49	6.34
China	1.40	0.91	0.91	5.88
Asia**	10.51	13.15	17.79	19.49
West Asia	0.64	2.26	10.55	4.29
Rest of Asia	9.87	10.89	7.24	15.20

Sources: Societé des Nations (1942); UNCTAD (1991, 2004).
* Dominican Republic, Haiti, Panama and the Netherland Antilles.
** Excluding China and Japan.

Latin American exports declined from 9.3 percent to 5 percent of world exports, while those of China and the Rest of Asia doubled from 11.3 percent to 21.1 percent of world exports. It is true that China and the Rest of Asia were in turmoil in 1928, but this is not relevant to explain more recent disparities. Since 1980, Latin America's world market share of 5.5 percent fell slightly to 5 percent, while the share of China and the Rest of Asia rose from 8.1 percent to 21.1 percent.

There is an enormous literature on export-led growth and on the causality between export performance and growth. Results are conflicting. There is surely a link between exports and growth. There might be a causality going from exports to growth.[5] But, as in the case of links between protection and growth, it is possible to make the distinction between necessary and sufficient conditions concerning export performance which might explain growth. That rapid expansion of exports does not assure a high rate of growth is exemplified by Mexico's mediocre growth performance and its very significant expansion of market share in world exports. Mexico's growth performance, of course, could have been even worse had its exports increased at a lower rate. But elsewhere in Latin America some good export performances have been accompanied by high growth since 1990, notably in Chile, but also in other good growth performers such as, for instance, Costa Rica and the Dominican Republic.[6] While it is difficult to be too confident on the power of export expansion as a growth engine, without the help of other policies it is unlikely that export expansion would hinder growth.

In a review of Latin American export growth performance, especially until the early 1990s, one should be aware that even the overall unsatisfactory export performance in economies such as Brazil was heavily dependent on direct subsidization which was either GATT or WTO-illegal. This took the form of direct tax exemptions, tax rebates exceeding the amount of indirect taxes paid, and tax rebates or other advantages dependent on export performance criteria. Decision making on export subsidies in fact was a simple variation of the pick-the-winner methods which had been consolidated under the import substitution industrialization regime, at first with good results until the early 1970s, then with decreasing success in the late 1970s and 1980s. It was only after the mid-1980s that a change of strategy started to take shape as disappointment with the deterioration of growth performance increased, together with the awareness of the limits imposed by both fiscal constraints and multilaterally negotiated rules.

Export of services may also be a source of growth, as the example of India suggests. But they are still of limited importance in Latin America and have expanded less than world exports of services. Brazil, and especially Chile, Costa Rica, and the Dominican Republic have expanded their exports between 5-fold and 7-fold since 1990, with performances above the region's average. This contrasts with between 8-fold and 15-fold in the case of China, India and the Republic of Korea. Exports of services in Latin America tend to be more concentrated in tourism and travel and less in more sophisticated items such as business services (see UNCTAD, 2004, Part 5).

---

[5]See, for instance, Giles and Williams (2000a, 2000b), and Love and Chandra (2004).

[6]The share of Costa Rica in world exports rose from 0.04 percent to 0.18 percent between 1990 and 2003, and that of the Dominican Republic from 0.06 percent in 1990 to 0.09 percent in 2001, UNCTAD (2004).

Table 10.3 Export structure by main categories and selected commodity groups, 1970–2003 (percentage of total exports)

	Food products	*Agricultural raw materials*	*Fuels*	*Ores and metals*	*Manufactures*
1970					
Argentina	74.3	10.9	0.4	0.5	13.9
Brazil	63.3	11.9	0.6	10.1	13.2
Chile	4.5	2.9	0	88.1	4.3
Mexico	39.7	9.1	3.2	15.5	32.5
Bolivia	2.7	1.7	4.5	88.0	3.0
Colombia	75.0	6.2	10.1	0.7	8.0
Peru	43.5	5.9	0.7	48.4	1.4
Venezuela	1.7	0	91.0	5.8	1.4
Costa Rica	79.0	0.8	0.4	0.1	18.7
Dominican Republic*	87.8	0.1	7.5	3.6	3.2
1990					
Argentina	56.3	3.9	8.0	2.4	29.3
Brazil	27.7	3.3	2.2	13.7	51.8
Chile	23.1	9.5	0.5	53.1	9.8
Mexico	11.6	1.6	37.5	5.7	43.3
Bolivia	18.9	7.6	24.6	44.1	4.7
Colombia	32.8	4.3	36.9	0.2	25.1
Peru	21.2	3.3	10.0	47.0	18.4
Venezuela	1.9	0.4	80.1	7.4	0.2
Costa Rica	58.2	5.5	1.0	0.9	26.8
Dominican Republic**	14.9	0.3	0.3	0	81.4
2003					
Argentina	45.7	1.2	17.1	3.9	30.7
Brazil	28.6	4.5	5.2	8.5	51.0
Chile	27.8	9.3	2.2	41.0	15.6
Mexico	5.5	0.5	11.2	1.2	81.4
Bolivia	29.6	2.0	30.1	17.7	16.1
Colombia	17.4	5.5	37.2	1.0	34.3
Peru***	20.7	2.1	7.6	29.4	17.0
Venezuela	1.1	2.2	82.2	4.1	4.3
Costa Rica	30.1	3.1	0.5	0.7	65.4
Dominican Rep. ****	18.7	0.4	0.1	0.3	76.2

Source: UNCTAD (1991, 2003).

* Dominican Republic total exports of US$ 214 million (presumably national exports). Data from UNCTAD (1991).

** Dominican Republic total exports of US$ 2,034.3 million. Data from WTO (1996a).

*** Unallocated Peruvian exports of 23.1% in 2003.

**** This structure is for 1995, data from UNCTAD (2002). Dominican Republic total exports in 2001 were US$ 5,290 million of which US$ 752 million not from free-trade zones. Data from WTO (2003).

Export expansion: taxonomies in Latin America

The economies of Latin America are heterogeneous from many points of view. Export structures and the geographical distribution of export markets are no exception. Different economies have widely different export structures, and contrasts have deepened since the 1960s. Until then, exports interests were wholly in commodities: fuels (oil), ores and metals (ores), food products, and agricultural raw materials. Since then, manufactured exports became significant in most economies. In many cases, these exports are concentrated in consumer goods and, especially, in textiles and clothing products. But in some industrially more mature economies in the region, exports of more sophisticated products have been gaining ground.

Of the largest economies of Latin America, Argentina is a relevant exporter of manufactures, but its share in total exports has been around 30 percent since 1990 and they are mainly exported to the rest of Latin America. It still is essentially a large exporter of commodities, mainly of food products and oil (see Table 10.3). Brazil has a more diversified export structure. The share of food exports has been drastically reduced and also its composition, as coffee gave way to new products such as orange juice and soy beans. Sugar exports became relatively more important. Success of Brazilian agriculture relied heavily on the development of new planting techniques, soil treatment, and seed varieties appropriate for tropical agriculture in poorer soils but with much higher insolation and humidity levels than in most competitors. Competitiveness in pulp, paper, and related products is also explained by such advantages. The share of exports of ores in total exports fell slightly in recent years, but the economy plays a major role in the world iron ore market with Vale do Rio Doce as the market leader. Market share of manufactures has remained at about 50 percent since the early 1980s, but, in spite of some success stories such as Embraer exports of regional jets, there is a heavy concentration in less technologically sophisticated products. Another important development was the consolidation of a prominent role as an exporter of iron and steel products. Mexico, in the later period, became essentially an exporter of manufactures and fuels, mainly to the United States. Its range of manufactured exports is more comprehensive than those of any other LACs.

Chile has been gradually increasing its export market shares in food products and manufactures to the detriment of copper. In the former case, much of the success has been due to product and process innovation, as exemplified by its increasing importance as a world exporter of fish and fruits. Fish, fruit, and wines answered for almost 12 percent of Chilean total exports in 2003. Chile also consolidated a significant share in world markets for pulp and related products, whose exports surged before 1990. Colombia reduced dramatically the share of food products in its total exports, increasing oil and coal exports before 1990 and rather diversified

Table 10.4 Export structure by main regions of destination, 1970–2003 (percentage of total exports)

	Developed economies					Developing economies				
	*Europe**	*Canada and US*	*Japan*	*Other developed economies*	*South-East Europe and the CIS***	*Total*	*America*	*Africa*	*West Asia*	*Other Asia*
1970										
Argentina	55.5	9.3	6.2	1.0	4.3	23.7	21.1	0.5	0.6	1.1
Bolivia	46.2	34.8	9.6	0	0.8	8.5	8.5	0	0	0
Brazil	45.5	26.2	5.3	0.9	4.5	17.1	11.7	1.6	0.5	2.5
Chile	60.9	14.4	12.1	0.5	0.1	11.9	11.5	0.2	0	0.1
Colombia	38.5	38.0	2.8	0.3	4.9	15.5	14.2	0.1	0	0.1
Costa Rica	25.5	43.1	4.8	0	2.9	23.6	23.5	0	0	0.1
Dominican Rep.	11.8	81.8	3.0	1.7	0	6.9	6.9	0	0	0
Mexico	11.1	71.2	5.7	0.3	0.3	11.3	10.5	0.1	0	0.5
Peru	48.8	33.4	13.6	0.5	3.1	9.5	6.5	0	0.1	0.9
Venezuela	15.1	46.6	0.8	0	0	37.5	36.7	0.5	0	0
1990										
Argentina	31.7	14.4	3.3	1.1	5.1	43.8	27.6	3.2	6.1	7.0
Bolivia	29.1	20.0	0.3	0	2.2	46.2	45.3	0	0.1	0.5
Brazil	33.7	26.3	7.5	0.8	1.3	28.1	11.8	3.2	3.7	9.3
Chile	38.5	17.9	16.1	0.4	0.2	25.8	12.2	1.3	1.2	10.3
Colombia	28.9	45.6	3.8	0.5	0.6	18.2	17.2	0.1	0.2	0.7
Costa Rica	29.7	49.6	1.0	0.3	0.1	18.2	16.4	0.1	0.2	1.3
Dominican Rep.	19.4	67.6	2.0	0	1.0	9.1	3.5	0.5	0	4.6
Mexico	13.4	70.2	5.5	1.0	0.1	8.6	6.6	0.3	0.2	1.2
Peru	33.0	23.2	13.4	0.2	3.8	24.9	15.7	0.7	1.0	7.5
Venezuela	14.0	54.2	2.8	0.1	0.1	27.3	14.5	0.3	0	1.6

continued

Table 10.4 Export structure by main regions of destination, 1970–2003 (percentage of total exports) – *continued*

	Developed economies					*Developing economies*				
	*Europe**	*Canada and US*	*Japan*	*Other developed economies*	*South-East Europe and the CIS***	*Total*	*America*	*Africa*	*West Asia*	*Other Asia*
2003										
Argentina	20.3	10.6	1.2	0.7	0.9	65.2	40.9	4.8	3.8	15.7
Bolivia	21.6	11.6	1.5	0.2	0.1	64.0	62.4	0.1	0	1.5
Brazil	25.4	24.2	3.4	0.7	2.6	41.0	19.1	4.0	3.8	13.6
Chile	22.8	18.1	10.5	0.6	0.5	41.0	18.2	0.5	1.4	20.8
Colombia	14.5	48.4	1.5	0.8	0.4	31.9	28.7	0.6	0.6	8.0
Costa Rica	21.2	26.6	1.4	0.1	0.1	22.0	13.4	0	0.2	8.4
Dominican Rep.	7.6	86.1	0.8	0.1	0	5.1	3.5	0.5	0	4.6
Mexico	3.5	89.4	0.7	0.2	0	5.8	3.5	0.1	0.1	1.4
Peru	20.2	28.6	4.4	0.7	0.8	31.9	17.9	0.4	0.5	13.1
Venezuela	7.2	46.2	0.2	0	0.1	33.2	31.7	0.1	0.1	1.1

Sources: UNCTAD (1991, 2004).

* In 1970 Europe excludes the Czech Republic, Hungary, Poland and the German Democratic Republic.

** In 1970 included the Czech Republic, Hungary, Poland and the German Democratic Republic as well as the Socialist Countries of Asia. But Latin America's trade with the latter was negligible in 1970.

manufactures in a more sustained way since then. The share of food exports decreased in Peru, as its manufactured exports increased between 1970 and 1990. But, since then, the latter remained below 20 percent. Venezuela is still essentially an oil exporter. In Costa Rica foreign investment in electronic products – massive if compared to the size of the economy – has radically changed the export structure towards manufactures, which now represent about two-thirds of total exports. The Dominican Republic and some of the Central American economies, as El Salvador and Honduras, are heavily dependent on clothing exports.[7]

To a large extent, export market orientation results from export product structure. Table 10.4 presents data on the destination of Latin American exports. Exporters of commodities tend to have a more diversified export structure by destination. Geography, of course, also plays a role. The closer is an economy to the United States, the higher the share of its exports directed there. The economies in the Southern region of South America and Peru being more remote geographically in relation to the United States and more important as world commodity suppliers of food and ores, tend to have a lower share of exports directed to the United States and Canada, typically in the 10–28 percent range. In the economies in the Northern part of South America this tends to rise to 50 percent and nearer to the United States in Central America and Mexico, to the 60–90 percent range.

The importance of the European market for Latin America has been generally decreasing since 1970. To a certain extent, this reflects the fact that Europe is not as important as the United States as a market for Latin American exports of manufactures. Intra-Latin American trade became increasingly important in the 1990s for almost all LACs listed in Table 10.3, with the exception of Costa Rica and Mexico, whose exports increased much above the regional average. This trend was reversed in the late 1990s, as a new crisis hit Latin America. Exports to other developing economies remained modest, with the exception of Other Asia where commodity suppliers such as Argentina, Brazil, Chile, and Peru increased their shares as the Chinese economy boomed.

Sources of export growth: Supply-related responses[8]

Export growth can be driven by improved competitiveness resulting from better domestic policies. Dissatisfaction with the performance of Latin American economies has prompted a quest for successful national experi-

[7]According to the WTO, the shares of clothing exports in total exports in El Salvador, the Dominican Republic, and Honduras were, in 2003, 62.6 percent, 51.4, percent and 38.3 percent, respectively (WTO, 2004, p. 156).
[8]This section is mostly taken from Abreu (2005c).

ences elsewhere, from which lessons could be extracted. The quest for paradigms of growth experiences, however, must take into account specificities both of economies selected as examples of fast growth and those that are seeking lessons that can serve to formulate more successful policies. Among those more relevant are: size of population and area, location in relation to major markets, conditions of access to those markets (FTAs), "cultural" factors (language, size of diaspora), factor endowments, savings ratios.

There are a few stylized facts which are common to successful Asian economies and are not often found in Latin America. Gross fixed capital formation in Asia has often been quite high. In 1990–2003 it was very high in China (39 percent), around 29 percent in most other Asian economies – Korea, Malaysia, Thailand, Singapore, and Hong Kong – and lower in India (23.1 percent) and Indonesia (21.9 percent), compared to the low 20 percent in Latin America. In Chile, it peaked at 23–26 percent in 1992–98. Growth in these high-performing economies has also relied on high rates of total factor productivity growth, which in turn depended on openness and/or the weight of manufactured exports in total exports. All these economies have substantially expanded their export/GDP ratios since the 1960s. It is now 56 percent even in Vietnam, contrasting with an average of 21 percent in Latin America. FDI to GDP ratios have been very high only in Hong Kong and Singapore, and to a lesser extent in Malaysia in the early 1990s. It was not above 3–5 percent in the other Asian economies. In Latin America it peaked at 5 percent in midst of the big privatization spurt, but it is back to 3 percent. The share of manufactures in total exports in the Asian paradigm economies is above 80 percent in most cases, higher than in Latin America, even allowing for the different resource-endowment bases. Research and development expenditures were and still are relatively high only in Korea – around 3 percent of GDP – compared to peaks in Latin America, in Chile and Brazil never above 1 percent. The role of the Chinese diaspora has been crucial to the widespread success of growth histories in most Asian economies. Hong Kong and Singapore, moreover, had the advantage of being English-speaking.

Asian economies have used a panoply of industrial policy instruments.[9] Some are now banned by upgraded multilateral disciplines or made difficult to use as global trade liberalization has been gaining ground. They have included subsidized credit targeting exporters, high protection of domestic markets and tax incentives to FDI conditional on export performance. An important aspect of the Asian success history has been openness to foreign technology in its several aspects: imports of capital goods; attraction of export-oriented FDI or active technology licensing (in most success histories); active technological policies concerning licensing, transfer

[9]This paragraph relies on World Bank (1993).

of non-proprietary technology, enhancing the role of returning nationals and the development of domestic research.

The Korean example is of great interest because the government played such an important role in selecting sectors as targets for its policies. And also, because Korea took off in terms of sustained high growth while Brazil, its often mentioned counterpart in Latin America, at least in the beginning of the period, practically ceased to grow after 1980. Brazil failed in its attempt to cope with acceleration of inflation and a major balance of payments crisis in the late 1970s, and faced recurrent macroeconomic crises between 1980 and 2002. Most of the Korean-type microeconomic policies have been tried and the very active export subsidization policy in the 1970s and 1980s did not result in the emergence of many competitive exporters, in spite of emblematic exceptions such as Embraer. Industrial policies in Brazil tended to involve more or less permanent subsidization rather than Korean-type histories of success of firms simply taking off.[10]

Export growth can also result from increased demand. This can take the form of either very high rates of demand growth in specific markets because of high growth of GDP, or increased market access in markets previously highly protected. The latter will be considered in the next section. The first case has been exemplified by China, but has also been relevant in the past to explain import demand of other high-growth Asian markets. What makes China important is the size of its economy coupled with its backwardness when compared to other economies in Asia whose GDP per capita levels increased at high rates in earlier periods, but lower than China's.

It is unlikely that Latin America will play a significant role as supplier of manufactures to China. And competition from Chinese products in third markets is a very concrete menace to Latin American exports. Much of the impact of Chinese competition is likely to hurt Latin American suppliers of clothing products located in the vicinity of the United States market, such as Mexico and most Central American economies.[11] But Mexico especially, could also be hurt by Chinese competition in traditional export markets of other types of manufactures. The picture is different for Latin American commodity exports. For some semi-manufactures, markets can be temporarily in disequilibrium as domestic demand surges outstrip domestic supply, generating an import surge. In this latter case, given time, domestic productive capacity can be increased, imports reduced and the country become an exporter rather than an importer of the relevant processed product. This has been the case of steel imports in China which have surged until quite recently, but have rapidly declined as domestic produc-

[10]See Moreira (1995) for a comprehensive comparison of Korean and Brazilian industrial policies.

[11]As shown in Inter-American Development Bank (2005), especially Chapter 5.

tive capacity started to come into production. The long-term behaviour of imports of commodities whose domestic supply is constrained by resource endowment – iron ore, soya, and copper – is likely to be different. Convergence of Chinese per capita consumption levels to those of more mature economies in Asia is the crucial element to explain the expansion of Chinese import demand of commodities and processed products such as iron ore, copper, soybeans, and soy oil.[12]

Sources of export growth: Improved market access

The interests of Latin American economies as *demandeurs* of trade liberalization are rather heterogeneous. Exports of ores and fuels are really not affected by obstacles to market access. These obstacles are very relevant in markets of agricultural products, mostly, but far from exclusively, in developed economies. They may take the form of extremely high tariffs or tariff quotas. Tariff escalation is also relevant, especially affecting tropical products. For many temperate agricultural products, domestic support policies and export subsidies adopted by developed economies contribute to lower world prices of food products – sugar, beef, pork, poultry, soybeans, dairy products – and also tobacco and agricultural raw materials as cotton. As agricultural protection and subsidization are progressively dismantled, sanitary and environmental standards will tend to be increasingly used as protection in the last resort.

A particularly perverse feature of agricultural protectionism in the European Union (EU) is that it creates vested interests in Asian Caribbean Pacific (ACP) economies in favor of the *status quo* as they have preferential access to the EU market as, for example, in the case of bananas and sugar. There are conflicting interests on the issue between the Caribbean producers and those in Central and South America. For sugar, ACP preferences serve as justification for heavily subsidized European exports. Efficient food producers – in Latin America notably MERCOSUR – would greatly benefit from trade liberalization and higher export prices for food products. Some net food importers in Latin America may be unfavorably affected by higher import prices, and thus be not enthusiastic about agricultural trade liberalization.[13]

Latin American exports of manufactures face relatively high tariffs in developing economies. In developed economies tariffs are generally low, but discretionary protection, especially antidumping, is very significant, affecting products such as iron and steel that compete with structurally

[12]See Abreu (2005a). China's per capita consumption of soy oil, for example, is still only 40 percent of Korea's.

[13]See Ingco and Nash (2004), Chapters 1 and 7, and Laird (2002).

inefficient domestic producers in mature economies. Exports of high-technology industrial goods, such as electronic components and regional jets, face no significant obstacles to enter markets of either developed or developing economies.

The end of the Multifibre Arrangement (MFA) and China's accession to the WTO are likely to have important consequences on Latin American exports of clothing. The end of MFA inertially-defined quotas in developed economies unfreezed constraints to the substitution of traditional less-efficient suppliers by new more efficient entrants, such as China. In the longer term, it is likely that these developments will deeply affect exporters in Mexico and Central America. Margins of preference resulting from regional agreements are unlikely to be sufficient to compensate the very significant difference in production costs. China's competition is likely to be also relevant in displacing other Latin American manufactured exports from third markets, including those in Latin America, but this is unlikely to be as important as the case of clothing, at least in the immediate future.[14]

Developed economies are *demandeurs* in relation to two sets of issues in Latin America. The first set of issues relate to market access. Market access for goods is relevant since the WTO-bound rate in most Latin American economies is 35 percent, but average MFN applied rates are around 13 percent, even in the more protectionist economies as MERCOSUR. There are, however, many applied tariffs above 15 percent and some even reaching 35 percent on products which are of interest for the developed economies as *demandeurs*: electronic products, electric and transport equipment. Market access for services is much more limited and much of it still dependent on discretionary decisions. Many of the demands by developed economies are in fact for a transformation of *de facto* into *de jure* market access.

The other set of issues is essentially on rules, and encompasses negotiations in relation to which there is much more reluctance by developing economies to make concessions: intellectual property, public procurement, labour and environmental standards, and competition. Size of an economy as measured by GDP, as opposed to market size as measured by trade flows, is particularly important here, since often what is at stake is access to the domestic market as a whole. The more active an economy has been in seeking preferential trade agreements with significant trading partners – which are likely often to be large developed economies – the less reluctant they will be, *ceteris paribus*, both to open their domestic markets and to agree to concessions on rules. The largest a given economy, the more comprehensive,

[14]See Part IV of Inter-American Development Bank (2005) for a comprehensive treatment of the impact of Chinese exports on Latin American exporters of clothing, and Chapter 5 for competition in third markets.

ceteris paribus, will be the range of industrial products which may be hurt by increased competition from imports entailed by trade liberalization.

Since NAFTA, Latin American economies – frequently as part of an existing FTA or "common market" – have been involved in a large number of bilateral trade negotiations with trade partners – also in many cases FTAs or "common markets" – within and outside the hemisphere. In terms of affected trade, the most important negotiations have been between the United States and many FTAs and economies in Latin America. Negotiations which have been concluded have included neither the more sensitive agricultural sectors in United States, nor antidumping. In varying degrees, LACs have accepted strengthened disciplines in relation to services and the rule-related other issues: intellectual property, public procurement, labor and environmental standards, and competition. In fact, with the important exception of sugar in Central America, the United States was in general in a comfortable position as a relatively efficient producer of agricultural products compared to most of non-MERCOSUR Latin America (especially if agricultural subsidies are not taken into account).

MERCOSUR itself faces, even if as a mere FTA, many problems whose analysis is outside the scope of this chapter. The persistence of the issue of automatic safeguards to cope with real or alleged import surges, coupled with the inability to devise equitable policies which could level the playing field among its member states, does not bid well for the future. This has had, of course, a significant impact on the likelihood of reaching favorable results in the negotiations with the European Union, the main example of ongoing negotiation of a Latin American FTA with partners outside the hemisphere. The obstacles have been, as expected, the difficulties in extracting concessions from the European Union on agriculture. Reciprocally, MERCOSUR has also proved obdurate in its refusal to improve on earlier commitments on protection on industrial goods, services, and rules-related issues. The indefinition of the Doha Round is not easy to circumvent, as it is difficult to have a clear idea of what could be the liberalization package finally reached multilaterally. The very limited results of the Hong Kong meeting of December have made this difficulty very explicit. A similar difficulty is faced in the FTAA negotiations. Many think that negotiations of MERCOSUR both with the European Union and the United States, in the FTAA context, will have to wait for the Doha results, especially on agricultural subsidies and antidumping. If so, the whole timetable of negotiations is likely to be postponed, as meaningful results in the Doha round are proving to be elusive.

It should not have come as a surprise that the FTAA negotiations have been stalled after the decision to have a two-tier process was reached. This architecture is to include a rather loose core of universally agreed weak disciplines and limited market access concessions, complemented by more exacting agreements covering access and rules agreed only by subsets of future members. This weak hybrid structure agreed in Miami, reflects mainly obstacles in MERCOSUR and the United States. On the one hand, MERCOSUR's reluctance to accept both a deep opening up of their market for manufactures and many of the US-sponsored demands on rule-related issues. On the other, it reflects the United States refusal to deal with agricultural subsidies and antidumping, and the marked reluctance to scratch agricultural protection. The geography of protection in the United States and Brazil indeed suggests that negotiations envisaging a scenario of comprehensive liberalization of trade in goods would face very significant political obstacles in both economies. Their removal would require a decisive commitment from both sides, which is really difficult to see as likely.[15]

Multilateral negotiations in the Doha Round are badly behind schedule, as shown by the Ministerial meeting at Hong Kong. There are many difficulties to face, in particular, those related to the balance between agricultural concessions from the developed economies and improved market access concessions for industrial goods to be made by the developing economies.

Conclusions: Domestic policies and improved market access[16]

It is important to recognize that macroeconomic stability, in general, has preceded the histories of growth success propped by specific industrial policies. Only in rare cases has there been significant and sustained growth without a substantial improvement of the previous record of investment and capacity of saving. This automatically raises issues related to the cost of investment, which affects the costs of both capital goods and construction, and also their quality. Microeconomic policies should target cost and quality to ensure that investment is cost-effective, that is, that addition to productive capacity is maximized given an investment ratio. Another related issue is also a grey area between macro- and micro-policies: the lower the

[15]See Abreu (2004a) for the political economy of the FTAA. See, for the regional impact of the FTAA on Brazil and the US, Abreu (2005b), where protectionist interests are shown to be concentrated in Brazil in the States of São Paulo and Amazonas. Major net interests against trade liberalization of Brazilian imports into the US are located in the States in the northern part of the Mountain Division in the West (Idaho, Montana, Wyoming, the Dakotas, Nebraska and Iowa), some States in the South (Arkansas, Alabama and Mississippi), Maine and West Virginia. For tariff protection, AD protection and agricultural support the States with more "protectionist" congressional districts are Pennsylvania (11 CDs), Georgia (9), North Carolina and Texas (8), Ohio (7), Florida and Illinois (6), California, Iowa and Virginia (5), Alabama, Arkansas, Kentucky, Louisiana and Michigan (4) and Indiana (3).

[16]Most of the conclusions on domestic policies come from Abreu (2005c).

variance of an economy's rate of growth, the lower the probability that investment plans will be affected by the economic cycle. Fluctuations in the rate of growth badly affect government's savings and its level of expenditure, as they generate revenue shortfalls. Projected rates of return are adversely affected as the conclusion of intended plants or infrastructure is delayed. This also affects private investment.

A good starting point when considering industrial policies is the recognition that international constraints, certainly for the more mature developing economies, prevent the use of instruments which have been effective in the past: preferential access to foreign exchange cover, subsidized credit, national content rules, export performance criteria. It is unlikely that the Uruguay Round decisions in relation to such "productive policies" – in particular, those on export performance criteria – could be reversed without rather expensive *quid pro quo* concessions by the main developing economies. For these, a meaningful development round is likely to hinge more on improved market access than on special and differential treatment. This naturally brings the focus onto policies that target market failures and are covered by WTO rules on non-actionable subsidies related to science and technology, aspects of regional disparities, and environment-related projects. On the other hand, since horizontal policies are non-specific, there is a strong argument for their defense, as there are no subsidies that can be targeted by dissatisfied trade partners.

There is scope for deeper horizontal structural reforms in almost every economy in Latin America, as for instance, furthering the creation of a strong long-term capital market. Some horizontal policies may lack focus and give room for merely disguising expenditures which are unrelated to science and technology development. But they avoid difficulties related to specificity that characterize vertical policies, even when they are targeted to address market failures. There is scope for policies at the intermediate level of aggregation between horizontal policies and vertical policies (which restrict their targets to firms in specific sectors or regions). There is much to be said in favor of a coordination of the several layers of intervention prompted by market failures, something which does not often happen. Opportunities created by WTO rules that allow regional subsidies should be used perhaps through a combination of science and technology and regional tax expenditures and vertical industrial policies. In spite of all well known difficulties involved in gathering the required information, vertical policies addressed to the improvement of distortions related to market failures still may have an important role in a comprehensive framework of industrial policies. In Brazil, such vertical policies have been applied in the past, taking into account a rational set of criteria targeting the risk entailed by specific projects, the importance of net externalities created, the ability of benefited firms to appropriate the results of their projects and the geographical location of projects in depressed areas. The record of success is not good even if there are some success stories.

The implementation of a meaningful package of such "industrial policies" requires political commitment at the highest level on the blueprint of such a set of policies. It is important that governments open a comprehensive debate on industrial policies and are able to win political support for rational policies. It is in this environment that "self discovery" should ideally take place involving full mobilization of science and technology institutions: government departments, academies of sciences, research institutions, universities, certification agencies, organizations of entrepreneurs and firms.

The implementation of a package of horizontal and vertical industrial policies will also require an overhaul of obsolescent government institutions. It is important to transform purely financial agencies into technological and scientific agencies with a high level of competence in the evaluation of technological alternatives, able to identify and mobilize state of the art technologies on a global basis, to gather meaningful market information, and undertake effective technological brokerage that will improve access of national industry to technologies adapted to their specificities.[17] It is also essential that robust evaluation machinery is put in place with the participation of acknowledged specialists recruited on a worldwide basis following transparent procedures. The objective would be to evaluate the results of previous efforts and offer a feedback that contributes to improve the "aim" of policy-makers in the selection of which market failures to target in the future. These vertical policies aimed at market failures still involve picking winners, but they are based on much more defensible criteria than the traditional policies favoring rent-seeking sectors with political clout and without any concern for market failure correction, which has been typical of most of Latin America in the past.

Past experience in many economies indicates that effective trade liberalization may be an important catalyst for the introduction of revamped domestic policies. Success in multilateral, regional and subregional negotiations on market access, or deepening of such initiatives, is important by itself due to the stimuli provided by increased exports and efficiency gains related to further opening up of domestic markets. But it is also important, as the mobilization of private interests required by the formulation of negotiating agendas in trade negotiations may have as byproducts – not necessarily less important – a reexamination of former "industrial policies", the discussion of their overhaul and improvement in their implementation.

---

[17]On the lines of TEKES, the main public funding organization in Finland. See Abreu (2005c).

The likelihood of trade liberalization playing such a positive role in different Latin American economies varies significantly as the prospects of success in the conclusion of different negotiations are very different. Based on past performance, one should expect that the United States would be able to complete its programme of negotiating FTAs with most of Latin America. The main exceptions would be where political aspects tend to prevail, as in Cuba and Venezuela.

So there are good prospects of improved market access playing a catalyst role for further reform and complementary policies in many economies of Latin America which may help them to face the menace of enhanced competition from exports of other developing economies, especially China. In the mid-term, the use of safeguards in the United States to protect CAFTA and Dominican Republic clothing imports by US-connected firms may extend the transition period required by the deep structural adjustment which is likely to occur. On the other hand, there is no reason to doubt that the success histories of Chile and Costa Rica can continue. There is also some inertia in good decision-making on economic policies.

In MERCOSUR, political difficulties may also play a role in trade negotiations, especially in the FTAA context, mostly by defining polar stances on rule-related issues. But even in more favorable political scenarios, there are important substantive obstacles, as mentioned earlier, to a significant improvement of access of agricultural products in the United States market which could be used politically by the Brazilian government to justify its own concessions. The solution, or even reduction, of present frictions within MERCOSUR is something which depends crucially on the course of political developments both in Argentina and Brazil. The same kind of political difficulties would probably affect the EU-MERCOSUR negotiations unless MERCOSUR governments are really hard-pressed for results in order to show something concrete. In spite of the better Brazilian recent macroeconomic performance in comparison with its recent past – with low and declining inflation coexisting with modest growth – and the relatively good performance of Argentina, there is a notorious lack of a catalyst to domestic reform in the format of a serious commitment to further liberalize imports coupled with new export opportunities.

But it is still more than likely that most developments in such partial negotiations hinge on what happens in the WTO. The only good thing that can be said about the present prospects of the Doha Round is that the world trading system cannot face a further failure after the stalemate in Cancún and the near failure at Hong Kong. There is going to be a lot of pressure on all quarters to reach an agreement. The problem, of course, is how to make sure that a balanced agreement, including a significant effort to liberalize agricultural trade, is reached within the initial timetable for the conclusion of the Doha Round.

References

Abreu, M. de Paiva (2005a) "China's emergence in the global economy and Brazil," Discussion paper, no. 491, Departamento de Economia da Pontifícia Universidade Católica do Rio de Janeiro, January.

Abreu, M. de Paiva (2005b) "The FTAA and the political economy of protection in Brazil and the US," Discussion paper, No. 494, Departamento de Economia da Pontifícia Universidade Católica do Rio de Janeiro, January.

Abreu, M. de Paiva (2005c) "Which 'industrial policies' are meaningful for Latin America?," Discussion paper, no. 493, Departamento de Economia da Pontifícia Universidade Católica do Rio de Janeiro, February.

Abreu, M. de Paiva (2004a) "The political economy of economic integration in the Americas: Latin American interests," in A. Estevadeordal, D. Rodrik, A. Taylor and A.Velasco (eds), *The FTAA and Beyond: Prospects for Integration in the Americas*, Harvard University Press for Harvard University David Rockefeller Center for Latin American Studies, Cambridge, Mass., and London.

Abreu, M. de Paiva (2004b) "Trade liberalization and the political economy of protection in Brazil since 1987," *Special Initiative on Trade and Integration*, Working paper SITI-08b, IADB-INTAL, Buenos Aires.

Clemens, M.A. and J.G. Williamson (2001) "A tariff-growth paradox? Protection's impact the world around, 1875–1997," *NBER Working Paper*, No. 8459, September.

Frankel, J.A. and D. Romer (1999) "Does trade cause growth?," *American Economic Review*, 89(3), June, pp. 379–99.

Giles, J.A. and C.L. Williams (2000a) "Export-led growth: a survey of the empirical literature and some noncausality results," Part 1, *Journal of International Trade and Economic Development*, pp. 261–337.

Giles, J.A. and C.L. Williams (2000b) "Export-led growth: a survey of the empirical literature and some noncausality results," Part 2, *Journal of International Trade and Economic Development*, pp. 445–70.

Ingco, M. and J.D. Nash (eds) (2004) *Agriculture and the WTO. Creating a Trading System for Development*, World Bank and Oxford University Press, Washington, DC.

Inter-American Development Bank (IDB) (2005) "The emergence of China: opportunities and challenges for Latin America and the Caribbean," mimeo, March.

Irwin, D.A. (2002) "Interpreting the tariff-growth correlation of the late nineteenth century," *American Economic Review (Papers and Proceedings)*, 91, pp. 165–69, May.

Laird, S. (2002) "Market access issues and the WTO: an overview," in B. Hoekman, A. Mattoo, and Ph. English (eds) *Development, Trade, and the WTO*, The World Bank, Washington, DC.

Love, J.J. and R. Chandra (2004) "Testing export-led growth in India, Pakistan and Sri Lanka using a multivariate framework," *Manchester School*, 72(4), July, pp. 483–96.

Moreira, M. Mesquita (1995) *Trade and Market Failures. The Role of Government Intervention in Brazil and South Korea*, Macmillan, Basingstoke.

O'Rourke, K.H. (2000) "Tariffs and growth in the late 19th century," *Economic Journal*, 110, pp. 456–83, April.

Rodríguez, F. and D. Rodrik (2001) "Trade policy and economic growth: a skeptic's guide to the cross-national evidence," in B. Bernanke and K.S. Rogoff (eds), *Macroeconomics Annual 2000*, NBER, MIT Press, Cambridge, MA.

Sachs, J.D. and A.M. Warner (1995) "Economic reform and the process of global integration," *Brookings Papers on Economic Activity*, 1, pp. 1–118.

Societé des Nations (1942) *Le réseau du commerce mondial*, Geneva.

UNCTAD (2004) *Handbook of Statistics 2004*, United Nations, New York and Geneva.
UNCTAD (2003) *Handbook of Statistics 2003*, United Nations, New York and Geneva.
UNCTAD (2002) *Handbook of Statistics 2002*, United Nations, New York and Geneva.
UNCTAD (1991) *Handbook of International Trade Statistics 1990*, United Nations, New York.
World Bank (1993) *The East Asian Miracle. Economic Growth and Public Policy*, World Bank and Oxford University Press, New York and Washington DC.
World Trade Organization (2004) *World Trade Statistics 2004*, Geneva.
World Trade Organization (2003) *Trade Policy Review. Dominican Republic 2002*, Geneva.
World Trade Organization (2001) *Trade Policy Review. Costa Rica 2001*, Geneva.
World Trade Organization (1996a) *Trade Policy Review. Dominican Republic 1996*, Geneva.
World Trade Organization (1996b) *Trade Policy Review. Venezuela 1996*, Geneva.
World Trade Organization (1995) *Trade Policy Review. Costa Rica 1995*, Geneva.
World Trade Organization (1994) *Trade Policy Review. Peru 1994*, Geneva.

Index

The manufacturer's authorised representative in the EU is Springer Nature Customer Service Centre GmbH, Europaplatz 3, 69115 Heidelberg, Germany. If you have any concerns regarding our products, please contact ProductSafety@springernature.com

Printed and bound by CPI Group (UK) Ltd, Croydon, CR0 4YY

30/10/2026

02242629-0012